ORIGINAL COPIES

Architectural Mimicry in Contemporary China

BIANCA BOSKER

With a Foreword by Jerome Silbergeld

spatial habitus

University of Hawai'i Press, Honolulu

Hong Kong University Press

First published in North America by University of Hawai'i Press
ISBN 978-0-8248-3606-1

Published in China by Hong Kong University Press
ISBN 978-988-8139-14-9

Printed in Hong Kong, China
18 17 16 15 14 13   6 5 4 3 2 1

Library of Congress Cataloging-in-Publication Data
Bosker, Bianca.
Original copies : architectural mimicry in contemporary China / Bianca Bosker ; with a foreword by Jerome Silbergeld.
p. cm.—(Spatial habitus)
Includes bibliographical references and index.
ISBN 978-0-8248-3606-1 (pbk. : alk. paper)
1. Architecture—China—Themes, motives. 2. Architecture—China—Western influences. 3. Architecture—China—History—20th century. 4. Architecture—China—History—21st century. I. Title. II. Series: Spatial habitus (Series)
NA1545.B67 2013
720.951'09051—dc23
                                                    2012017567

Printed on acid-free paper and meets the guidelines for permanence and durability of the Council on Library Resources.

Designed by Cynthia Ng

Printed and bound by Paramount Printing Co., Ltd.

CONTENTS

Foreword by Jerome Silbergeld   vii

Acknowledgments   xi

1. Into "the Land of Courtly Enjoyments": An Introduction to China's Architectural Mimicry   1

2. The Fascination with *Faux*: Philosophical and Theoretical Drivers of Architectural Reproduction in China   20

3. Manifestations of Westernization: The Anatomy of China's Simulacrascapes   37

4. Simulacra and the Sino-Psyche: Understanding the Chinese Motivation for Replicating the Alien   67

5. Residential Revolution: Inside the Twenty-first Century Chinese Dream   93

Conclusion: From Imitation to Innovation?   118

Notes   133

Bibliography   147

Index   155

FOREWORD

Whatever one may have read about or expects to see in a visit to today's Beijing, Shanghai, Guangzhou, Xi'an, Chongqing, Chengdu, or half a dozen other Chinese metropolitan centers, the traveler there is likely to be dazzled by the pace of urban development, by the lightning-like speed of Westernization, by China's sudden surpassing of the cities of Europe and North America at their own "game." The New York or London or Tokyo that the traveler returns to can only seem like a dated and relatively downtrodden city. This phenomenon raises all sorts of questions about the new and the old in China, including the wholesale abandonment of China's two thousand-plus-year-old tradition of architectural engineering and urban design—a tradition so thoroughly systematized by the early centuries of the first millennium CE and so deeply integrated into Chinese systems of thought and culture that little room existed for improvement or individual architectural creativity and only slow, almost invisible evolution in basic form took place before the modern encounter with the West.

What isn't well known is the collateral Chinese tradition of thematic appropriation, dating back to the unification under the First Emperor in the late third century BCE. According to official Chinese histories, as Qin Shihuangdi successively conquered the last six kingdoms holding out against unification, he replicated each of their local palaces (probably in miniature, perhaps two-thirds scale) along the banks of the Wei River outside his own capital city of Xianyang. Before unification, when variations in regional culture were still considerable, in everything from writing script to architectural style, the diverse architecture arrayed along the Wei must have been quite a sight to residents of the capital and may well have rivaled the contrast between old and new seen in today's urban centers. The underlying nature of this appropriation was manifest as well in the early royal parks: exclusive preserves that later gave rise to China's private gardens but that were paradisical microcosms stocked with all the beasts, horticultural varieties, and man-made replicas of geography from throughout the known world that the ruler could manage to gather in one place as both symbol of his hegemony and a reality that he could draw upon to enhance his own earthly powers. As a classic example of this, when still in the early planning stages of his invasion of the Dian Kingdom in the deep south (now Yunnan Province), the Han emperor Wudi (reigned 141–87 BCE) made a small-scale replica of Dian's Kunming Lake, upon which his naval assault would be launched. Down through the ages, such appropriation continued. Reduction of scale of alien landscapes and architecture facilitated control; possession of the replica made it real. The modern historian of architecture should realize that the appropriation of Soviet-style architecture in the 1950s—no less a transformation than the current one—served in the Chinese mind to vault China into leadership of the international socialist movement.

The Chinese appropriation of "other" types of architecture results from all kinds of negotiation. Professor Ning Qiang recently showed me photographs of the city hotel of Tumushuke (Tumxuk), a town just east of Kashgar in China's westernmost, Islamic province, built in an eighteenth-century northern European style found anywhere from Hanover north to Sweden and Finland. When a major hotel was proposed in an Iranian style appropriate to the region and its ethnicity, Han members of the provincial administration blocked it; if there were to be a local Muslim uprising, they protested, rioters would naturally flock to such a site and fortify themselves there. The designer relented and produced a traditional Chinese-style building instead. But now the Muslim-Uyghur members of the administration protested against this as a violation of their territorial culture. In a third go-round, the politically savvy architect produced the northern European design. Everyone was happy with it: nothing was lost, something was gained.

More or less alike in principle, each example of architectural appropriation is different in its particulars. But none is more astonishing than the one presented here by Bianca Bosker. Designed for China's newly risen upper-middle and upper classes, a new brand of suburb has recently sprung up surrounding many of the modernist cities, serving as gated communities that provide simulacra of foreign towns and cultures— not modernist but retrograde, like the Tudor-style Thames Town outside of Shanghai. Providing the benefits of a life abroad without one's having to go abroad, these themed suburbs allow their residents to globalize while avoiding the challenge of foreign languages and cultures, while China avoids the brain-drain of its educated elite. "What distinguishes the Chinese simulacra cities from Disneyland, Renaissance Towns, Las Vegas, and other theme-park-like environments," the author writes, "is that the suspension of disbelief is temporary in the latter and permanent in the former."

If the theme-park atmosphere here seems *faux* and superficial, Ms. Bosker's study of this urban phenomenon most decidedly is not. She explicates the motivation behind it and details the reality of it through careful architectural and anthropological investigation, in both image and word. In her own words:

> What this exploration will reveal is that the factors impinging on the
> decision to simulate alien townscapes are not merely exogenous but
> lead deep into the cultural character of contemporary China: the rise of
> its newly minted middle and upper classes and their desire for branded

luxury consumer goods and, more important, symbols of self-cultivation; the flexing of the national soft-power muscle; a "yes-we-can" boosterism bloated on a decade of unprecedented economic growth and increasing prestige and power in the global arena; and a deeply rooted tradition of celebrating cultural achievements by constructing gigantic monuments.

Accordingly, she translates this architecture into a study that ranges widely from Chinese concepts of originality and copywork—in Chinese ontogeny, *everything* in the material realm is but a replica of its ur-concept, or *xiang*, residing outside of this realm; multiples, regardless of scale, are equals—to a characterization of what these suburbs say about the latest in taste, emergent class differentiation, business methods, and ecology in today's China. Those viewers who would be astonished by the sight of these new towns (Thames Town here, Fontainebleau Villas there, Bauhaus architecture somewhere just up the freeway) will be even more astonished when they read what this book has to say about them, as Ms. Bosker opens the gates and takes us inside.

Jerome Silbergeld
P. Y. and Kinmay W. Tang Professor of Chinese Art History
and Director, Tang Center for East Asian Art, Princeton University

ACKNOWLEDGMENTS

Those who claim writing is a solitary craft are stretching the truth. This book would not have been possible without the help of many individuals, to whom I am indebted for sharing their time, energy, advice, and expertise.

Boots on the ground are a must. In this regard, I am grateful to all those individuals who assisted my research efforts in China—among them architects, scholars, journalists, officials, developers, and homeowners. These people opened up their homes to me, welcomed me into their offices, offered their impressions, and shared their photographs. Two individuals in particular provided vital assistance that has been indispensable to this book's execution: Sophia Miao, who has given valuable consultation and research assistance throughout this project, and Haiyao Zheng, a source of enlightened guidance, moral support, and lively company.

I am especially grateful to Professor Jerome Silbergeld of Princeton University, whose wise counsel and engagement with the subject matter laid the foundations for an intellectual adventure that would not only span several years, but would also culminate in a more profound understanding of what it takes to bring a book such as this one to fruition. I am also deeply appreciative of the insights, academic excellence, and editorial rigor that have been generously offered by Professor Ronald Knapp, Professor Xing Ruan, and Patricia Crosby, each of whom demonstrated a deep interest in the topic and in the fine art of bookmaking. They have been dedicated, valuable, and thoughtful collaborators through the process of preparing and submitting this work. When inspiration was required, I was fortunate to have been able to call upon Professor Martin Kern, Christian Hubert, Roger Cohen, and John McPhee, who shared lessons from their craft and guidance on how to move forward.

I would like to acknowledge the enduring support I received from my friends and family: Dorka Bosker, Karen Brooks, Joey Foryste, Michael Goodall, Tak Inagaki, Bibi Lencek, Katrina Lencek-Inagaki, Misko Lencek-Inagaki, Nina and Rado Lencek, Ari Lovelace, Christine Miranda, Daphne Oz, Richard Pine, Tanya Supina, and Ali Sutherland-Brown, all of whom showed an indefatigable interest in China's remarkable simulacrascapes and my work. I am especially grateful to Matt Nguyen, whose patience knew no bounds, whose support has been unrivaled, and whose constructive criticism, manuscript reviews, and encouragement helped take this work over the finish line. Finally, I would like to acknowledge my parents, Lena Lencek and Gideon Bosker, for showing me the way with their own works, encouraging me to take risks, and reminding me that the trajectory from facts to story is a long, lonesome—sometimes even tortuous—road, but a road worth taking nevertheless.

1 INTO "THE LAND OF COURTLY ENJOYMENTS"

An Introduction to China's Architectural Mimicry

Within an astonishingly compressed term of two decades, China has catapulted its architectural universe years into a future in which the laws of physics no longer seem to hold: skyscrapers fold in half, buildings hover over water, and steel twists like silly putty. Architects have been breaking world records constructing mega-metropolises with the "greenest," biggest, fastest-built, tallest, and most daring structures on the planet. But while the centers of Chinese cities now flaunt cutting-edge style, engineering, and technology, the suburbs and satellite townships are giving way to an entirely different breed of architecture: not innovative but imitative and backward-looking. Chengdu, the capital of Sichuan Province, has constructed a residential complex for nearly two hundred thousand that is the twin of Dorchester, England, from its Poole Promenade down to the cobblestone paving on the streets. In the Yangtze River Delta, a 108-meter replica of the Eiffel Tower graces Champs Elysées Square in what has been branded the "Oriental Paris," a faithful reconstruction of Georges-Eugène Haussmann's City of Light. Shanghai officials devised a plan for "One City, Nine Towns" that calls for ringing the metropolis with ten satellite communities, each housing up to three hundred thousand and each built as a full-scale replica of a foreign city.

On the peripheries of its first-, second-, and third-tier cities, China appears to be inverting the paradigm of the "Middle Kingdom." While it once considered itself to be the center of the world, now China is making itself into the center that actually contains the world.

The suburbs of China's megalopolises, larger cities, and even smaller towns in provinces throughout the country—such as Beijing-Tianjin-Tangshan, Guangzhou-Hangzhou-Shenzhen, Anhui, and Sichuan (among many others)—are a surprising quilt of European and American Grand Tour destination sites. Tracts recently occupied by collective farms now boast sparkling versions of Paris, Venice, Amsterdam, London, Madrid, and New York. In homes, civic buildings, and government offices cast in historical revival styles from Europe and the United States, upwardly mobile Chinese go through the familiar paces of life in unfamiliar settings. Their alien homes are part of a

Overlooking the "Fountain of the Chariot of Apollo," a copy of a fountain at the Palace of Versailles at the Tianducheng development in Hangzhou. Beyond it, a replica of the Eiffel Tower punctuates the center of one of several housing areas in the development. Photograph by author.

mammoth trend of "duplitecture" that is striking both in the minuteness of its attention to detail and the ambitious scope of the replication. Western-style structures are found not in isolation, scattered throughout the existing urban fabric, but in dense and extensive themed communities that replicate identifiable Western prototypes. Entire townships and villages appear to have been airlifted from their historical and geographical foundations in England, France, Greece, the United States, and Canada and spot-welded to the margins of Chinese cities.

The target of the replication program goes beyond architecture and construction techniques. In fact, the agenda is all-encompassing: to re-create not only the superficial appearance of Western historical cities, but also the "feel"—the atmospheric and experiential local color—of the originals through such devices as foreign names, signage, and lifestyle amenities. In such communities, millions of China's new economic elite shop in markets selling Western foods, dine in Western restaurants, navigate streets bearing Western names, congregate in parks and squares with monuments to heroes of Western

culture, and celebrate festivals and holidays lifted from alien traditions. Hundreds of "theme park" suburbs—meticulously reconstructed versions of the most iconic cities of the West—now constitute an archipelago of the alien "other" within the geographically and historically integrated, coherently "Chinese" urban habitat. The Chinese housing industry has rewritten the capitalist real estate mantra "location, location, location" into the motto "replication, replication, replication."

    The comprehensiveness of these copies has elicited criticism and derision on the part of Western and Chinese intellectuals alike, whose instinct is frequently to reject these themed communities as "kitsch," "fake," "temporary," or "unimaginative and cliché."[1] But as this book will probe through analyses of these simulacra-spaces and the people within them, these themed landscapes should not be so easily dismissed. Far more than shelter, these homes are, in subtle but important ways, shaping the behavior of their occupants while also reflecting the achievements, dreams, and even anxieties of their inhabitants and creators.[2]

Gondolas are a common sight along man-made canals running through Venice Water Town, which takes its design inspiration from Italy's "Floating City." The pink, orange, and beige townhouses, with windows all framed by ogee arches and balconies framed by white balustrades, overlook bridges and cobblestoned streets lined with shops. Hangzhou. Photograph by author.

In the grip of a massive and comprehensive transition, the Chinese have seized on the iconography of Western architecture as a potent symbol for their ascension to—and aspiration for—global supremacy and the middle-class comforts of the "First World." They have selected Western, rather than indigenous, residential and suburban prototypes as their pragmatic solution to the problem of housing a swelling, newly affluent urban populace. Rich with implications for the political future of China, as well as its role and "national personality" in the global arena, the massive "knockoff" residential industry is emerging as a vibrant experimental frontier and a means of adapting to the opportunities and obstacles of China's new market economy. Sociologically, the Westernized homes and communities may well be the place where the gears of state mesh with the cogs of individual ambition, newly awakened consumer desire, and spirited bids for self-determination, at least in the arena of quotidian life.

This book is about these themed communities in China: the residential developments of the last two decades that replicate alien and anachronistic models targeted at Chinese home buyers and their place in the nation's modernization and globalization. This phenomenon will be examined from both historical and contemporary perspectives. It is historical in that these new communities—which will be referred to as "simulacrascapes"—are manifestations of cultural constants that include deeply rooted attitudes toward replication and a long-standing tradition of the imitative appropriation of the alien. The "culture of the copy" can be situated within traditional Chinese philosophy, value systems, and power relations. And this phenomenon is contemporary in that the architectural and urbanistic imitation will be examined in relation to the emergence of the "New China" and a new social order. It will be argued that it is, in part, within these communities that the Chinese are beginning to stage sites of "otherness" where a rising middle class lays claim to economic and cultural power and even incubates an embryonic political identity.

More, Bigger, Faster

The construction of life-sized themed enclaves has gained momentum since its initial development in the early 1990s, emerging as one of China's most popular and perplexing architectural trends. This breed of building initially took root in China's southern Special Economic Zones, catalyzed by new economic policies in the post-Reform era (1979–present) that restored private control over land use, established housing as a free-market commodity, and opened the nation to foreign investment, with initial real estate investors made up of Taiwanese and Hong Kong financiers, as well as overseas Chinese.[3]

The simulacra movement has grown in tandem with a threefold increase in the number of cities since the late 1970s.[4] In 2009, fully 45 percent of China's population, or about 570 million people, were estimated to be living in urban areas.[5] Residential construction, investment, and sales have likewise increased at a breakneck pace during the past two decades, fueled by economic reforms, the privatization of housing, cheap credit, and the increasing affluence of the Chinese. Twenty-eight billion square feet of new housing, equivalent to one-eighth the housing stock of the United States, was erected in 2003 alone, and the pace has not slowed since.[6] The total area of new residential construction has climbed steadily, increasing by nearly 16 percent year-on-year in 2009.[7] An estimated 40 percent of the world's cement and steel is consumed every year in new housing alone.[8] Annual expenditure on construction projects has also ballooned: in 2009, China's investment in the real estate industry swelled over 16 percent to 3.6 trillion RMB.[9]

An expansive display of model homes in the Weimar Villas community stands at the center of a salesroom in Anting Town. A combination of villas, townhouses, and high-rises surrounds the town center, which includes a chapel, commercial units, and a school. Shanghai. Photograph by author.

Consumers have kept pace, taking advantage of increased income and loosened credit to snap up newer, larger, and more luxurious homes. China's Ministry of Construction estimates that by the end of 2005, 80 percent of urban Chinese owned their homes.[10] The average per capita housing space for urban Chinese has more than tripled in the past twenty years, from less than eight square meters in the early 1980s to over twenty-eight square meters in 2008.[11] Even amid the turmoil that struck the international financial markets in 2008, government statistics indicate China's residential property sales jumped around 80 percent to approximately 3.8 trillion RMB in 2009,[12] as individual home mortgage lending rose nearly 50 percent over the previous year.[13] Real estate prices have been increasing no less quickly: the average cost of a home has more than doubled since 2003, from around 2,212 RMB per square meter to 4,518 RMB per square meter in 2009.[14]

Significant portions of China's billions upon billions of square feet of new housing are contained within enclaves modeled on Western sites. In 2003, 70 percent of Beijing property developments emphasized Western architectural motifs, according to market research conducted at the time.[15] Li Yan, a designer with China's largest real estate developer, China Vanke, estimates that in 2008 the firm built approximately two-thirds of its residential properties in a European theme.[16] Real estate advertising and industry events directed to the newly affluent confirm the dominant position of these "fantasy" residences. Wallpapering the thoroughfares of Chinese cities, billboards advertising local residential developments are all but exclusively dedicated to airbrushed renderings of velvet and chandelier-bedecked living rooms and coax with promises of "royal living" in "the land of courtly enjoyment" or "the experience of seaside life of California in

A billboard in Beijing advertising a new residential development trumpets, "We will never be second." Photograph courtesy of Yan Zhang.

America."[17] Housing fairs, bustling expositions where developers promote their real estate, are carpeted with booths showcasing miniature dioramas of "Spanish" apartment complexes, "Mediterranean" villas, and "Rococo" townhouses.

Originality in Replication

To be sure, architectural mimicry often goes hand in hand with periods of cultural change, and comparable exercises in imitation are not unique to China. Japan produced its own collection of Western-style developments, such as Huis ten Bosch in Nagasaki Prefecture, a theme park opened in 1992 with an adjacent residential area that includes full-scale replicas of Dutch buildings such as Queen Beatrix's palace.[18] Indonesia, Cambodia, Singapore, Egypt, the United Arab Emirates, and other rapidly developing nations are likewise experimenting with using Western architectural and structural paradigms to construct their own themed residential suburbs.

Moreover, these contemporary "plagiarists" are only the latest in an ancient and venerable line of borrowers from the archive of historical architectural styles. Within the last three centuries alone, Russians, Americans, and Emiratis, among others, have shown a penchant for cross cultural "code switching" in architecture. In the United States, for example, immigrants, driven by nostalgia for their homelands and by a desire for ready-made cultural markers of status and gravitas, became exceptionally adept at transplanting European townscapes to the new continent. The nineteenth century saw revivalist architecture blossom in the Hudson River Valley outside New York City, where wealthy landowners such as the Rockefellers sought to fashion the "Rhine of America."[19] They drew their inspiration from Dutch city dwellings, Spanish monasteries, Italian piazzas, and English Gothic designs.[20] To showcase their industrial, agricultural, and scientific prowess, Americans selected Greek and Roman templates, as in the case of a full-scale replica of the Parthenon constructed in Nashville for Tennessee's Centennial Exposition in 1897. Several decades later, in the 1910s and 1920s, American colleges and universities, including Princeton and Yale, modeled their scholarly utopias on the Gothic architecture of Britain's Oxford and Cambridge Universities in order to convey their parity with England's oldest and most respected centers of learning.[21] More recently, in 2002, developer Fred Milani built a full-size copy of the White House, itself based on the British Georgian style, in Atlanta, Georgia.[22] And just as the Chinese reference foreign locales in the names of their developments, so too did Americans call their cities, towns, and roads after foreign notables and landmarks. "Deities, places, famous personalities

of the ancient Greek, Roman, and biblical world"
lent their names to towns in upstate New York such
as Ithaca, Rome, Troy, Pompey, Homer, Aurelius,
Athens, and Cicero.[23]

While the device of architectural and urban
mimicry is typologically not unique, the uses to
which it is put by a given culture at a given time
are often distinctive in the sense that they satisfy a
specific set of symbolic and pragmatic agendas and
are symptomatic of shifts in the "deep" structure
of the society in which they circulate. What might
distinguish China's current and fervid simulacra-
building movement? This book proceeds from

The Breakers, Cornelius
Vanderbilt II's Italian Renaissance
style mansion (completed
1895). Newport, Rhode Island.
Photograph by author.

the paradoxical premise that in the way it copies the West, contemporary China
manifests its tremendous originality. This originality stems, first of all, from historical
precedent in theory and in practice. The ontological status and value of the copy in
China differ substantively from corresponding Western notions. The copy in China is
not stigmatized, as it is in the West, and this lack of stigma is manifested in a number of
cultural institutions and practices and is supported by a philosophical system.

China's simulacrascapes are also differentiated by the foreign origins of the
originals from which they take inspiration. While cultures commonly appropriate alien
architectural and urbanistic schemes to serve nostalgic or prestige functions, historically
they tend to borrow from within the same civilizational matrix with which they identify.
In the United States, for example, the "fakes" have been based on Anglo-Saxon (British
Tudor, Queen Anne, Gothic), Mediterranean, or Teutonic models and the architectural
styles and morphologies of peoples who share the same geocultural genealogy. The
United States has yet to produce on American soil full-scale residential communities that
replicate Thai villages or Chinese *siheyuan* courtyard homes. The various "Chinatowns,"
"Germantowns," and "Little Italies" that do exist in many American cities are the
products of immigration, rather than imitation, and reflect the cultural roots and
traditions of their primary residents. Similarly, the Beaux Arts or Art Deco enclaves
in East Asian cities, for instance, were the product of Occidental colonial settlement
and were not intended to house the indigenous colonized subjects. By contrast, in
contemporary China, the dominant target of appropriation for residential enclaves
housing the Chinese is a geopolitically, temporally, and culturally alien and remote
civilization. This drawing on "another's" past, then, appears to be one peculiarly Chinese
approach to housing its indigenous population or, more precisely, certain segments of its
own population.

Dutch colonial style townhouses, with commercial space on the ground floors and windmills just beyond, line a main street in Holland Village dotted with planters containing plastic tulips. Shanghai. Photograph by author.

Another distinctive feature is the sheer number of these "alien" simulacrascapes and the proportion of the total new housing stock that they represent. Where other nations—India, the United Arab Emirates (UAE), or Japan, for instance—may have only a handful of themed developments for the ultra rich, China has billions of square feet dedicated to such projects, some already completed and others under construction, offered in a range of price-points that make ownership accessible to the increasingly economically nuanced emerging middle class. "The aggressiveness with which these [architectural] issues are playing out, the number of projects that you see, and the unprecedented pace of all these phenomena are what distinguishes China," argues urbanist and historian Thomas Campanella, an associate professor at the University of North Carolina.[24] Fueled by rapid economic growth, a population of over 1.3 billion, and a muscular government apparatus, China's importation of "prestige" historical architecture from the West is occurring on an unprecedented scale.

In its present iteration, the originality of these landscapes consists also in the novel circumstances of the historical moment in which this architectural mimicry is occurring. Specifically, China is seeking to reposition itself within a dynamically changing world in which forces of economic consolidation and interrelation, environmental degradation, and technological advance are accelerating global interdependence, redrawing the balance of power among the superpowers, and redefining notions of economic, political, and strategic superiority. The technology available to China for copying alien lifestyles is unprecedented: it has the mechanical and infrastructural capability to create cities virtually overnight. It has the financial resources to underwrite massive housing projects, recruit foreign consultants, and import expensive materials. It has a powerful government able and willing to support urban planning projects of extraordinary scales. And it has a client base for these simulacrascapes—a growing middle class that includes a population of between 100 million and 247 million consumers and that is projected to encompass 40 percent of China's total population by 2020. (Estimates for the size of China's "middle stratum" vary depending on base income for the middle class, which the National Bureau of Statistics has pegged at between 60,000 and 500,000 RMB per year).[25] With one of the highest savings rates of any major country and an ever-expanding group of over 300,000 millionaires, this fiscally robust client base increasingly has the resources to invest in the new-style housing.[26]

A Tradition of Cross-Cultural Exchange

Within Chinese civilization, architectural mimicry is only one manifestation of cross-cultural fertilization. As one of the world's key manufacturers of consumer goods, the New China not only produces but also vigorously and energetically re-produces everything from high-end couture to cutting-edge electronics and patented pharmaceuticals.[27] But while the massive scale on which China is in the business of intercultural brokering may be peculiar to the post-Mao era, the phenomenon itself is characteristic to all periods of Chinese history, even the "isolationist" Mao years.

For thousands of years, since the country's earliest interactions with Western merchants along the Silk Road beginning in the second century BCE or Jesuit priests on missions in China in the sixteenth and seventeenth centuries, China has engaged in robust exchanges of goods, technologies, and ideas with the West, selectively taking inspiration from foreigners for everything from dishware to dwellings. Through the centuries, China's architecture has provided a continuous record of Western influence, starting with Han dynasty period (206 BCE–220 CE) tombs, which scholars have speculated show the traces of Roman architecture.[28] Sometimes, the impetus for cross-cultural fertilization originated with the Chinese themselves. This was the case, for instance, during the early years of the People's Republic, when Mao Zedong invited

Soviet architects, artists, writers, and planners to help design "Red China."[29] At other times, as in the aftermath of the Opium Wars, foreigners imposed their architectural traditions on the Middle Kingdom.

Starting in the sixteenth century, the Chinese had already begun to selectively adopt certain scientific methods from the West. Dynastic officials were interested in the innovations but often reluctant to welcome the technology of the "foreign devils," which they feared might undermine ideologies that served as the basis for imperial authority. But following China's defeat at the hands of the British in the First Opium War (1839–1842), the doors to the once-isolationist Middle Kingdom were flung open to the West, and the trickle of Western ideas, settlers, and goods turned into a flood. Before long, the influence of foreigners was writ large on the urban plan and buildings of China, particularly in the country's concession territories. Under the Treaty of Nanjing, signed in 1842, the British gained access to five Treaty Ports (Xiamen, Fuzhou, Ningbo, Shanghai, and Shamian Island), which they could use for foreign residence and trade. The European settlers imported their own approaches to urban planning—applying Western standards for population densities, street layouts, spatial orientation, and building forms—that resulted in neighborhoods with an urban fabric completely distinct from the traditional Chinese city. Qingdao and Tianjin were among the foreign concessions in China controlled by European powers during the nineteenth and early twentieth centuries, and the architectural DNA of these locales still records the presence of the Westerners, who brought with them churches, alien planning principles, and neoclassical design.

During the early years of the "Mao Era" (1949–1976), Mao Zedong and his young government developed close ties with the ideologically compatible Soviet Union and invited consultants to become intimately involved with the planning of Chinese cities. The architecture of the Soviet Union was "seen in China as an appropriate way of celebrating the socialist revolution and a newfound sense of nationalism. . . . Some prominent buildings . . . were even designed by Russian architects."[30] Until the chill in Sino-Soviet relations in the early 1960s, China took a great deal of its urban planning and architectural cues from the Soviet Union. Over eleven thousand Russian advisers, particularly those with technical knowledge, arrived in China to share their expertise with the new socialist society, and more than thirty-seven thousand Chinese traveled to the Soviet Union for training, especially in technical disciplines.[31]

Between the bookends of the Han dynasty's integration of Roman architectural elements, and the Maoist adoption of Soviet neoclassicism and concrete apartment blocks, China has a long-standing tradition of appropriating alien architecture. Although familiarity with Western building forms informs China's choice of a replication model, it is only one factor contributing to the current movement in architectural mimicry.

The Euro- and America-centric orientation of China's residential communities signals a rupture with both traditional indigenous housing design and the most recent socialist residential typologies. It also—and more suggestively—represents a marked departure from China's previous engagements with foreign architecture on home terrain. Unlike earlier examples of architectural appropriation, the copycat communities of the present take the incorporation of Western design to new extremes.

Chateau Zhang Laffitte, Zhang Yuchen's $50 million replica of the Château Maisons-Laffitte, was constructed using over ten thousand photographs of the seventeenth-century castle and the same Chantilly stone used in the French original. Beijing. Photograph by Ophelia Chong.

The "epigonic" architecture of the past is characterized by more selective and partial appropriation of Western typologies and styles. By contrast, the contemporary examples of architectural mimicry duplicate both discrete buildings or building types and the very communities within which these were originally embedded. In addition, the current wave of appropriations is distinguished by its anachronisms. While earlier appropriations strove to emulate the most advanced architectural motifs, the simulacrascapes of the present draw on historical Western styles. For example, Holland Village (Shanghai) and Venice Water Town (Hangzhou) specifically focus on mimicry as a conscious and deliberate antiquarianism. They duplicate European sites that enshrine the past. Moreover, these Western forms, as opposed to, say, the French concessions in Shanghai or Tianjin, were built by and for the Chinese, not for overseas Europeans. Although the first Western-style communities in post-Reform China were initially aimed at foreign expatriates, since the late 1990s these residences have enjoyed a surge in popularity among Chinese consumers, who are now able to afford and eager to acquire these homes. The residential developments considered in this analysis will be those targeted at, and inhabited by, local Chinese rather than foreigners.

Beyond "Backward"

Despite the nation's history of cross-cultural exchange, these latest manifestations of Western form have not been wholeheartedly accepted. Within China itself, opinion on the merits and value of these simulacra is divided. The Chinese intellectual elite—the nation's more progressive urban planners, scholars, architects, and journalists—have followed these developments with confusion, criticism, controversy, and no small amount of disbelief. Tong Ming, a professor of architecture at Tongji University puzzles, "Why should we have foreign styles in these new towns? Why not Chinese? It's not a good feeling for some Chinese people, primarily those from cultural fields and intellectuals."[32] In an article on urbanization in China, journalist Zhou Jian remarks that in the case of "French-style" and "British-style" garden cities, logic and reason do not seem to factor into decision making and that these "theme park" habitats not only leave observers feeling befuddled, but also, more important, fail to take into account Chinese citizens' lifestyle needs.[33]

Fountains line the entrance to the English County development in Kunshan, which boasts to potential residents that its homes incorporate "classical English architectural concepts." Photograph from SouFun.com.

Unable to decipher a rationale for a vision that seems anathema to the modernizing impulses that drive so much of Chinese urban planning, Chinese and foreign observes alike have criticized and even ridiculed these residential "theme parks." The writers of *Urban China* magazine dismiss the theme-towns as manifestations of "trash culture."[34] The journal *Shanghai and Hong Kong Economy* describes British-style Thames Town, in Shanghai, as a "controversial landmark" and criticizes these theme-towns as representing a failure to cultivate a local architectural dialect and slavishly imitating the West at the expense of local culture.[35] "A lot of people were quite against such an idea [building developments in a European style]," observes Tong.[36] Indeed, the *Architectural Journal* discusses the controversy simulacra-building projects have generated among architects and townspeople, who frown on the theme-towns for imitating Western identities instead of creating their own and examines how city planners have grappled with the problem of ensuring that these developments had a suitably recognizably Western feel.[37] Many architects working in China say that despite being consistently approached to design themed "fantasyscapes," they decline the commissions. "Life is too short to be copying someone else's work," says architect Rossana Hu of Neri and Hu Design. "We refuse to do these copycat types of designs."[38]

To Western observers, these communities appear quaint and droll at best and kitschy and sinister at worst. To architect Alex Chu, a partner at the firm Enclave, this themed architecture is "silly" and "uninspired," while K. M. Tan of Shanghai's KUU Architects dismisses it as "backward," "inauthentic," and "insecure."[39] *Washington Post* architecture critic Phillip Kennicott deems it "terrifying."[40] Yet these homes, which have been embraced by developers, policymakers, and home buyers alike, merit more nuanced and balanced scrutiny. Far from "trash culture" and "unenlightened" imitations, to many Chinese these freshly minted, stylistically alien communities can be read as "ultra modern" and connoting progress. [41]

The simulacrascapes represent an enigmatic complex of meanings. For all their prominence and pervasiveness, China's "theme park" residential communities have received little critical attention outside of documentation and descriptions of their physical properties and economic underpinnings.

A large bell tower stands at the entrance to the Mediterranean-style Goya development in Hangzhou. The community is landscaped with palm trees, colorful mosaics, and terracotta tiles. Photograph by author.

Considering their scope and cost, the footprints these projects have made, and the impact they have on the quotidian experiences of ever-growing numbers of Chinese, it is valuable to deconstruct the drivers, semiotics, and telos of what may be among one of the most mass-based architectural exercises of the present.

Analyzing the Neuro-Architectural Matrix

In an attempt to decipher the origins and implications of these simulacrascapes, this book will draw on architectural theory and criticism, historical attitudes toward imitation in China, and original, on-site research at the themed towns. Information about these themed developments, which consists of marketing materials, details on sales and prices, urban master plans, house designs, blueprints, and prospectuses about community life, was collected on multiple visits to these sites between July 2006 and October 2008. Descriptions and analysis of these environments are based, in part, on photo documentation undertaken during these visits and in-depth interviews with employees and residents of these towns; developers, architects, and officials who played an integral role in the execution of these projects; and informed analysts and observers, including university professors, architects, journalists, and critics.

In order to account for the generators, precedents, and purpose of China's "derivative" communities, this book will investigate these issues within the framework of four overlapping contexts: (1) the indigenous Chinese tradition of replicating alien landscapes and iconic elements in multiple formats; (2) the architectural and cultural manifestations of Westernization in the themed towns; (3) the marriage of pragmatic and symbolic determinants that gave rise to these developments; and (4) the sociopolitical implications of these transplanted territories, as well as what these themed communities reveal about the makeup of the twenty-first-century "Chinese dream." With this itinerary through China's urban, historical, and cultural landscapes, it will be demonstrated that while the forms in these simulacrascapes may be foreign, the desired functions are indigenous and driven by autochthonous demands, both functional and symbolic. These theme-towns stem from a confluence of social, philosophical, economic, and political forces unique to China and, in this way, capture and reflect the essence of contemporary China.

The next chapter examines Chinese attitudes toward duplication and traces the evolution of replicated landscapes in China from the imperial parks of the Han dynasty through the private gardens of the Qing (1644–1912). From an exploration of the form and function of these man-made replicas of alien locales, parallels between past and present simulacrascapes emerge, suggesting novel ways of viewing these theme-towns.

For the Chinese, the culture of the copy has a distinct value. The West, on the other hand, has embraced the "culture of the original" in the modern era, trusting the original as legitimate and connoting technological supremacy while rejecting the copy, which is viewed as inferior, tainted, and subversive. As will be argued, Chinese philosophical systems have conferred a different sense of the worth of the copy and the original, one that offers insight into how architectural imitation emerged. Though originality is prized, at the same time replication is not only permitted, but also praised as testament to cultural and technological achievement. This cultural esteem for the copy is rooted in the cyclical imperial worldview, in Zen cosmology, and in imperial politics. The stylistic choices for replication are alien and anachronistic (i.e., European historicist idioms of architecture), but the impulse to re-create the past and duplicate the alien is deeply Chinese. China's traditional perspectives on the replication of the alien have, even in the present day, fostered a permissive climate for such copycat constructions.

Chapter 3 analyzes representative theme-towns from provinces throughout China in order to illustrate how the Western character is adopted and incorporated into the

landscape. As will be discussed, these foreign enclaves rely on urban planning principles, architecture, landscaping, promotional materials, and controlled consumer processes to create a credible Western themescape. China's developments emulate many of the design principles of theme parks, such as their being organized around "closed spaces . . . with controlled access," presenting "atmospheric forms of entertainment (musicians, characters or actors who perform in the streets 'free of charge')," having an "important commercial vocation (fundamentally food and beverages and shops)," and containing "one or more themed areas."[42]

But at the same time, China's themed communities are designed as permanent homes to hundreds of thousands of Chinese, who here raise children, wash cars, cook dinners, and live out their daily routines. What is distinctive is the extent to which the planned communities immerse their residents in alien lifestyles, alien values, and alien quotidian rituals. The chapter investigates how the transformative remodeling of the home and the communal setting for the rituals and rites of domestic life produce

A re-creation of the Amsterdam Central Station, which has since been demolished, stood near a windmill located in the town square of New Amsterdam in Shenyang. Photograph by Eli Dickison.

The Shanghai Minhang People's Court courthouse takes its inspiration from both the U.S. Capitol and the White House. Photograph by Gao Bo.

an urban theater in which the residents are coaxed into constructing a new Chinese identity. By so doing, the themed communities serve an important function of inculcating "global" urban behavioral modes and norms in a population fresh from the isolationist cultures of a discarded socialism.

Chapter 4 probes the motivations driving the construction of these new towns. It does not attempt to reduce these to a single, global catalyst but instead delves into a matrix of heterogeneous contributing factors, both pragmatic and symbolic. This chapter explores the proposition that China's simulacrascapes represent a stage in the nation's transition from imitative to innovative. In resorting to Western building forms, the Chinese have found a solution that allows them to both meet the challenges of urbanization and capitalism and learn from the architectural expertise of the West.

These factors, however, are only half the story. What may seem on the surface as a form of self-colonization or "West worship" is actually, to the Chinese, an assertion of China's supremacy. Symbolically, these themed communities are perceived

Brightly colored paint, wrought iron balconies, and white columns lend a European air to the Baroque-style townhouses at the San Carlos community in Shanghai. Photograph by author.

as monuments to the nation's wealth and technological prowess and as markers of its progress since the days of Maoist communism. As such, they encapsulate a key cultural narrative: they signal China's phenomenal ability to catch up to and surpass the West and to establish itself as a First World power.

Chapter 5 investigates how these copycat communities offer evidence of China's "residential revolution"—the nation's transition from a top-down to a bottom-up, consumer-driven system. They testify to the economic empowerment of the increasingly affluent Chinese, who, for the first time in decades—if not ever—are able to choose, rather than to submit to, the dictates of a ruling cadre or the force of tradition and who have won a measure of freedom and the means to shape an individual identity.

Chapter 5 also chronicles the dream of the "good life" that has a Western hearth at its heart. China's bureaucrats have extolled the nation's "peaceful rise"—but what does this rise look and feel like for China's hundreds of millions of homeowners? How does it play out in the domestic sphere? These Westernized enclaves provide a more intimate, individualized perspective into what China's increasing wealth and status have meant for the lifestyles and aspirations of its populace. For the Chinese consumer searching for ways to display wealth and sophistication, the Western brand has cachet, and Western consumer culture has come to stand as a marker of progress, civility, and prestige. Through interviews, profiles, and notes from visits to the homes of residents in the themed developments, a composite narrative of the domestic life within the Western-style enclaves will be constructed. The perspective of the Chinese homeowners in these communities deepens and complicates our understanding of the rationale for and future of China's Westernized landscapes.

Although China's themed enclaves are, broadly speaking, economically homogeneous (to afford residence in these Westernized developments homeowners must have, at a minimum, attained a "middle-class" income), the residents come from a diverse array of backgrounds, professions, and geographies. They are professional ping-pong players, factory owners, professors, bankers, government officials, architects, lawyers, and interior decorators, hailing from a variety of locales. Some have fully grown children, others are rearing toddlers, and still others have only recently entered the workforce. Residents in the more expensive enclaves tend to be slightly older, but young couples are an equally common sight within these stylized communities. For many, these homes are second residences—often serving as weekend getaways—and a good number of residents profess to have visited or lived abroad.

Unavoidable Obfuscations

Anyone studying complex social phenomena in today's China inevitably encounters nation-specific obstacles to the search for answers. Some of these—such as the lack of transparency in official and private sectors—are endemic to China. Others—such as self-interest, chauvinism, and the importance of "saving face"—must always be reckoned as potentially contributing to bias in the responses of sources. Given the great number of actors involved in these complex projects, from developers and investors to landowners and bureaucrats, the competing, often conflicting, agendas that emerge in their stories resist being distilled into a single, coherent, and internally consistent narrative. Finally, the full significance, meaning, and implications of these developments have yet to ripen with the passage of time. At present, many of these developments are too new to have played out the nuances of their impact; the depth of their significance; and the dimensions of their cultural, political, and economic ramifications. As of this writing, of those communities that are complete, some are still ghost towns, empty stage sets, snapped up by eager speculators waiting for residents to animate them. Still others, despite having attracted a bustling community of full-time residents, are too new to have attained their projected maturity. For these reasons, there is a greater focus on the roots than the fruit of the phenomenon and only speculation regarding the future direction and significance of these simulacra communities.

It remains for the future to tackle a number of crucial and deeply important questions: How will living in a replica of Germany or Beverly Hills affect Chinese citizens and their lifestyles? Will this trend continue into the future, or is it a passing fad? How will history treat the simulacra townships? Will the popularity of these foreign building types choke the growth of a national, distinctly Chinese, architectural style—or will it inspire it?

The current state of knowledge about these simulacrascapes may not be sufficient to allow for more than tentative hypotheses about their long-term effect on China. But from seeking to understand these developments from the "front end"—by investigating what they look like, what they mean, and how they relate to China's traditional culture, history, philosophy, and politics—we can come closer to demystifying a significant phenomenon in the daily lives of the world's newest—and oldest—superpower.

2 THE FASCINATION WITH *FAUX*

Philosophical and Theoretical Drivers of Architectural Reproduction in China

Towers and terraces emerge from the piled-up flowers,
The entire universe hides in a single seed.[1]

The "authentic" and the "fake" are categories that face off against each other in philosophically and culturally complex ways. Their definitions and distinctions vacillate, depending on the vantage point from which they are considered: idealist or empirical, psychological or anthropological, esthetic or ethical. Some societies lay great stock by these distinctions; the same societies, at different periods of their development, may be blind to their differences or find them irrelevant in various ways. As critic Lionel Trilling suggests in his cultural history of "authenticity," the concept acquires an ontological status or comes to be equated with "the real" and "the real" with "the original" rather late in the history of the West, emerging at the transition from medieval to modern culture.[2] Meanwhile, China has long had its own classification system for copyworks, one that handles different types of replication, from "tracings" to "imitations," in distinct ways depending on the meaning, manner of execution, and value of each form.[3]

Articulating the distinctions between the "authentic," in the sense of the "original," and the "fake," or the "copy" or "simulacrum," is central to determining the motivations that drive the conception and execution of China's themed residential landscapes. With a preliminary understanding of the premiums and cachet that are potentially embodied in "counterfeited" environments, it is possible to fully appreciate the benefits and collateral power that champions of these contemporary Chinese "theme cities" might have anticipated from their venture into architectural duplication.

Deciphering China's contemporary architectural laboratory, with its focus on replicating the alien, requires that we first define the terms and lexicon that will be used to analyze this phenomenon. What should we appropriately call these structures and communities? What is their aesthetic status and value? Should they be stigmatized as fakes? Celebrated as careful copies? As Wen Fong, professor emeritus at Princeton

University, notes in his essay "The Problem of Forgeries in Chinese Painting," the Chinese distinguish among several different forms of "forgeries," employing discrete terms to describe each one. The Chinese copywork system, Fong writes, differentiates among "*mu*, to trace; *lin*, to copy; *fang*, to imitate; *tsao*, to invent."[4] Tracing aims to "produce an exact replica of the original."[5] A copy is looser, and, as Fong notes, a Sung critic likens it to "a wild goose which flies along with its companion."[6] An imitation is more of an "adaptation." An "invention," likened to a pastiche, has the impression of "creative inspiration and wild abandon" but, upon further reflection, appears "confused and exaggerated," "devoid of any true emotion," and plagued by a "strange feeling of contradiction."[7] In the Chinese framework, forms of "forgeries" lie along a spectrum, with each "category of copy" produced, received, and valued in its own way. To be certain, China's architects are not alone in duplicating forms: Chinese filmmakers, artists, and writers are also engaged in repurposing ideas and models, "adapting" earlier works to suit their purpose. Yet what sets apart China's "imitation" communities is, to a large extent, a matter of degree: they are not "freehand copies" (*lin*) but more developed "forgeries."

Bearing these distinctions among *mu*, *lin*, *fang*, and *tsao* in mind, this study adopts the term "simulacrum" to designate the residential communities in China that model themselves on historical Occidental prototypes. The term, to be sure, comes with its own baggage of associations but will be found to be most amenable for the phenomena under consideration, not only because it defines the Chinese communities relationally in a way that always implies the prior existence of a phenomenon to which the Chinese residential unit relates, but also because it suggests a competition between two autonomous systems, each claiming superiority by virtue of its own standards of excellence. The term, which has its origins in the late Middle Ages, was initially used to describe religious icons believed to embody great functional potency. Since the late 1980s, Western postmodern theory has engaged the concept of simulated space as a novel phenomenon. Such topics as the "hyperreal" and "simulacrum" have been in vogue among Western postmodernists, who claim we have entered a "borderless age" in which meaning, identity, and reality hover on the verge of extinction.[8] The arguments of these theorists have informed central concepts, such as the "simulacrum," with new meanings and potency. Each of these words is charged with distinct connotations, and, as noted, the meaning of "simulacrum" is especially nettlesome. Is the Chinese construction of a "fake" Britain or Germany just another example of the hyperreal, à la Disneyland, or the wax museums the Italian humanist Umberto Eco visited on his search for the "Absolute Fake" in the United States?

Understanding the postmodernist argument can bring us closer toward understanding the significance of the Chinese experiment in city making because the postmodern analysis of the relationship and intersection between "what is original" and "what is derived from the original"—or "what came first" and "what is *faux*"—shares several key elements with the philosophical perspectives promulgated by ancient Chinese belief structures. The proposition that the authentic and its reproduction run fluid is not novel but dates at least as far back as the fifth century, when Chinese scholars, artists, and philosophers began to offer compelling arguments in support of replicating landscapes. Their views helped shape what would become a tradition of landscape re-creation that has been documented as early as the Han dynasty in the form of royal hunting parks.

As New York University professor of fine arts Jonathan Hay observes, because elements of Chinese belief structures have remained consistent over time, many of the principles that underlie these systems of thought are applicable to modern thinking.[9] According to Hay, the Chinese tradition has been consistently "reprocessing" itself, giving an elastic quality to its historical evolution.[10] And while historical analysis has revealed these traditional belief systems and narratives of the past to be far more complex than allowed by conventional accounts, certain principles persist and may inform present perspectives. Is it possible that long-standing attitudes about creating simulacrum landscapes have not disappeared but rather have evolved to better suit contemporary pressures and needs? Although Chinese philosophical conceptions have morphed considerably over time, the classical Chinese thinking on landscape re-creation represents a valuable portal for analyzing contemporary events.

The lens through which the Chinese have viewed these replicated micro-territories, combined with their explicit endorsement of replication as providing experiences that foster "communion" with the power and spirit of the authentic, is crucial to understanding how and why such projects as the theme-towns may exist at all. Moreover, these are fundamental to mapping the difference between the Western "historicist" or "ethnic" architectural stylization and its Eastern iteration. While not positing a definite and direct link between ancient traditions and contemporary practices, this argument submits that at the very least, these classical Chinese beliefs illuminate the philosophical and perceptual infrastructure that has created a cultural climate that is permissive with respect to the replication of alien prototypes and that is uniquely hospitable to the unprecedented explorations into simulacrum construction taking place in the present day.

Philosophy of Fakery

For Jean Baudrillard, Frederic Jameson, Umberto Eco, and other theoreticians of the simulacrum, transformations in both the physical and virtual spaces of the twentieth and twenty-first centuries have merited a closer examination of how—

or whether it is even possible—to distinguish between an "original" and its perfect "copy." These scholars argue that world cultures have entered an age in which the technological prowess that permits the generation of copies virtually indistinguishable from the originals is producing a dissolution of borders, identities, and distinctive markers of authenticity. Marxist political theorist Frederic Jameson notes the present postmodern age is defined by a "new depthlessness, which finds its prolongation both in contemporary 'theory' and in a whole new culture of the image or simulacrum."[11] Fashion designer Yoji Yamamoto observes in Wim Wenders's 1989 documentary *Notebook on Cities and Clothes*, "With the electronic and digital . . . the very notion of original [becomes] obsolete. Everything is a copy. All distinctions have become arbitrary. Identity is out, out of fashion."[12]

Baudrillard, Eco, and philosopher Gilles Deleuze are among the theorists who have proposed that the simulacrum, also known as the "hyperreal," copies the real so completely and exactly as to nullify the distinction between the two. In other words, the simulacrum, for all intents and purposes, stands in as a substitute for the real. "Simulation threatens the difference between 'true' and 'false,' between 'real' and 'imaginary,'" writes Baudrillard.[13] Postmodernist theorists consider the simulacrum to be a contemporary phenomenon that is the product of a world characterized by a breakdown in distinctions between literal and figurative borders and by the interchangeability of signs that denote the original and the derivative. The consequences of this competition reach into all areas of contemporary experience. Baudrillard, for one, finds this unsettling because it implies that something "catastrophic" has occurred and that a major disruption has fractured the continuum that extends from the real to the fake. This disruption has upended the traditional concept of the world as a system with absolute markers of the "real," and "reality has imploded into the undecidable proximity of hyperreality."[14] The note of panic and even hysteria in Baudrillard's observation arises from his fear that the simulacrum thrusts us to the verge of meaninglessness, which is to say, chaos: moral, legal, economic, social, and political. Postmodernist theorists ask, "How are we to maintain our laws and uphold order when there is no difference between actual behavior and simulated behavior? How do we know what is real if the image of the simulacrum is the same as the image of the real?" Baudrillard is sounding the alarm that we teeter on an unsteady precipice, on the verge of collapsing into a messy imbroglio of twisted meanings and uncertain authenticities given that "illusion is no longer possible, because the real is no longer possible."[15]

This Occidental anxiety about the emergence of the simulacrum needs to be factored into the responses of Western observers and critics to the proliferation of "fakes" in China. With Chinese factories churning out copies of Western designer fashion, films, technology, prescription drugs, art, and architecture, the world is being flooded with products that continually challenge the consumer not only to detect difference, but also to consider why the distinction between the real and the fake might even be meaningful. The proliferation of a universe of simulacra, made possible by technological advances that are unprecedented in human experience, destabilizes such sacrosanct and foundational notions as national supremacy, status, ownership, and priority. All this is profoundly disquieting and might go some way toward explaining the discomfort—expressed as condescension, dismissal, or mockery—that Western observers register in the presence of the simulacra towns in China.

A second possible reason for the perception that the simulacrum exercises an unsettling subversive effect is suggested by Eco. When he visited Walt Disney's theme parks in the 1970s, he speculated that our pleasure might derive, among other things, from the fact that "we not only enjoy a perfect imitation, we also enjoy the conviction that imitation has reached its apex and afterwards reality will always be inferior to it."[16] The key point that is relevant to this discussion is not the hedonistic element that Eco finds in the visit to the theme park, but rather his identifying this pleasure with what might be seen as a Promethean moment in the creation of a perfect copy. The engineering of a flawless simulacrum represents an advance of culture above nature, human ingenuity over the "felt fact" of a recalcitrant material world. In this respect, the generation of perfect copies of Western achievements—be they in the realm of architecture, urbanism, fashion, or pharmacology—can serve as a potent symbol of the civilizational superiority of the "counterfeiters." To be able to make a perfect copy is to be able to take control of the world.

Counterfeiting, Copying, and Qi

The West, committed to the "culture of the original," regards the copy as a marker of creative and technological inferiority, stamped with dishonesty and consequently anarchic, subversive, and threatening to the status quo that equates power, legitimacy, ownership, and order with originality. This position vis-à-vis the "double" has not always held true. Historically, the market value of the "original" emerges during the Industrial Revolution in response to the birth of a technology that facilitated reproduction, as well as the philosophical and aesthetic ideology of Romanticism, with its premium on originality.[17] In the wake of such cultural shifts, the "paternity" of objects, ideas, and buildings is deeply valued and is enshrined in the institution of the copyright and a legal mechanism for establishing and protecting the prestige and authority of the "original."

But do the Chinese buy into this cosmology of priority? It has been argued that the Chinese worldview holds a different opinion of the relationship and relative value of the original and the copy. "Art forgery in China has never carried such dark connotations as it does in the West," Fong observes. Certainly, "originality"—synthesizing tradition and innovation to transform models and "produce something unprecedented"—has great value in China too.[18] Yet concurrently, the ability to render a good copy has, historically, been taken by the Chinese as a marker of technological and cultural superiority, and the coexistence of an original and its virtually indistinguishable double does not trigger the ontological crisis that is characteristic of the West. For example, the evolution of *shanzhai* culture in contemporary China reflects the skill and zeal with which the Chinese replicate, as well as the widespread tolerance for the practice. The term, which translated literally means "mountain fortress," refers to the production of counterfeit name-brand goods, from cars to television shows, apparel to electronics, that often offer features the originals lack (there are *shanzhai* versions of Apple's iPhone called the "HiPhone" and "SciPhone"). Though some authorities have expressed concern with intellectual property issues, these copycats are hardly taboo. "Once a term used to suggest something cheap or inferior, *shanzhai* now suggests to many a certain Chinese cleverness and ingenuity," Sky Canaves and Juliet Ye note in the *Wall Street Journal*.[19] The director of China's National Copyright Administration, Liu Binjie, even praises *shanzhai* as a practice that "fits a market need" in China and is "a sign of the cultural creativity of the common people."[20] Furthermore, in *The Future of the Past*, Alexander Stille, a journalist and professor at Columbia University, cites lexicological evidence for the existence of a distinctive Chinese attitude toward the copy. He points out that "The Chinese language has two different words for copy. . . . *Fangzhipin* is closer to what we would call a reproduction—a knockoff you would buy in a museum store—while *fuzhipin* is a very high quality copy, something worthy of study or putting in a museum."[21]

This cultural trend and lexical duality alert us to the critical need to consider the practice and the principles of constructing simulacra-spaces in China against the backdrop of classical Chinese readings of the simulacra, inasmuch as these not only offer a more "Chinese" way of looking at the themed communities, but also preempt the postmodern validation of the authenticity of the reproduction. Classical Chinese scholars appear to concur with the postmodernist theoretical view that there is no distinction between the real and the image of the real (the replica). However, in sharp contrast to the Western perspective, the Chinese have considered the interchangeability of the two as consistent with the "natural" order of things. Ontological and axiological distinctions between the original and the counterfeited were seen as artificial, even irrelevant, for the boundary between the real and its replica was deemed neither essential nor absolute. In contrast with Baudrillard's position, the simulacrum did not bode a "breakdown" or an assault to the order of the cosmos. Instead, the real and the simulacrum were taken as being virtually undifferentiated, and their interrelatedness was considered acceptable. It can be argued that these two optics—the Western postmodern and the traditional Chinese—while leading to somewhat different conclusions about the implications of the breakdown of the conceptual barriers between the original and the reproduction, also share certain attitudes about the status of the two.

A seminal essay, "Preface on Painting Mountains and Water," by Chinese scholar Zong Bing, represents one of the earliest surviving texts outlining Chinese attitudes and perceptions of replication. In this short composition, Zong a "distinguished Buddhist scholar and painter of the early fifth century," addresses the issue of landscape paintings.[22] His philosophy on the two-dimensional medium of painting can be applied to three-dimensional architectural constructions since, as Lothar Ledderose of Heidelberg University explains, the Chinese did not impute significant differences between constructed landscapes in two-dimensional forms (i.e., paintings) and three-dimensional forms (i.e., imperial parks).[23]

The capacity for replicating and transferring the sensory, visual, and emotional characteristics of on-site experiences to fabricated simulacra representations in the form of art is proposed in Zong's essay. Eager to visit the mountains but prevented from doing so by old age, Zong describes a remarkable journey into the natural world through his paintings:

> I long for the Lu and Hong Mountains, and [being ill] I feel cut off from the regions of Jing and Wu. I tend to "forget that old age is coming on," but I am ashamed that I cannot concentrate my vital energies and attune my body. Distressed at the thought of repeated failure, I now draw images and lay on colors to construct these cloudy peaks.
>
> Those secrets, which were already lost by the period of middle antiquity [the Shang dynasty], may still be pursued in one's imagination a thousand years later. Those subtle mysteries beyond the power of words to describe may be drawn forth by the mind from writings and documents. How much more so when dealing with the mysteries of what one has traveled through and inspected visually, where the form may be copied down and the original color may be rendered with color.
>
> Mt. Kunlun is so massive and the pupil of the eye so small that from close up its form cannot be perceived, but retreat several miles and it will all be contained within the eye. Truly, as one goes farther from it, the smaller it appears. Today, as I spread out the plain silk to capture its distant image, Mt. Kunlun may be enclosed within a single square inch. A vertical stroke of three inches captures several thousand feet in height; a few feet of ink spread horizontally embody a panorama of several tens of miles. So, when we examine paintings, we should be troubled only by a failure of representational skill, not by the fact that the scale is reduced and the features generalized, for that is a natural occurrence.

And so the magnificence of the [sacred Daoist] mountains Song and Hua and the spirits [*ling*] of the Dark Valley can all be captured in a single painting. Taking visual correspondence and mental accord as one's principle, then given skill at rendering the various types of things [*lei*], [the viewer] will visually respond equally [to paintings as to real landscapes] and will be fully in mental communion [with the spirit lodged in the painting].[24]

This passage explicitly suggests that if one exploits the synergies between "mental accord" and "visual correspondence," one can produce reactions to a simulacrum or representation that are as deep as those elicited by the original. It helps illustrate that within the classical framework, the Chinese were inclined to make only minor distinctions between the "original" object invoked in a work of art and its referent, the "artificial" representation of this original.

Princeton University professor of Chinese art history Jerome Silbergeld, in his essay "Re-reading Zong Bing's Fifth-Century Essay on Landscape Painting: A Few Critical Notes," understands Zong's composition to suggest that a good simulacrum—one that manages to capture the essence of the original—will be imbued with a "life force," or *qi*, making the sign a perfect substitute for the "original" referent on which the sign is based:

Just as the landscape "seduces the Dao," so must the painting; and just as the Dao responds by investing the landscape with its essence, so will it respond to a skilled miniaturization. Everything, after all, is but a replica of some original type housed immanently in the Dao, and each thing according to its own type possesses some vitiating essence, some particular variety of *qi*, supplied by the Dao and differentiated by that typology, be it mountain or water *qi*, human or dog, whether great in quantity or small.[25]

As Silbergeld notes, Zong's manifesto on perception supports a strategy of belief in which any sign or simulacrum has the potential to become "real." By channeling *qi* ("seducing the *Dao*"), the image can easily become the substitute for the real.

In his study of container gardens, historian Rolf Stein of the Collège de France offers several anecdotes from Chinese history that lend additional support to the view held by Chinese that there were no fixed boundaries distinguishing the real from its representation. A story from the *Yi xian zhuan*, written by Wang Jian during the Qing dynasty, explains how an image of a landscape drawn by two Daoist women transforms into a "real" landscape. According to the text, there was once a hermit, Dongfang Xuan, who

lived at the foot of a mountain in a cottage along with a woman who taught him the Daoist arts (*shu*). Another Daoist woman visited them to play chess. The hermit was busy and told the two women to entertain each other for a while. So with their fingers they drew a design on the ground in front of them. This then changed itself into a great lake edged with high pine trees and green bamboos. There was a boat in the middle. One of the women got into it. The other woman threw a shoe into the lake. It also turned into a boat, and she got in. The two magicians traveled around, singing. Finally they made everything disappear with the help of a spell.[26]

In this case, a representation or image of the real was capable of generating real-life action. As Wang's story demonstrates, the realms of the real and the representational are not clearly defined but overlap and intermix, one as accessible and valid as the other. The duplicate or simulacrum can offer the same experience as the original, even if its literal appearance is completely different; in this case, even a drawing of a landscape can aptly capture the essence of the original so that it effectively can become that original landscape. As Ledderose notes in his discussion of miniature container gardens, "In front of the tray landscapes it becomes evident that in Chinese aesthetics there is no simple border line between objects created by nature and works of art created by man: they are both considered natural."[27]

Traditional Chinese views of energy and life-creation help explain how miniatures or replicas could become "real" simulacra—that is, replicas that are perceived as equally "real" and "authentic" as the original. "Over against the idea of a stable, finite, and heterogeneous world, the Chinese set at once a world homogeneous and evolving, in a space and time which are without fixed limits."[28] For the Chinese, the sign and the real are seen as "evolving" and "without fixed limits." Yet in the Western mind, not only are the sign and the real fixed, but also the question of beginning and origin is central to distinguishing between the two—between the "real," "authentic," or "original" and the "sign," "image," or "simulacrum." Hay notes, "In the Western tradition . . . the question of beginning . . . has long been foremost."[29]

Classical Chinese theories, in contrast, did not seek out or expect "real" things to have a clear origin or beginning, and such theories are central to understanding the perceived fluidity between the original and its copy. Referring to a third-century passage by the philosopher Zhuangzi on creation and existence (what Hay calls "process and product"), Hay observes, "The classical tradition in Chinese thought did not generally regard the 'non-beginning of the beginning' as a paradox to be explained, but rather as a fact to be accepted. . . . Reality is a state of flux and thickening [coming into being] is always matched by thinning. Its patterns are constant only through change, as they pass through phases of materialization and dematerialization."[30]

According to this traditional Chinese view of existence, there is no absolute. Existence and reality are defined not according their origin but consist of partaking in the universal, continuous process of "coming into being." Hay explains: "Resonance initiated in the universal, macrocosmic state of energy gives birth to negentrophic patterns of assonance, the coming into being of which . . . is the nature of existence and life. This is reality."[31] The cosmos is ordered and arranged according to the binary system of heaven and earth. This system is based on the belief allegedly articulated by Laozi in the *Dao de jing*: "*Dao* gives birth to one, one to two, two gives birth to three; and three gives birth to the ten-thousand phenomena."[32] Origin, existence, and reality are not static, finite, or whole. In such a universal order, where "ten-thousand" things are each interconnected by the joint process of coming-into-being, where there is no "beginning" or even a "non-beginning," the real and the simulacrum, the authentic and the forgery, the referent and the image are unified, overlapping, and interconnected.

In resonance with positions staked out by the postmodernists, traditional Chinese scholars perceived the simulacrum—its impact, spirit-generating powers, and meaning—as virtually indistinguishable from the original it replicated. With respect to China's themed cityscapes, these micro-territories, while being neither precise replications of foreign spaces nor perfect examples of place mimesis, do qualify as examples of simulacra when viewed in relief of traditional Chinese attitudes. The townships we will investigate need not be cookie-cutter replicas of the European, alien originals in order to "succeed" (that is, replicate the original in a convincing way) but need only capture the "essence" of the referent space.

Deconstructing the Authentic

If one applies the philosophical and perceptual principles that are part of long-standing Chinese belief systems to the practice of architectural mimesis, we can begin to understand why such bold and unprecedented undertakings in urban design have entered the brick and mortar mainstream of Chinese city-making. Viewed through a traditional Chinese lens, such landscapes may not be experienced by the Chinese as forgeries or fakes, as they are by most Westerners. The simulacrascapes may instead offer a deeper, more profound experience; although copies, to the mindset of the Chinese, their impact provides something more equivalent to the experience made available by originals in Germany, Britain, and other European outposts.

Classical Chinese theory offers evidence that the Chinese may have embraced a more "fluid" position on distinctions between the real and fake. In this worldview, duplications and their originals may not be so different since all are connected by energy (*qi*) that merely mutates among different iterations and informs both forms. The Chinese have erased many distinctions between the "authentic" and the "copy," and as a result, their perspective allows for the essential *dao*, or life force, that informs the original to percolate with like intensity through the simulated copy. The spiritual energy lodged in the replicated facsimile can be as powerful as that embedded in the original. In other words, what this traditional philosophy suggests is that the Chinese may see these simulacrascapes as in themselves authentic and as equally "real" in every sense as the "original" metropolises situated in distant, even unreachable outposts abroad.

The Chinese belief that the *qi* and "authenticity" of things are fluid and dynamic explains why there may exist in China a permissive attitude toward accepting, executing, and placing a premium "value" on simulacra-building projects. To be sure, other factors shape the conception and appetite for projects of this kind and will be analyzed further in a subsequent chapter. Whatever the underlying drivers for replication of the alien, this analysis of Chinese attitudes toward reproduction helps us understand how a cosmology that posits that the real is interchangeable with the "fake" has laid the foundation for the creation of three-dimensional simulacra-spaces, both during antiquity and in modern times. The philosophical underpinnings of these attitudes are buttressed by a venerable historical architectural tradition of Chinese dynastic imperial and private gardens that translated these abstract notions of life, reality, origins, and the *dao* into the construction of actual replicated landscapes.

Chinese Garden Building: Planting the Seeds of Replication

Although unprecedented in size and scope, the simulacrascapes currently under construction in China are not the country's first exercises in landscape replication. Beginning in the third century BCE, the Chinese used the flora, fauna, topography, and architecture of alien places to remake remote environments in local settings. In these earlier iterations, many of these man-made duplications took the form of imperial gardens, private gardens, and temple gardens.[33] The contemporary replication of foreign landscapes on domestic soil can be informed and better understood through this ancient Chinese architectural legacy devoted to the simulation of alien spaces.

The private gardens of Chinese officials, intellectuals, and merchants, the construction of which reached an apex during the Ming (1368–1644 CE) and Qing dynasties, may well be a kind of predecessor to the modern-day simulacrascapes. Even these "natural" gardens are themselves descendents of imperial hunting parks, an earlier iteration of constructed landscapes that date back to at least the Han dynasty and generally exemplify what is referred to as the "paradise garden" type.[34] Ledderose draws a minor distinction between the earlier and latter forms, arguing that the paradise garden was designed to "look like" or "represent" something specific (often a microcosmic replica of the universe) while the natural garden was less formal and grandiose, yet also sought to be a "small model of an ideal sphere."[35] In order to understand the motivations for and underlying philosophy of the more recently constructed landscapes of the Ming and Qing, as well as the simulacra cities of twenty-first-century China, we will examine these two garden types and trace certain parallels between today's replicated landscapes and earlier forms.

Imperial Gardens

Built on a massive scale, often on several hundred hectares of land, the hunting parks of Chinese emperors were grandiose constructions where rare plants, exotic animals, and stones from far-off lands were meticulously assembled into miniaturized replicas of the cosmos. These dynastic "zoological, botanical, and geological" gardens were microcosms that "figuratively and literally were understood to represent the entire terrestrial realm."[36] In addition to assembling flora and fauna from all over the Middle Kingdom and the known world, these parks replicated natural and man-made monuments within an enclosed space.

Chinese historical texts are replete with lengthy and vibrant descriptions of these imperial paradise gardens. The "Western Capital Rhapsody" in the *Wen xuan*, an anthology of classical Chinese literature dating back to the third century BCE, for example, offers a laundry list of the rare and varied species assembled in the First Emperor's Shanglin Park, including "Unicorns from Jiuzhen, / Horses from Dayuan, / Rhinoceroses from Huangzhi, / Ostriches from Tiaozhi, / Traversing the Kunlun, / Crossing the great seas, / Unusual species of strange lands, / Arrived from thirty thousand li."[37] Ledderose describes the "Supreme Forest" of Emperor Wu, who reigned under the Han dynasty (141–87 BCE), offering insight into how these microcosms were created:

> The park contained thirty-six "detached palaces and separate hostels" (*ligong bi guan*) with "divine ponds and numinous pools" (*shenchi lingzhao*). It was populated by rare and precious animals that had been brought together from the corners of the world, from places as far away as Mesopotamia, India, and northern Vietnam. The range of plants was equally inclusive. According to one source there were more than three thousand species. Moreover, valuable and exotic stones had been gathered there, among them a coral tree with four hundred and sixty-two branches. With these tangible specimens of every kind of thing in the universe, the park was not merely an image of the cosmos, but its replica: a microcosm.[38]

These confined spaces boasted magisterial landscapes and offered a place where the emperor could retire during his leisure time.

In these parks, emperors would come to hunt, to entertain, and to offer sacrifices, but these spaces also served the symbolic purpose of legitimizing and strengthening the emperor's authority. An apocryphal anecdote from the second century helps illustrate how, in their first iterations, these landscapes served a powerful and symbolic function that was reserved only for the emperor, one he "did not like to share with common people."[39] Although the legitimacy of this story has since been disproved, the tale was for a long time taken to be true and aptly represents a broadly held view of history. As the story has it, a wealthy merchant, Yuan Guanghan, built his own personal hunting park that, like the emperor's, was lavishly stocked with imported beasts of all types and sizes and replicated natural landscapes. Later Yuan was sentenced to death—Ledderose notes, "apparently the possession of an artificial earthen mountain was a privilege which rulers—at least until the Han dynasty—did not like to share with common people"—and his park was "confiscated and turned into an official garden, its birds and beasts, plants and trees were all transferred into the Supreme Forest."[40]

The act of "landscape appropriation" via these parks could serve multiple social purposes, such as honoring the emperor and even controlling future events.[41] Yang Ziyun's "Rhapsody on the Tall Poplars Palace" in the *Wen xuan* presents a debate between two interlocutors, Plume Grove and Sir Ink, that includes a defense of the emperor's imperial park and highlights its importance as a symbolic marker of imperial clout. Plume Grove argues that the "primary function of these spectacles is to impress non-Chinese visitors with the might and power of the Han empire."[42] He describes the parks and the hunts they house as "a way/To uphold the glories of the Grand Ancestor,/ To venerate the measures of Wen and Wu,/Revive the hunts of the Three Kings,/ Restore the preserves of the Five Emperors."[43] In response to Sir Ink's argument that the emperor's extravagant gardens impose hardships on the peasants living nearby, Plume Grove tells Sir Ink, "You, my guest, merely begrudges that the Hu are catching our birds and beasts;/And does not know that we have already captured their kings and lords."[44] The emperor's "capture" of the unusual animal, mineral, and plant species contained in his park is synonymous with his "capturing" the loyalty of subject "kings and lords." The imperial park is defended as a place of supreme importance for maintaining order and upholding the leader's status.

The strength and power earned by replicating the alien is derived from several sources: first, from the act of conceiving, designing, and fabricating an elaborate facsimile of the original; and second, from the act of possessing the miniature itself. Demonstrating his ability to duplicate the universe is also a way in which the emperor confirms the preeminence of his expertise and skill across all disciplines. Cary Liu, an architectural historian of China, explains that the replicated landscapes of the Qing dynasty emperors were likewise intended to augment imperial ascendancy: "This condensed potency through duplication . . . allowed the ruler as dynast and archon to embody the mandate of heaven."[45] The ability to assemble the alien and arrange the world according to his own will legitimizes the ruler, who is so powerful he can "move mountains" (or houses or landmarks, as the case may be in the present day) and alter the order of the cosmos as he sees fit.

In addition, the impulse to re-create space is no doubt also linked to the "magical belief that by artificially making a replica of something one wields power over the real object."[46] Stein notes, "To set up a park holding specimens of all the typical things and beings of the universe is already a magical act, concentrating the universe into its center, the capital, the residence of the king."[47] The process of building is significant, as is that act of possession, and in sum, we observe that the Chinese endorsed the act of duplicating landscapes as an affirmation of power and control. These replicated microcosms, a kind of premodern "theme park," were built in order to fulfill social and political end goals, and throughout multiple dynasties, these constructed "scapes" have been integral to establishing the emperor's authority and power.

Private Gardens

Beginning in the Six Dynasties period (220–589 CE), emperors lost their monopoly over construction of these gardens, and a new type of man-made landscape, the natural garden, came into being. The majority of these replicated landscapes were built adjoining the private residences of high-ranking Chinese officials, wealthy landowners, and successful merchants, as well as the Chinese literati, and came to represent the refined lifestyle of the elite.[48] These private gardens were much smaller than the imperial parks, often covering no more than six or seven hectares of land, although similar construction techniques and layouts were employed as those used in the royal hunting parks.

Here too the emphasis was on the imitation of nature. Many gardens would use small rocks or hills to symbolize famous peaks or well-known mountains.[49] While this natural garden type was "less formal and less ostentatiously stuffed with rare animals and plants" than royal parks, private gardens also relied on similar strategies to re-create natural landscapes—such as the careful construction of hillocks; painstaking digging of pools; meticulous planting of bamboo, pine, and other greenery; and scrupulous consideration of layout and orientation.[50] The classical gardens of Suzhou are among the most famous remaining examples of this garden type.

As they passed from the hands of the emperors to the non-imperial elite, these simulacrascapes took on not only new forms, but also new meanings. For some, these private gardens became centers of leisure and entertainment enjoyed by the educated elite, while for others, they were places of escape that promised a haven away from the banality of the everyday. Officials and the literati could enjoy a secluded life basking in a natural environment of mountains and streams. Replicating a "place beyond the confinement of the common world," these gardens offered the possibility of quick withdrawal and spiritual fulfillment in a natural setting.[51] The fabricated landscapes served as a "small model of an ideal sphere," a "spot that suits the mind" and a "place for political retreat."[52] Representing the cosmos in the form of a built miniature was not just a demonstration of power, as it had been for emperors, but also a status symbol through which the Chinese elite could express and confirm their attainment of a certain rarified level of refinement. Liu Dunzhen, a Chinese architectural historian, explains that beginning in the Northern and Southern Dynasties (420–589 CE), re-creations of iconic mountains, peaks, and aquatic pools in private gardens symbolically implied that the officials and literati who had built the parks were like the scholars and recluses who had chosen a noble life of hermetic seclusion and retreated to these distant natural habitats.[53]

Appropriating Power through Mimesis

The concept of appropriating power, internalizing bourgeois sensibilities, and enhancing personal prestige via the act of replicating either natural landscapes or, as in the present, foreign environments appears to be an underpinning of the history of Chinese architecture. Although contemporary theme-towns do not share the identical purpose or design elements of the imperial and private gardens of ancient dynasties, there are several important likenesses between both replicated landscapes. These similarities may help illuminate possible explanations for why this act of architectural "imagineering," founded entirely on duplicating a foreign and distant "other," could have crystallized in China.

First, not only do the imperial gardens and current townscapes manifest the instinct to replicate alien and remote locales, but also the past and present techniques for accomplishing such mimesis are similar. In both, sophisticated architectural reconstructions, spatial planning, and extra-architectural elements, such as ornamentation and naming, are used to re-create the alien "scapes," whether from the Western or the natural world. And whether ancient or modern, the Chinese who constructed these replicated landscapes also put a premium on the authenticity of the materials; in various instances we note that contemporary developers, and likewise both dynastic emperors and the bourgeois nobility, made an effort to construct their replicas out of the same materials as the original referents.[54] Moreover, the layout of the landscapes would in each case, premodern and contemporary, attempt to replicate the spatial qualities of the foreign location, first through the mapping of the gardens' orientation and later through urban planning.[55]

Naming also played a major role in the process of replication. In a similar manner that Swedish-themed Luodian Town (in Shanghai) labeled its artificial body of water "Malaren Lake" (after a lake by the same name in Sweden), so too did the Chinese of the Han dynasty recognize the power of place names in helping to create the simulacrum. As Ledderose points out in his description of Emperor Wu's Supreme Forest, "Certain spots were given the names of famous places far away in the empire or even beyond its borders. An artificial lake dug in 120 BCE was called Kunming lake. It had a circumference of forty *li* and was a replica of a lake measuring three hundred *li* in the southern kingdom of Kunming or Tien."[56] In short, there was a certain logic and order behind the arrangement of these imperial and private gardens—a kind of visual and architectural language through which the replicated spaces communicated certain meanings and were imbued with a symbolic significance. Similar methods continue to be employed in the creation of replicated cityscapes.

It should be noted that the historical Chinese hunting parks and gardens are not strictly analogous to the contemporary Western-style developments in every dimension: importing plants and animals in order to re-create natural environments is not equivalent to importing a culture and its artifacts in order to replicate a foreign habitat. The Han dynasty imperial parks or Ming and Qing dynasty private gardens re-created the natural world, while the modern simulacrascapes replicate a Western space. Yet the themed landscapes of the past and present are conceptually and functionally alike in key ways. Specifically, in the imperial gardens, powerful Chinese rulers assembled a mix of organic and inorganic elements, collected from afar, within an enclosed space that served the symbolic purpose of legitimizing and affirming their authority. In modern day simulacra-cities, many of which were conceived and funded by Chinese officials, the Chinese display their ascendancy through a similar process of replicating the iconic alien—in this case, the built environment of rival cultures. In both instances we witness the Chinese borrowing elements from the "other's" landscape and assembling these into a confined and controlled space situated within their own domestic setting. Beneath the surface variations in selection and execution, there is an underlying, continuous mechanism to empower and appropriate through the curation and imitation of an original. These historical relationships are important to articulate, as the parallels bring to light new explanations for the origins and success of China's contemporary simulacrascapes.

History Repeats Itself

In the final analysis, evidence suggests that the Chinese interest in landscape replication may have historical roots in traditional attitudes toward copyworks and copying, as well as a long-standing practice of re-creating alien landscapes. The teleological rationale for these European- and American-style projects comes into clearer focus when one appreciates that similar goals may form the basis for both the dynastic and modern replication projects: to faithfully re-create an existing part (or whole) of the outside world within the local domain as a means of legitimization and self-aggrandizement. More broadly, China's classical theories, techniques, and attitudes linked to the practice of place-duplication in particular provide a valuable historical and semiotic rationale for why a society would invest such energy, resources, and faith into the constellation of perplexing themed residential communities that have emerged throughout China. Although China's premodern "culture of the copy" did not directly give rise to the theme-towns of the present, the relatively open, positive view of replication that it embodied may have fostered a culture more accepting of copying.

Given the long-standing tradition of place-mimesis in China's past, the view of these landscapes as symptoms of the West spreading its influence eastward is called into question. Although the building form, construction, and style may be entirely Western, the philosophy and traditions that inform the nation's cultural makeup suggest that the act of replicating alien-scapes may be fundamentally, endemically Chinese.

3 MANIFESTATIONS OF WESTERNIZATION

The Anatomy of China's Simulacrascapes

Come into Thames Town. Taste Original British Style of Small Town. Enjoy Sunlight, Enjoy Nature, Enjoy Your Holiday & Your Life. Dream of England, Live in Thames Town.[1]

The above inscription was written on a banner hung outside the sales office of Dreams Come True Realty in Thames Town. Inside, a real estate agent, Song Yucai, used a laser pointer and a small model of the British-themed housing development to take prospective buyers on a virtual tour of the town. She recited a rehearsed sales pitch.

"Your house is your castle," Song said, quoting a line from the Thames Town brochure. "Have you ever been to England?" she asked. "Here, we have a church, good air, and the Thames River. It's just like in England."[2] Song, a native of Anhui Province, had never been farther from home than Shanghai, but she was not mistaken. With its red telephone booths, security guards dressed like the Queen's Foot Guards, and statues of Winston Churchill, Thames Town might almost have passed for the English original.

Within an afternoon in Shanghai, visitors can tour the Weimar Villas of German-style Anting Town, stroll the granite piazza of Italian-themed Pujiang Town (or rather the "Citta di Pujiang"), and go boating on Malaren Lake in the Scandinavia of Shanghai, Luodian Town. This feeling of traveling Europe in the suburbs of Shanghai is captured well by Pujiang Town's slogan: the entire experience is "Out of expectation within common sense."[3]

These European themed communities are not unique to Shanghai but range far beyond the outskirts of the metropolis. They can be found peppering suburban landscapes throughout the nation's first-, second-, and third-tier cities; its inland and its coastal provinces; its poorer and its wealthier districts. Developers have constructed housing estates of varying prices and levels of luxury in order to put the theme homes within the reach of more than an elite few. Buyers with a range of incomes, from the

Security guards, dressed in uniforms inspired by those of the Queen's Foot Guard, patrol Thames Town's main square. In the background, a couple poses for a wedding portrait. Shanghai. Photograph by author.

ultra-wealthy to those of more modest means (earning around 70,000 RMB per year) have all been targeted.[4]

Although statistics recording the exact prevalence of these themed developments are hard to come by, research and anecdotal evidence confirm that the seeds of China's simulacrascape-building movement have spread throughout the country, giving rise to Romanesque villas, Swedish towns, British villages, mini-Versailles, and Californian communities in the environs of cities from Beijing to Wuhan. Chongqing boasts landmarks from two of America's signature cities: a replica of the Chrysler Building, called "New York, New York," stands not far from the Beverly Hills luxury villa development, home to "facsimiles of the gold stars of Hollywood Boulevard set into the paving stones."[5] Fuyang officials built themselves their own "White House" in the form of the U.S. Capitol building, as did wealthy individuals in Shenzhen, Guangzhou, Nanjing, and Hangzhou.[6] Nanjing boasts Roman Vision and Hyde Park, Suzhou has Germany Villas, Guangzhou is home to Le Bonheur, and Foshan has The Paradiso. The title given to each development hints at the foreign fantasy that has been created within.[7]

In name, architectural design, branding, landscaping, management, and amenities, these simulacrascapes attempt to replicate for their residents and visitors the experience of living abroad in the interest of exploiting the cachet of Western lifestyles. This chapter will examine the components of China's branded communities to define which Western elements are selected for replication and outline the strategies that are used for convincingly realizing the foreign theme.

Constructing a Story through Space

One of the most puzzling and fascinating aspects of China's contemporary counterfeit cityscapes is the thoroughness and extent of the duplication of foreign landscapes. "It's both stunning and extremely perplexing," observes Harvard University professor Peter Rowe.[8] How does the "foreignness" manifest itself? Through what mechanisms does the copy become convincing and recognizable? Where does the Chinese version diverge from the original? Finally, what does this divergence suggest about the way China views the West?

A representative sample of developments that range in price, geography, form, and theme will serve as case studies to elucidate the composition of these communities. China's average home price in 2009 was estimated at 4,518 RMB per square meter, and this analysis will address both upmarket and mid-range themed communities, from the 34 million RMB villas on the outskirts of Beijing to the more modest Hangzhou residences priced at 4,000 RMB per square meter.[9] "Mission-style" Rancho Santa Fe in Shanghai houses only two hundred families in villas that sell for 30,000 RMB per square meter, while Tianducheng in Hangzhou, built as a full-sized town intended for a population of over two hundred thousand, offers apartments in a "French" milieu for around 4,000 RMB per square meter.[10]

Although the inspiration for the foreign inflection of each town varies from one to the next—some taking their cue from Spain, others from Scandinavia, for example—most regularly rely on a consistent combination of material and nonmaterial stratagems to create a credible, coherent, and coordinated theme. The foreign enclaves establish their non-Chinese identity through three principal elements: the form of the individual structures (the architectural style of both commercial and residential units); the master plan (the layout and geometry of streets and structures); and nonmaterial signifiers that create a certain atmosphere (including promotional materials, controlled consumer processes, and recreational activities).[11] Interpretation goes hand in hand with replication, and even those developments that replicate Western originals with the greatest fidelity are ultimately a hybrid of Chinese and foreign elements, adapting Western forms to local preferences and tastes.

At the same time, however, indigenous routines are evolving and shifting within these themed territories. In part, what is so distinctive about these enclaves is the extent to which the planned community immerses its residents not only in an alien architectural form, but also in an alien style of life with alien quotidian rituals. The Western theme extends beyond the building frames, floor plans, and fixtures and into the rhetoric used to brand the enclaves; the landscaping of the development; and the activities, routines, and lifestyles choreographed for the residents and visitors. To what extent this cultural

Brick-covered storefronts alternate with timber-framed buildings along a street in the Scenic England development in Kunshan. Storefronts are hung with English signs. Photograph from SouFun.com.

molding by architectural *dépaysement* can be viewed as a force for potential social change or political reorientation is a matter for future provocative speculation.

The Building Blocks of Similitude: Architecture in the New Towns

Each simulacrascape—from the most to the least expensive—features a walled perimeter that is patrolled by security guards and that separates it from the more public area beyond. Thus isolated, these private enclaves bear little resemblance to their surroundings. Windsor Gardens, for instance, a pristine British-themed gated community in a suburb of Shanghai, is just a stone's throw from the Panda Machinery Corporation, but its cobblestone streets and lavish gardens are a continent away from the soot-coated factory and the dusty Songjiang Science and Technology Park.

Within their tall, secure walls these townships are marked by a striking stylistic homogeneity. In the West, as a result of private property laws that allow homeowners the liberty to remodel their property, neighborhoods by and large blend a potpourri of architectural styles and landscaping themes that evolve over time as owners and tastes change. In China, however, the themed homes are part of tightly regulated communities and are subject to rigid design codes imposed by real estate developers to maintain the integrity of the Western style. Like "residential covenants" imposed in the United States and elsewhere by homeowners' associations or boards of owners, these rules are strictly enforced by a property's management and concern everything from structural changes to a home to where and how residents can hang their laundry. Yet the overarching similarity between the U.S. and the Chinese systems conceals a more fundamental and suggestive difference, which is that Chinese restrictions extend to any modifications that might detract from the foreign theme and introduce a discordant Chinese note into what would otherwise be a seamless field of the cultural fiction. "It's a European concept, and the developer and government wanted to keep it as European as possible," explains the head of one street committee with regard to the community's restrictive covenants.[12] The management at China Vanke's British-themed Stratford community in Shanghai explains that homeowners can "change nothing on the outside of their house" because the developer "wants to keep the style united and preserve the English 'feel.'"[13] Most enclaves prohibit residents from altering the façades by painting, mounting external air conditioner units, installing new windows, planting vegetables in the gardens, hanging wash outdoors, or enclosing balconies with glass panels, practices common among Chinese homeowners. As a general rule, the more expensive the community, the more vigilant the management is about enforcing the policies. When San Carlos, a mid-tier development in Shanghai, first opened, it banned laundry from windows. But "everyone was upset," a property manager recalls, and the management compromised by allowing the use of removable metal rails for hanging the washing, though it prohibited the more traditional bamboo supports.[14]

Laundry hung from a wooden pole dries outside a home in the San Carlos development in Shanghai. Though San Carlos property managers banned residents from setting up bamboo rods from which to dry their clothes, not all homeowners chose to follow the mandate. Photograph by author.

Such stringent ornamental censorship works to preserve the primary appeal of these homes and justify their price. After all, it is precisely the foreignness that is their principal selling point. The white balustrades, Corinthian pilasters, and shingled dormers are the lure that draw prospective buyers to whom the neoclassical, Palladian, or Queen Anne homes beckon. The implicit promise that the strict codes protect is that nothing will detract or distract from the total illusion of being at home in the alien.

No element of the original is too small or too incidental to be ignored in the pursuit of "authenticity." The marketing material of Chongqing's Beverly Hills explains that the three-story mansions are "modeled on the sumptuous and classical U.S. West Coast villas," and indeed, the illusion is sustained by a staggering number of details:

Beijing's Palais de Fortune villas, as shown in a sales brochure. The villas are each named after French locales, such as "Louvre" and "Alsace." Image by Fortune Real Estate Group.

faux family crests mounted on taupe-colored pediments; French doors with white trim; wrought-iron balconies; terracotta roof tiles; small palm trees planted next to impeccably groomed lawns.[15] In Beijing, a residential development with the moniker Palais de Fortune takes *haute* French living as its theme. Enclosed within a gold-tipped fence, nearly two hundred Versailles-inspired châteaux with names such as "Louvre" broadcast capitalist *luxe* through ubiquitous cherubs, black-shingled roofs, circular dormers, broad archways, cupolas, and Palladian windows. The French Baroque styles here function exactly like luxury-brand logos on clothing. These architectural "tags" are as instantly recognizable as the Nike swoosh or the Chanel "C's," which is precisely their appeal.

Palais de Fortune is only one of many developments that has opted to use authentic foreign construction materials in their stylistically foreign structures. A member of the Palais de Fortune sales team points out that the chandeliers, roof tiles, and outdoor sheetrock were all imported from France. At the nearby Orange County development, the architectural plans originated in southern California, and the appliances, tile, wood siding, and wall sconces were all manufactured in the United States.[16] The Orange County realtor boasts that even the carpets, milled in America, "are similar to ones in the White House."[17]

A subset of communities even goes so far as to adopt European urban planning principles in order to ensure that the spatial layout of a town is true to its Western referent. In these cases, there is an emphasis on creating a space that not only looks foreign, but also feels foreign. Shanghai's Holland Village, dotted with plastic tulips, windmills, and oversized wooden clogs, went beyond adopting urbanistic paradigms of the West and instead replicated, whole cloth, the urban plan for Kattenbroek, a section of the city of Amersfoort in the Dutch province of Utretcht. Both Kattenbroek and Holland Village have been laid out within a circular perimeter that has been divided into quadrants separating commercial and residential areas. Within the residential areas of the development, building height was limited to six stories (and five to six in the commercial zone at the center) to emulate the scale of traditional European villages and bring the population density in line with that of the Dutch average.[18] As a result, the two towns have a comparable density of about fifty-five homes per hectare. Moreover, the urban plans for both locales were designed by the same architect, Ashok Bhalotra, of the firm KuiperCompagnons (KCAP).[19] Holland Village's scheme was "obviously the application of the Kattenbroek formula," writes researcher and KCAP senior architect Shiuan-Wen Chu, while the sales booklet boasts of "absorbing the essence of Holland architecture" and integrating "residential arrangements that are of typical Holland style."[20] Adopting an urban plan based on the layout and density of European town models—rather than the linear, grid-like orientation typical of contemporary Chinese developments—can signal and emphasize a development's foreign character and has been embraced by some developers keen on enhancing the Western theme.

A final point about the siting of these Westernized dwellings is easy to overlook but worth noting for the contribution it makes to the "authenticity" of these simulacrascapes. Traditionally, the Chinese have situated residential dwellings in the landscape differently from their Western counterparts. In the typical Chinese *siheyuan* courtyard home or even *shikumen* stone townhouses, for example, the home occupies the periphery of the property so that a private courtyard is contained within the home, and the outermost walls of the residence line the outermost edges of the building site. The floor plans of villas in Kunshan's English County, as well as those of a multitude of other residential communities, seem to follow a template adapted from American suburbia, where the dwelling stands in the center of a plot of land and is frequently surrounded by a lawn or garden. The courtyard that for so many centuries defined the Chinese home has been eliminated from many residences, and outdoor space has been moved from the center to the periphery of the home. As the English County floor plans

A sales brochure for Holland Village in Shanghai compares the Chinese development's urban plan (*right-hand column*) with the design and layout of Kattenbroek (*left-hand column*), a section of Amersfoort, The Netherlands, which served as the inspiration for the Chinese copy. Image by Shanghai New Gaoqiao Development Co. Ltd.

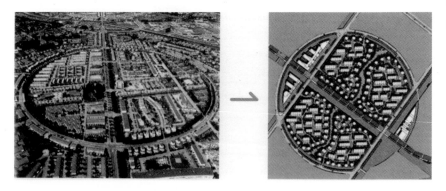

(*Far right*) The floor plans for a villa in the English County development illustrate in detail the intended purposes for each of the rooms in the spacious house. The basement (*bottom*) includes a personal gym, home theater, game room, and balcony; the first floor (*middle*) highlights the house's kitchen, maid's room, two dining areas, two living rooms, two bathrooms, two-car garage, and spare bedroom; the second floor (*top*) includes three bedrooms, each with their own private bathroom, balcony, and sizable closets. The siting of the home borrows from American suburbia, with the lawn situated around the residence itself. Kunshan. Images from Kunshan City Real Estate Development.

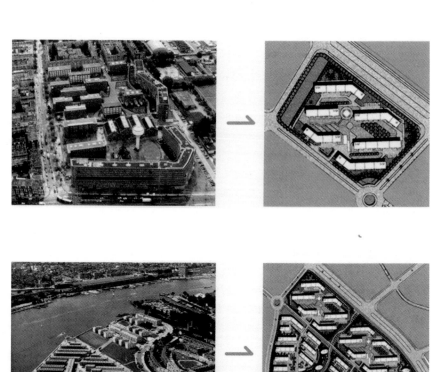

show, the single-family homes in these theme-towns also break with the traditional Chinese design in that they are built as multi-story structures of pre-cast concrete or masonry (rather than timber or stone) and include basements. For all their efficiency—allowing for taller structures and greater square footage—basements have traditionally been considered abominations, for in Chinese lore, the act of digging into the ground is associated with death and burial and, moreover, is discouraged by the rules of *fengshui*, the Chinese spirituality of place, which forbid excavation on the premise that it will disrupt the flow of *qi*.[21] The amenities that are de rigeur in these homes are identical to those that are standard in upper- and upper-middle-class American suburban homes: a two-car garage, home theater, personal gym, and two dining areas, one formal and one in the kitchen. English County homes also offer walk-in closets, private balconies, and full bathrooms for each of the three bedrooms housed on the top floor, as well as a second kitchen, an additional feature foreign to most American homes. Taken together, the features of these residences indicate that the traditional Chinese principles determining the relation between a structure and its site have been recast in numerous themed developments and replaced by an alien order.

Another popular approach to creating the experience of living abroad without leaving home lies in replicating a foreign site (Paris, Venice, Orange County) rather than a specific period's style. Such enclaves establish their identity by selecting key iconic landmarks for literal reproduction and using these as the conceptual anchors. They then rely on a small set of architectural devices—highly recognizable building types, characteristic colors, fenestration, roofing materials or shapes—to fill in the residential areas in an approximation of the original locales. The idea is to establish identity by referencing touristic monuments and vistas and producing the equivalent of three-dimensional and fully habitable picture postcard habitats.

Venice Water Town in Hangzhou, for example, draws on familiar images and architectural "props." As in the original Venice, the townhouses are painted in warm shades of orange, red, and white. The windows feature balustrades and ogee arches and are set into loggias framed in stone. The structures blend Gothic, Veneto-Byzantine, and Oriental motifs and overlook a network of canals on which "gondoliers" navigate gondolas under stone bridges. The property's crown jewel is a replica of Saint Mark's Square and the Doge's Palace

in the town square, complete with Saint Mark's Campanile; a pair of columns topped with gilded statues of the lion of Saint Mark and Saint Teodoro of Amasea, the patrons of Venice; and ornate patterned tiles on the façade of the "Doge Palace."

New Amsterdam in Shenyang, which has since been demolished, took its inspiration from The Netherlands, re-creating entire streets, canals, bridges, and canal houses from Amsterdam and its surrounding areas. This 545-acre complex in the north of China had true-to-scale replicas of significant Dutch structures, including the Peace Palace of The Hague, the Muiderslot (Castle Muiden), the Noordeinde Palace, Amsterdam City Hall, and Amsterdam Central Station, as well as numerous windmills, houseboats, and a "facsimile of a corvette with iron cannons."[22] Critic Dieter Hassenpflug from the Bauhaus-University Weimar marveled at the "original street lighting, trash cans, and street signs" that were re-created in New Amsterdam to create a "facsimile of urban scenes."[23]

Chinese developers in Huizhou are also at work duplicating the Austrian town of Hallstatt, population eight hundred. Minmetal Land, the company spearheading the project, is projecting that the replica of this UNESCO World Heritage site will occupy nearly five acres of residences in a "European architectural style" and a "commercial street built with the characteristics of an Austrian-style town." Hallstatt's most noteworthy landmarks will be rebuilt, practically stone for stone, in Guangdong Province. These will include the central marketplace, the famous lake, and a four-hundred-year-old hotel. Hallstatt mayor Alexander Scheutz says he was "definitely a bit stunned" when he saw Minmetal Land's plans.[24] "I saw these pictures, the most in-depth documents with the most detailed plans of houses, balconies, gables, windows everything. Even the Trinity-Column behind me, all the same as here," says Scheutz. "Let's just say I was a little bit surprised."[25]

For all their literal renditions of famous landmarks, statues, and street signs, the Chinese copies strike the Western observer as fake. Not every feature has been replicated exactly: China's reproductions have failed to reproduce the "correct" scale of the buildings, the proper relative placement of landmark structures, and the architectural diversity of the "original" landscapes.

These doubled cities are being built to house only a fraction of the population that lives in their Western referents, so some adjustments to scale, while discordant to Western eyes, are no doubt part of the logic of the projects. Yet it is striking that the Chinese copies often reimagine the towns to be bigger than the originals. Although China's themed developments are smaller than their Western referents—in population as well as in total area—the size of the structures and layout of the themed towns make them in many respects "larger than life." Many Euro-style enclaves in China have abandoned the more intimate scale of Western towns. Forgetting the small, meandering streets of cities like Florence or Madrid, developers embrace taller structures situated along broader avenues. The wide streets and eight- and nine-story buildings in Venice Water Town dwarf the medieval passageways and five-story structures of the "real" Venice. However, not every duplicated landmark has been enlarged equally: while the residences of Venice Water Town are considerably taller than those in Italy, Saint Mark's Campanile in Saint Mark's Square is but a fraction of the size of the original. Since the scale of China's copied theme-towns is frequently inconsistent with that of the original locale, buildings appear mismatched in their height, size, and layout. In addition, not only do Chinese developers often fail to situate the reproduced landmark to match its position in its original site, but they also are not beyond combining in a single community monuments and buildings that in the original are located in different towns. In China's "Paris" at Tianducheng, for example, the Eiffel Tower borders a *parterre* garden taken from Versailles and a reproduction of the Arena of Nîmes, a historic amphitheater

Prior to the demolition of Shenyang's New Amsterdam, a large boat built in a traditional style stood next to a replica of the Peace Palace in The Hague. A copy of Amsterdam's Central Station was visible just beyond. Photograph by Eli Dickison.

located in a city far south of Paris. Tianducheng's developers have helped themselves to French icons from throughout the country and assembled them next to each other without concern for geographical accuracy.

Finally, what contributes to the sense of pastiche is that the buildings of the simulacrascapes are both too new—the pristine Doge's Palace in Venice Water Town lacks the discoloration, irregularities, or character that come with age—and too old—the replicated models are chosen from a specific historical period, and little, if any, of the contemporary architecture that in Europe has been inserted among the antiques is imported. New Amsterdam reproduced only the archaic stratum of Dutch icons. The Dutch capital's Millennium Tower, Python Bridge, or Nemo Science Center were nowhere to be found. The Dutch-style townscape of New Amsterdam, like Chengdu's copy of Dorchester or Hangzhou's duplicate of Paris, was asynchronous with the present: it was the monarchical, aristocratic Netherlands of the past, rather than the twenty-first-century metropolis, that the Chinese captured through their replications of sculptures and Baroque buildings. Significant architectural editing and curating has gone into creating these "Venices," "Amsterdams," and "Dorchesters" of China, yielding reproductions that appear, at best, as interpretations of the original. Yet this mismatch is not for lack of ability or resources. Rather, it is a deliberate customization: the Chinese are less concerned with an exact copy and more interested in replicating the aspects of the European or American "other" they find most iconic, attractive, and desirable.

Western architects are sometimes unable to capture China's vision of what a "European" or "American" town should look like, and developers will frequently turn to Chinese architects to design these facsimile townscapes. "Western architects cannot design these, but the Chinese-born architects can design these very well. They know the proportion and the detail that developers are after," Zhou Rong, a professor of architecture at Beijing's Tsinghua University, explains. "Spanish people don't know what the 'Spanish style' is."[26] Chinese architect Xie Shixiong, general manager of the firm France KM, sums up the dilemma simply: "Foreign designers won't design the type of foreign architecture the Chinese want."[27] Lisa Bate's experience as an architect in China confirms Xie's conclusion. The Canadian, a principal with B+H Architects, was hired to design a Canadian-style residential development in Shanghai, Canadian Maple Town, and recalls a major controversy with her client on how the "Canadian" theme would be made manifest: "The client was insistent on a Canadian character, but we got into huge issues on whether that meant Canadian design or theming. They wanted something more thematic, more Disney-ish. We tried to tell them that's not what 'Canadian' is."[28] Furthermore, in their efforts to ensure a convincing copy, development companies will not only turn to Chinese designers, but they will also frequently mandate that Chinese architects supplement their knowledge of the West by studying the "original" architecture firsthand on location in Europe or the United States. "Our designers went to France several times in order to draw the entire district that today covers one million square meters," says Wang Xufei, the subdirector of Tianducheng.[29] Prior to constructing his California-style estates, Weighdoon Yang, vice president of SinoCEA, which owns such Beijing properties as Orange County and Watermark-Longbeach, organized several trips to southern California to research home designs and neighborhood layouts in communities such as Coto de Caza.[30] The team behind Huizhou's copycat Hallstatt also spent considerable time in Austria collecting data about the village, much to the dismay of some locals. "I don't like the idea of knowing that a team was present here for years measuring, and photographing, and studying us," says a Hallstatt business owner. "I would have expected them to approach us directly—the whole thing reminds of a bit of 'Big Brother is watching.'" Yet even after firsthand study, developers end up with a generalized view seemingly drawn from tourist postcards, Hollywood films, or glossy magazines.

Tianducheng's yellow "Hilltop Castle" stands perched on a hill above the development's "Little French Town," a collection of shops, entertainment venues, and cafés. Hangzhou. Photograph by author.

These Western-style territories may be unconvincing to foreigners, but many Chinese visitors and residents find the architectural mimesis both credible and enchanting. "Strangers who come here feel like they're in Paris," says Fu Min, who works in the real estate office of Tianducheng. "When I first came here, I felt like I was going to a foreign country every day for work."[31] For less affluent homeowners, the standard of comparison is limited: many have not traveled to the West, and the only knowledge they have of what these landscapes should look like comes from promotional tourist materials, as well as television and film interpretations. "Chinese people see a lot of movies and TV shows from Western countries, so they feel quite familiar with the image of Western styles," observes Zhou.[32] A visitor to one of Shanghai's British-style developments explains she was impressed with the authenticity of the English town because it looked "just like what I've seen on TV."[33] Such comments suggest that these "transplanted cityscapes" are versions of Venice and Amsterdam that were curated by the Chinese to resemble *their* vision of these locales rather than to accurately and comprehensively present them as they stand, today, in their respective countries. Wen Fong's observation on how copies are received holds true: "Since the essence of a good forgery concerns primarily the subtle question of taste, it is often possible that a fresh and carefully made fake with all its desirable trimmings appears, in the eyes of its intended audience, even more appealingly 'authentic' than the authentic."[34] Although these simulacrascapes diverge from the originals, to Chinese audiences, they are persuasive and impressive replicas. As noted in chapter 2, the Chinese perceive "authenticity" differently from their Western counterparts, and the elements required to produce a copy that is credible to the Chinese eye are not the same as those for Westerners. They also perceive the "West" differently from their Western counterparts and are interested in some European and American cultural forms while preferring to ignore others. The developers are more concerned with re-creating a town that satisfies the Chinese conception of "France" than they are with duplicating twenty-first-century France as it appears today. A degree of interpretation, appropriation, and customization occurs in the construction of these Western theme-towns, yet the overall objective is to create a place that potential Chinese home buyers can identify as foreign—and more often than not is recognizable as an antiquarian version of Europe, emphasizing the greatest, most recognizable, and trademark cultural accomplishments of the West. For all their "kitsch factor," these simulacra towns may be informative for European and American observers: they can serve as a key or map to how China sees the "other" and what parts of the West it chooses to appropriate.

Seeing China in the West: Lingering Local Influences

Although the planners, designers, stagers, and promoters of China's replicated enclaves have controlled so many aspects of replication, these simulacra do not entirely disassociate from their home turf. Developers have selectively reproduced elements of European and American architecture while also ensuring that they incorporate key living features that Chinese residents refuse to relinquish. These often "non-negotiable" Chinese elements concern the extended family (which includes multiple generations, as well as live-in help); the home's inner courtyard; the hearth (i.e., kitchen); and *fengshui*. Many of these elements and their architectural *mise-en-scène* were compromised during the Mao years, and some Chinese homeowners now yearn to restore them. These subtle Chinese architectural and urbanistic influences ensure that while Western, the simulacrascapes will also remain Chinese in key ways.

Although Western in most respects, the floor plans of villas in the themed townscapes are often altered to better meet the needs of Chinese residents. The homes in Shanghai's Scandinavia Stroll, for example, include a small bedroom and bathroom off the kitchen intended to be used by the hired help—who are nearly ubiquitous among upper-class Chinese families—and also include enough bedrooms to accommodate the traditional Chinese *san dai tong tang* (three generations living together) domestic arrangement. On tours through the model or unfinished houses in Scandinavia Stroll, real estate agents were careful to point out to potential buyers which bedrooms would be best suited for grandmothers and grandfathers (typically those on the ground floor, near a bathroom), making explicit the intended purpose of an extra bedroom as a place for relatives, rather than a guest room or other type of living space.[35]

Some communities have incorporated traditional Chinese courtyards into the layout of the home. "Courtyards, for Chinese people, are one thing that is hard to give up," explains a sales brochure. "Our ancestors were born and grew up in compounds. Therefore, to return to life with a courtyard is the hope of countless families."[36] In the San Carlos community, Rococo-esque façades and patios flanked by Grecian statues give way to open-air courtyards at the core of the townhouses.

The kitchens in many of these homes have also been tailored to suit Chinese lifestyles. By contrast with the open-plan arrangement typical of Western dwellings, these kitchens, which Xing Ruan, professor of architecture at the University of New South Wales, describes as "distinctively modern Chinese," are enclosed and fully separated from dining areas.[37] Many come equipped with appliances customized to Chinese cooking needs: ovens are often omitted, and stoves are outfitted with wok ranges topped by large, stainless steel hoods designed to filter grease and smoke.

Principles of *fengshui* frequently determine the siting, layout, and landscaping of Western-style residences. In keeping with the *fengshui* prescription that south is the most auspicious orientation and that water is the carrier of wealth-bearing *qi*, south-facing residences fronting artificial canals are common features of these communities. In developments such as Tuanbo New Town in Tianjin or Original Mediterranean Villas in Shanghai, residences face south onto man-made bodies of water.[38] Dai Yin, a property manager at Luodian Town, explains that homeowners find the small artificial lake within the enclave to be the "most attractive" feature of the property. "The businessmen love water: they think it will help them make a lot of money and have good luck," she says.[39] While some estates, such as Weimar Villas, replicate the curvilinear layout of European towns, others follow typical contemporary Chinese principles of land use that maximize the number of south-facing units. By lining up homes in parallel rows, planners minimize the number of north-facing units, which are less desirable and fetch correspondingly lower prices.

With the landscaping, developers often try to cater to both indigenous and foreign design elements, such that sculptures of mythical Greek deities and European royalty crop up in gardens of traditional Chinese inspiration. At Malaren Class Villa in Luodian Town or Shanghai's Jiande World Villas, small pagodas and rock fountains frame

Bamboo, rocks, a pond, and a small gazebo are nestled together in the garden of a gated community in Shanghai's Jiande World Villas. Photograph by author.

the European townhouses and villas, which nestle in bamboo groves that traditionally are thought to ensure happiness and good fortune. Curving, rock-hewn pathways, which are typically found in classical, Chinese gardens, snake through the plantings. In such subtle but important ways, the designers and managers of the properties diverge from a strict adherence to European stylistic imperatives and make concessions to indigenous beliefs and traditional practices.

Although a strictly Western design unadulterated by such "local inflections" might be the initial draw to prospective buyers, once they take up occupancy, these features often come to be perceived as undesirable. Chinese residents frequently find them to be inconvenient, uncomfortable, or unworkable. Some buyers complain that the architects and planners—frequently foreigners—failed to take into account specifically Chinese modes of using space. In a number of instances, a too strenuous adherence to Western plans and a failure to respect the four values of Chinese residences—hearth, family, layout, and *fengshui*—have been liabilities for the developers. For example, villas in Luodian Town initially did not sell well because the European architects had neglected to shape their designs according to *fengshui* principles. A major stumbling block for Chinese buyers was the treatment of entryways. Doors had been placed on the incorrect side of the house, lacked symmetry, and did not include an appropriately constructed entranceway. Property sales in the enclave picked up only after the developer relaxed the restrictions on alterations owners could make to the exteriors of their homes.[40] In

One of numerous homes being remodeled in Luodian Town. In many cases, the entrances to the homes have been altered to make them more in keeping with principles of *fengshui*. Specifically, front doors are being relocated to the south-facing side of the residence, with porticoes and columns used to create greater symmetry at the entrances. Shanghai. Photographs by author.

2008, nearly every home in Scandinavia Stroll was being remodeled to adhere to *fengshui* standards. New entrances, with columns and porticos, were being installed on the southern face of residences, and both existing and new entryways were redesigned to be more symmetrical and unobstructed.

The interior disposition and layout of rooms also proved problematic for a significant number of buyers and residents. Xing Lei, a real estate agent at Anting Town, complained that after nearly four years on the market, certain apartments still had not sold because their layout was not amenable to Chinese homeowners. "When they decided to build Anting, they not only wanted to try to make the outside look German, but the interiors were also definitely not Chinese," he says. "The designers forgot to take into account how Chinese people like to live; the layout of the rooms and their direction were inappropriate."[41] Residents at Blue Cambridge in Shanghai report that although they were attracted to the Western style of neighboring Thames Town, they considered the floor plans of villas in the development "quite poor." Typical upmarket

Chinese homes have a single large multipurpose space, whereas Western villas carve up the floors into a number of small rooms dedicated to single functions like eating, entertaining, sleeping, and working.[42] One Blue Cambridge couple felt the layout of the British-style villas was spoiled by a "waste of space": poorly placed corridors and stairways turned what might have been spacious rooms into cramped and awkward spaces.[43]

Whether preferring bigger rooms, more windows, or an orientation not typical of Western homes, many Chinese have found that the ways of the West are not always best. More specifically, these Chinese homeowners have begun to map out, through the concrete choices they make in purchasing and remodeling their homes, their ideal of the "new" Chinese in the post-Mao era as a synergy of East and West, adopting or preserving elements from each civilizational matrix as they respond to dynamically evolving cultural, political, and economic pressures.

The Double Is in the Details

Among the most distinctive of the devices used by the simulacra towns to enhance their "Western feel" are the cultural amenities. These include features that in their original context serve three functions: to orient the indigenous community in a cosmology (i.e., houses of worship); in a collective historical time (monuments to nationally significant events or figures); and in a community (food markets, public events and rituals, festivals, attire). In many instances, the Chinese simulacra communities appropriate these markers but deploy them in significantly selective ways. When these elements are transferred into the simulacra communities, they are voided of original meaning and are put into the service of branding the community, as well as delivering on the promise of enabling homeowners to live like the middle and upper classes in the developed world. They offer residents cultural ambidexterity, allowing them to be well versed in Chinese traditions as well as Western comforts and culture. Unlikely structures such as Gothic cathedrals, Greek statues, and British pubs reveal an important mechanism at work in the towns: the replication not only of architectural styles, but also of cultural elements and architectural "props" that help present a coherent theme.

This section examines the extra-architectural features of the developments to see how these play a role in creating convincing simulacra of Western habitats. They include the types of businesses situated in the commercial sectors of the towns; public fixtures; promotional materials that contribute to shaping a coherent brand and identity for the locales; the names of streets, neighborhoods, and businesses; and controlled recreational activities, personnel attire, and manners.[44]

Tianducheng borrows French images, landscaping, names, and even customs to spin a convincing fantasy. Entering this "Oriental Paris," visitors are met by a 105-meter Eiffel Tower—the second largest replica in the world—rising out of the Hangzhou smog.

A view of the myriad buildings that make up Tianducheng's "Little French Town." An amphitheater modeled after the arena of Nîmes and bordered by *parterre* gardens of the type that decorate the grounds of the Palace of Versailles are visible in the distance. Hangzhou. Photograph by author.

The development's main square, named the "Champs Elysées" after the *grande avenue* in Paris, boasts a nearly true-to-size replica of the Fountain of the Observatory (or the Fontaine des Quatre Parties du Monde) from Paris's Luxembourg Gardens, while statues of "Seine and Marne river goddesses" stand just beyond.[45] Carefully manicured *parterres*, their tightly clipped hedges and ornate patterns mimicking the sixteenth-century French knot gardens, blanket the residential and public areas of the development. A driver in a top hat and tails drives a horse and buggy to a yellow church at the top of a hill, where a Chinese "priest" in black robes and white clerical collar stages Western wedding ceremonies at an altar hung with a cross.

In Jiande World Villas and Chengdu's British Town, similar accessories enhance the impression of being abroad. British Town, built as a replica of England's Dorchester, evokes "Ye Olde England" with black metal street lamps modeled after the boxy gaslights of days past and statues in the public square that include a horse-drawn carriage manned by an attendant in top hat, red hunting coat, and riding breeches. Narrow

lanes leading off the Old Town Square are lined with storefronts, which, even though empty, sport signage with fanciful names printed in Roman characters. Townhouses and apartments are named after Dorset landmarks, such as Poole Promenade.[46] Likewise, in Jiande World Villas, the street names are lifted from famous foreign locales: "Toronto Road" crosses "New York Road," which leads into "Washington Garden" and beyond that, "Berlin Garden," "London Garden," and "Madrid Garden." Each house has a mounted placard that identifies the origins of its style—"Tudor," "Queen Anne," "American," "Colonial," or "German"—and educates visitors with a detailed description of the characteristics of each.

A central plaza in Chengdu's British Town, modeled after Dorset England's Dorchester, is flanked by timber-framed buildings with pitched roofs and the columnar billboards typical of European streets. Photograph from Chengtu.com.

The interiors of the buildings in these the simulacrascapes seamlessly preserve this "other culture" experience, rigorously adhering to Western conceptions of interior design. The model units of Long Island Villas in Wuhan and HNPoly Villas in Changsha, for example, are furnished to suggest that affluent, successful Continental couples have taken up residence. The Long Island living rooms feature silk brocade sofas, curtains heavy with ornate tassels and layered fabric, and sparkling gold-tipped chandeliers. In the bedrooms and libraries of the "British Royal" model homes, portraits of Thomas Jefferson and Napoleon stare down at burgundy Oriental rugs and velvet pillows, while the bookshelves are lined with classic English-language works.[47] The homes in HNPoly Villas reflect a British countryside-chic ethos, with colorful wallpaper emblazoned with ferns, fruit, and hunting scenes; toile curtains; heavy oak furniture; and dark still-life paintings mounted in antique wooden frames.

Wicker baskets, English-language books such as "Big Surprise," and ruffled pillows are on display in a model home at the HNPoly Villas development. Changsha. Photograph by Poly Real Estate Group.

The model units function as lifestyle narratives, three dimensional "conduct books" that shape the experiences prospective home buyers can hope to have by living in the themed towns. As the buyers glide from room to room, they catch glimpses of themselves reflected in the generously and strategically positioned mirrors and reflective surfaces. They are encouraged to insert themselves into the Euro stage sets and to imagine themselves playing starring roles in "pseudo-reality" real estate, impersonating affluent, cosmopolitan members of a Chinese-cum-European bourgeoisie, the new masters of the universe.

The pedagogy of these model homes appears to be succeeding. The Chinese owner of one Thames Town villa faithfully reproduced the model rooms in his own house and followed all the suggestions laid out by the real estate agent and the promotional brochures. The ground floor was outfitted to include a bar, game room, home theater, miniature garden, piano, karaoke, and home gym and was decorated with wall-to-wall carpeting and plaid curtains. Er Xiaohong, an interior decorator who has been living and working in Anting Town for over a year, explains that the most popular curtain fabric for residents of the German-themed community is an off-white silk brocade with gold highlights in a fleur-de-lis pattern, trimmed in gold tassels.[48] Asked whether this is a Western or Eastern look, she replies that it is a "definitely Western, . . . very European style" that people like best.[49] She notes that this material is her personal favorite as well and that she has used it for all her own curtains.[50]

These small glimpses into people's homes suggest that the appeal of the theme-towns is not only the exterior architecture or quality of the buildings, but also their European character, which residents hope to embrace because it seems to be presented as synonymous with wealth and modernity. They thus extend the mimesis from the façade of their homes to the interior domestic space.

Branding Soul

The promotional sales materials of China's themed communities come in the form of glossy, five-color booklets that do double duty as agitprop (agitational propaganda) and "users' manuals" inspiring and educating potential Chinese home buyers. Chock full of cultural factoids, they speak to the Chinese hunger for information bites about the "First

THE GARDEN OF
MONET
Impression of the mediterranean sea
莫奈的花园
进福景苑
户型单片
69759666

A sales pamphlet for the Garden of Monet development in Shanghai, which claims to deliver the "impression of the Mediterranean sea." Image by Shanghai Jin Fu Real Estate.

World" that will allow them to instantly master the cross-cultural context in which their future homes are rooted. Only the highest achievements of Western civilization are included as antecedents for a residential experience that promises comfort, luxury, and status. In short, these simulacra developments offer the Chinese a glimpse at why, as Deng Xiaoping allegedly noted with encouragement, to "get rich is glorious"—and how to flaunt it. The cult of Mao and his ubiquitous Red Book has given way to the cult of branding.

With their names and slogans, the residential communities package themselves as symbols of the acme of European and American achievements in "high culture." Estates such as Top Aristocrat (Beijing), Glory Vogue (Beijing), Eaton Town (Suzhou), the Garden of Monet (Shanghai), Galaxy Dante (Shenzhen), and Majesty Manor (Guangzhou) trumpet the triumph of money, Epicureanism, erudition, and aristocracy. To the average upwardly mobile Chinese, these names, although far-fetched and hyperbolic, must seem to bestow prestige on the residences and their inhabitants.

At the same time, there is more at stake in the appropriation of names that designate sacrosanct Western cultural icons than a form of branding. The pastiche names are actually the product of careful marketing that capitalizes on the aspirations and psychographics of a nascent middle class. As such, they are only the preliminary trumpet blasts of a carefully orchestrated media campaign that is effecting a social and cultural revolution through advertising. An entire corpus of promotional materials expands on the implications and benefits, tangible and intangible, of buying into the themed communities. In florid prose and dramatic pre-enactments, brochures and videos help clarify, define, and set lifestyle agendas for a society trying to find its way out of a socialist past into a yet uncertain order. The promotional literature traffics in sanitized cultural clichés calibrated to the inherited biases of the pre- and post-Maoist Chinese.

Perhaps the most striking thing about the carefully worded texts is the degree to which they steer clear of the democratic, individualistic, liberal traditions of Western cultures. Instead, they focus almost exclusively on recalling anachronistic aristocratic traditions, privileges, and pageantry. Beverly Hills invites home buyers to a "land of courtly enjoyment."[51] Coming into contact with the architectural scenery of Thames Town, the brochure claims, you enter "the territory of the aristocracy, and a world of prestige."[52] Tianducheng reminds buyers that the "European-style living space" that its homes offer is "one of the necessities of aristocratic life."[53] The brochure for Beijing's Palm Beach Villas lays out the equation between architectural style and social status and sophistication: "The simplicity of neoclassicism still reflects nobility and luxury" and, "the meaning of a house far exceeds the place to shield against wind and rain: Palm Beach Villas is the ultimate embodiment of our inner feeling."[54] As tempting as it might be to dismiss claims such as these as unadulterated hype, it would be wrong to ignore their underlying message: that living in a Western themed home is about claiming personal power and prestige.

Sales materials assure that buying into a gated compound is a ticket to high social standing and the best the world has to offer. Palace on Rare, in Shanghai, woos with the promise that you can "live here to touch the world." Palais de Fortune assures the residents of its Versailles mansions that they will "construct a legend of fortune, steer the world's power," while residents of Air Garden Babylon in Chongqing are guaranteed they will "live for pleasure and win the world."[55] In short, the "ideal" seems to consist in a seamless merger of high class, high touch, and high think, a combination irresistible to the up- and outwardly mobile Chinese. The Western landscape is presented as the fundamental component of a civilized, refined lifestyle, as a domesticated, miniaturized version of the global arena, with the resident occupying the highest position attainable.

The sales pitch scripted for the realtors peddling the "foreign" residences, as well as the rhetoric contained in print, online, and in video materials, relentlessly foregrounds the Western theme. When met by a sales agent, a prospective buyer is immediately told that the units were designed by a European firm, embody a European style, and re-create the atmosphere of a European town (or American, Canadian, or even Australian, as the case may be).[56] Prospectuses, brochures, maps, and Web sites prominently feature Caucasian models to draw attention to the authentic European character of the offerings. "The blonde, blue-eyed person sitting next to you at the coffee shop could be an American schoolteacher," Stratford suggests in its brochure. "The people pushing the baby carriage in the park could be a British couple that lives next door." Stratford's slogan promises, "This is Shanghai, but it is also the world."[57]

Visits by foreigners with even the most remote "celebrity potential" are scrupulously documented and publicized on the Web sites of these estates.[58] For example, on the Weimar Villas site there are notices of visits by Herald Maass, a China correspondent from the German newspaper *Frankfurter Rundschau*; by an unnamed mayor of a satellite city outside Moscow, and by French architect Jean-Marie Charpentier.[59] In a press release for its Oktoberfest celebration, British Town dedicates a full paragraph to detailing the number of foreign business owners, officials, and individuals who will be attending the event.[60] Prospective buyers are thus encouraged to infer that these simulacrascapes are endorsed by those who are most familiar with the "authentic" versions of these spaces. Moreover, by living in the development, residents too can become "attractions," "tourist destinations" inspiring the awe and admiration of representatives from the West, while also coming in close, regular contact with members of the "global elite."

High *Faux*-lutin'

With a compulsiveness rivaling Gary Ross's 1998 suburban utopia *Pleasantville*, the master planners have minimized the possibility that the Chinese residents of their communities will ever suffer the culture shock of lapsing from their European fantasy. In addition to tightly controlling the appearance of the architecture, they provide amenities and services such as clinics, schools, fitness centers, restaurants, and convenience stores that offer a seamless "aristocratic" experience—and total convenience—from front gate to doorstep.

Most "estates" have small town centers, in essence outdoor shopping malls, within the confines of the development to service the needs of the inhabitants. Shenzhen's Mediterranean-style Vanke Town, for example, has a wide range of restaurants—from Kentucky Fried Chicken to hot pot—clothing boutiques, small supermarkets, and repair shops on site. The more upscale communities go even further in providing for their residents, assigning each household its own butler to assist with chores, reservations, directions, repairs, and other tasks.

In some developments, the vendors harmonize with the theme of the Western brand in question. Their merchandise, ambiance, and service contribute to the overall credibility of the illusion of living abroad and serve to enhance the status of the community. The Thames Town commercial area, for example, is dominated by businesses catering to European food and entertainment. The two coffee shops serve exclusively Western cuisine, including steak, poached eggs, coffee beverages, and European pastries. IMP Bar markets itself as a destination for fine foreign liqueurs served by Russian waitresses and mixed by a German bartender, while at the Rock Music Pub, patrons can enjoy cocktails, a wide selection of wines, and live music in a wood-paneled

bar largely inspired by the décor of British pubs.[61] The shops in the town, which include an overwhelming number of wedding photography studios, feature European products, such as top-of-the-line imported red and white wines at the Chateau Bacchus wine cellar. Universal Marine, on the other hand, specializes in nautical paraphernalia, from antiqued compasses to maps of the British Isles. Although European cuisine and cafés are beginning to make inroads into the restaurant scene of major Chinese cities, in Thames Town they represent by far the lion's share of the food concessions. In fact, there is only one Chinese restaurant and one Chinese teahouse, with no signs of the noodle stands, dumpling carts, or congee restaurants that are a universal feature of every Chinese settlement.[62] This guarantees that even the air has an alien smell, lacking the characteristic aromas of Chinese neighborhoods.

Through developer-sponsored festivals and celebrations, residents of the themescapes are recruited into cultural experiences that familiarize them with Western customs, food, and leisure activities. For several consecutive years, Anting Town has hosted a three-day German lifestyle festival that includes exhibits on German art, architecture, and culture—food for the mind—and a full lineup of Teutonic foods and beverages: sausage, cheese, schnapps, and beer.[63] According to a *Shanghai Star* article, this event is one of many that Anting Town's developer, SIACRE, designed with the aim of "developing a German lifestyle . . . in the town."[64] A SIACRE employee in charge of organizing the festival told the *Shanghai Star*, "Now that most of the infrastructure facilities have been put in place, we believe Anting Town is set to become an important platform promoting German culture and lifestyle in Shanghai and in China at large."[65] Tianducheng has hosted similar lifestyle festivals. For instance, a recent press release on the Tianducheng Web site described a "Hangzhou French Culture Week" celebration that showcased "French distinguished guests," such as a delegation of officials from Nîmes, and hosted activities that included sessions of "red wine tasting and appreciation" led by "Mr. Christian, the chairman of the French Red Wine Association"; a "French cars tour" featuring Peugeot, Renault, and Citroen automobiles; an exhibition of artwork from the Louvre (replicated by artists from Zhejiang Province); and musical performances by a troupe of musicians from the Loire region.[66] These "courses" on French culture went so far as to "educate" Chinese attendees on what kind of perfume or cologne to wear, the subtle differences between a "bistro" and a "brasserie," and the evolution of French cinema.

The Chinese, of course, have not invented these "cultural immersion" events. They are part and parcel of generic commercial "mall" culture in the United States and, increasingly, throughout Europe. What is distinctive is the manner in which these "courses" in American and European culture are being embraced in conjunction with such a complete immersion into Western architecture. Surrounded by Baroque

The exterior of Small Town Coffee, a café in Thames Town located kitty-corner to Chateau Bacchus, a wine store and wine bar. Shanghai. Photograph by author.

Towers and gingerbread trim lend this pink Queen Anne–style home in Shanghai's Forest Manor a more European character. Photograph by author.

buildings, paintings of Napoleon, and replicas of European squares, the Chinese in these simulacrascapes have earnestly welcomed these Western cultural events as opportunities to learn foreign ways, as well as to show off their mastery of the alien cultural idioms and Western standards of high culture. At festivals and celebrations such as these, the Chinese residents spill out into their public spaces, staging themselves as Europeans for each other's—and visitors'—benefit. Upwardly mobile Chinese, while not abandoning local traditions, will "try on" foreign habits as they perform Western rituals, ingest Western foods, and appreciate Western artistic traditions.

Although Chinese homeowners are not abandoning their native culture as they transition into these themed towns, even within the domestic sphere there have been adjustments in the quotidian routines of the residents. The spaciousness and privacy of the homes, as well as the upmarket clientele these communities attract, have recast relations among neighbors and even relatives. Whereas people in more traditional Chinese communities are more engaged with community life—participating in "street committees," performing community service with other residents, attending town meetings—many simulacrascape homeowners prefer to be left alone and demand much more privacy. "The management concept is much more Western, not Chinese," an official says of Thames Town. "People who live in old compounds are more likely to get involved with group activities, like meetings, but people here don't want to get involved; they don't want to be disturbed. They want to live a more European life; they have high expectations."[67] Most developments have street committees, but few are as vital and active as those in typical Chinese neighborhoods. Some families in these themed enclaves observe that moving to larger homes can also alter the family dynamic, a change that threatens to distance relatives as well as neighbors. "Due to the large area, each family member has more space. That subtly changes the relation between each family member," explains Zhang Xiaohong, who lives in the Galaxy Dante development in Shenzhen with her husband and teenage son. "I can't say whether it is positive or negative, but the large space definitely affects the closeness of family members."[68] The Western cultural practices being fostered in the simulacrascapes concern not only domestic activities, but also more public interactions between homeowners within the same community. The Chinese in these locales are embracing new ways of participating in community life, as well as socializing, as they engage in activities that center around mastering Western food, drink, art, autos, and traditions.

Imitation as Incubator

An examination of these simulacrascapes reveals that these towns have replicated not only the architecture and urban plans of alien townscapes, but some aspects of the culture of these locales as well. From street names to the uniforms of the security guards, pub fare to type of entertainment, a set of non-Chinese cultural referents has been built into the theme-towns in a manner that is as thorough and purposeful as the architectural replication. The town plans are set up to enable Western patterns of consumption, socialization, and recreation both within the individual household and within the community. The infrastructure includes components such as Christian churches, historical monuments, ethnically authentic foods, vendors and festivals, and class-pegged leisure activities that make the cities into incubators of new, Western-style aspirations and life "plots."

It should be noted, however, that the target lifestyle for emulation belongs, broadly speaking, to the upper-middle class of these national groups. The wine drinking, charity functions, classical music concerts, and golf lessons are practices specific to the Western bourgeoisie. The focus on this particular lifestyle template suggests that in immigrating into the foreign-themed communities, the Chinese are experimenting with one ready-made model of the "good life" that is now becoming available to them in the era of increased personal affluence. The European and American templates come with the globally acknowledged and recognized cachet of privilege, election, and power. It is not that the Chinese forsake their own culture or native values when they enter these landscapes. They aspire to the more luxurious, comfortable lifestyle of the global elite, which they can now afford and which their own post-socialist world has not yet elaborated, while also incorporating and adapting Chinese cultural practices. They are behaving in ways similar to their Western counterparts not because they want to be Western but because they are, and want to enjoy being, rich, and customs such as drinking fine wines or living in large homes go hand in hand with privilege. The implied statement of these simulacrascapes is twofold: first, "culture," refinement, and social prestige are as covetable as cash; and second, for the Chinese to live like the British or Germans in their homes is not enough; one must be like the global elite as well: in habit, in custom, and in manner.

What distinguishes the Chinese simulacra cities from Disneyland, Renaissance towns, Las Vegas, and other theme-park-like environments is that the suspension of disbelief is temporary in the latter and permanent in the former. For theme park visitors, the escapist unreality the imagineered landscapes provide ends as soon as they leave the park. For the Chinese residents of these themed enclaves, the fantasy is lived—yearly, daily, hourly. The consequences of living within developments that replicate both the structural templates and cultural templates of the West have yet to be fully realized. It remains to be seen how Chinese homeowners will fuse the foreign customs with their own and whether they will become dexterous in the "high" culture of both civilizational matrices.

4 SIMULACRA AND THE SINO-PSYCHE

Understanding the Chinese Motivation for Replicating the Alien

Baroque rhetoric, eclectic frenzy, and compulsive imitation prevail where wealth has no history.[1]

At no time during the roughly three millennia of its history has China had as many stylistic options for its residential architecture as in the thirty years since the shift from a command economy toward the open market. Yet in the remarkable building boom that has deposited broad swaths of suburbs around Chongqing, Chengdu, Changsha, and other cities, among all the directions Chinese builders could take—from indigenous antiquarian to cutting-edge futuristic—one of the leading stylistic imperatives has been Western historicism.

The transformation of China into the factory of the world and the ideological shift to the policy of "socialism with Chinese characteristics" have put money into the hands of more Chinese than ever before. These two developments have also seeded consumer aspirations and spurred spending habits that mirror those of the capitalist West. In housing trends, this translates into an exceptionally strong and historically unparalleled preference for housing stock of European and American provenance among upwardly mobile and affluent Chinese.

The migration of Chinese *nouveaux riches* from crowded, inner-city apartments to detached housing with landscaped lawns, amenities, and security guards manifests a desire to "trade up" as means allow. The proliferation of gated communities and villa residences is a predictable consequence of China's increased prosperity, just as the spread of malls, McDonald's restaurants, and movie theaters has gone hand in hand with enhanced spending power. Yet meeting the demands of new consumers need not have taken the form of replicas of Western homes. Why, then, have developers and city planners gravitated—and done so to such an astonishing degree—to European and American prototypes? Is this copycat consumerism just a by-product of China's conversion into a "sweat shop" for Western designs and a symptom of its creeping

A row of homes in the English County community in Kunshan. The development promises residents "exclusive" access to a stable and boats, among other perks. Photograph from SouFun.com.

globalization? An instance of bravado? Or is it also an expression of something deeper and more complex?

This chapter will tease out the complicated and often contradictory motivations that drive the Europeanization and Americanization of China's satellite suburbs. Rather than focusing exclusively on the pragmatic or "hard" dimensions of the phenomenon—such as who gets to decide what to build and where—the chapter will also examine the "soft" sociocultural and symbolic elements of the question. What this exploration will reveal is that the factors impinging on the decision to simulate alien townscapes are not merely exogenous but lead deep into the cultural character of contemporary China: the rise of its newly minted middle and upper classes and their desire for branded luxury consumer goods and, more important, symbols of self-cultivation; the flexing of the national soft-power muscle; a "yes-we-can" boosterism bloated on a decade of unprecedented economic growth and increasing prestige and power in the global arena; and a deeply rooted tradition of celebrating cultural achievements by constructing gigantic monuments.

Inspiration for Replication

Generally speaking, three sectors have been responsible for the construction of simulacra communities: privately owned real estate firms, public real estate companies, and state-owned enterprises. Real estate firms are either owned and financed by private interests or, as in the case of public companies such as China Vanke, are listed on China's stock exchanges and are accountable to their shareholders, which may include government-held entities. State-owned enterprises (SOEs), such as Beijing Capital Group Limited, have also played a key role in developing the simulacrascapes. SOEs are largely or entirely owned by the central, provincial, or city governments and, in some cases, may be created in order to execute a specific project.[2] Thames Town helps to illustrate the role of a SOE in the construction process. In August 2000, the Shanghai Songjiang New Town Construction and Developing Company was founded under the sponsorship of the Shanghai municipal government and the direction of the Songjiang district government. This newly formed company, charged with contracting and overseeing the construction of Thames Town, then received from the government an infusion of 1 billion RMB to be put toward constructing the themed community.[3]

Unfortunately, however, this rather simple outline, while accurate in the main, is overly straightforward when it comes to describing actual conditions on the ground. China's real estate sector is more accurately represented as a tangled web of affiliations where the division between private and public interests is not always so clear. The relationship between state and private enterprise, entrepreneurs and investors, and consumers and bureaucrats is often murky and ridden with unspoken codes of corruption, favoritism, and *guanxi* (connections). For example, the publicly held Zhejiang Guangsha Development Company built Tianducheng "under the guidance of the [Hangzhou] government," which reportedly offered the developer "preferable policies" for the project.[4] In effect, the city government is said to have rigged the auction of the land so that Guangsha could purchase the property for a price below the going rate.

Government ownership of all land frequently requires that real estate developers, both private and state-owned, liaise with local governments to finance, gain approval for, and complete their ambitious theme-towns. In the course of these partnerships, officials who stand to gain from the property development all too frequently rely on nefarious and illegal means to secure land for these ambitious endeavors. The corruption trials in Chongqing of legislator Li Qiang and top judicial official Wen Qiang brought to light the frequently brutal means by which local officials may evict homeowners and forcibly seize their properties. In Chongqing alone, there surfaced tales of women who were "roughed up" after they protested vacating their homes to make room for a redevelopment project; of dozens of people from a neighborhood transported via government-owned buses to the outskirts of town, only to return home to find their residences demolished;

and of a local Communist Party chief watching as thugs attacked with cleavers a couple who refused to relinquish their farmland.[5] Bribing bureaucrats with money and gifts in order to secure a real estate contract is routine, and not even large, multinational corporations are blameless. In early 2009, a "star deal maker" at Morgan Stanley (an international financial services firm) was embroiled in scandal and accused of bribing Chinese officials to acquire hundreds of millions of dollars worth of property holdings.[6] Separately, the deputy minister of the Ministry of Supervision acknowledged in May 2010 that over three thousand officials, among them several mayors, had received penalties of up to life in prison for construction project abuses such as embezzlement, bribery, and graft.[7] These residential developments—expensive and expansive—often necessitate the complicity of developers and local bureaucrats, as well as business practices of dubious legality.

These actors—a complicated and diverse cast of private consumers, business interests, municipal governments, and Communist Party functionaries and policymakers—have all contributed to the conception and materialization of the theme-towns. With so many competing agendas and actors and such acute regional differences and market fluctuations, no singular, linear storyline emerges to account for the rationale driving the themed environments. In each instance, the decision to create simulacrascapes stemmed from a confluence of pragmatic requirements and symbolic needs. Among the former was the nuts and bolts imperative of learning construction techniques, design options, and planning solutions that China, during a decades-long moratorium on innovating residential construction, had neglected. The existing housing stock with which China entered the Reform period was simply inadequate with regard to hygiene, comfort, space, and availability to meet the needs of a population migrating in vast numbers to established and new urban centers.

Moreover, a significant portion of the population exerting pressure on the housing market was moving into a new socioeconomic niche and was anxious to improve its standard of living to match that of the middle classes in the developed worlds. The top priorities for both the government and the private sectors were to meet the most pressing housing needs while simultaneously satisfying the newly developing taste of the emerging consumer for Western comfort and style. By constructing these communities as knockoff Western prototypes, they were able to tap into existing Western architectural expertise, and using Western engineering and technology, they could complete developments as rapidly and cheaply as possible.

The simulacra movement was also a readily visible means by which the Chinese could demonstrate—to themselves and to other nations—that they had attained a certain level of sophistication, wealth, and modernity. Appropriating cutting-edge Western technology for the construction of nostalgia and Grand Tour residential

communities provided a way for the Chinese to exhibit their accomplishment in that it allowed them to instantly duplicate the originals that in the West had taken years to complete. Yet even as they embarked on pharaonic construction projects that transformed significant tracts of Beijing and Shanghai into stunningly futuristic zones, Chinese developers were ringing these visionary vertical urban cores with horizontal retro suburbs. Working on both fronts simultaneously enabled the Chinese to showcase their competitive edge in the real estate market: when it came to building the metropolis of the future or the quaint burg of the past, the Chinese proved they could do it faster and more literally than anyone else.

Clockwise from top left: Four views of Luodian Town, Shanghai: the center of the town, viewed from across a small river that intersects the community; the chapel's brick-colored steeple seen through trees in a square; empty storefronts hung with posters advertising Nike and Reebok stores "coming soon"; another view of the chapel, pictured here surrounded by townhouses and a park lined with benches. Photographs by author.

A Great Leap Forward

The wholesale gravitation of the newly urbanized and newly wealthy population toward the foreign architectural styles of simulacra cityscapes has been linked to an identity and creativity crisis in Chinese architecture. This state of "arrested development" or "creative block" is the fallout from decades of Communist rule, when individual designs were seen as an unnecessary luxury, indulgent, and rightist. With architecture and city building still dominated by the industrialization programs and urbanization schemes based on Soviet models that were put in place during the Mao years, Chinese architects have been struggling to catch up to twenty-first-century planning principles since the nation's "Opening and Reform."

During the years when other countries were experimenting with new theories for urbanization and city growth (i.e., the rise of the suburbs in postwar America, the New Urbanism movement), the Chinese government all but neglected the fields of architecture and urban planning in favor of promoting heavy industry and transforming China's cities into production-based enclaves.[8] In *Architectural Encounters with Essence and Form in Modern China*, Peter Rowe and Seng Kuan explain how, under Mao, Chinese architects were not free to practice their craft: "In this extreme ultra leftist political environment, little building of note was undertaken; even the term 'architecture' was denounced as being too far removed from a direct reckoning and engagement with the real needs of the people for shelter, an attack that showed just how far theorizing in the direction of 'production and life had gone.' "[9] As the authors observe, China's political policies have left its architects unqualified to tackle the sudden imperative to design cities, infrastructure, and homes. Zheng Shiling, a director with the Shanghai Urban Planning Commission, likewise bemoans a sterility in China's architectural inventiveness, and he too blames the past for this paucity of artistic ingenuity: "Though ideological liberation and political reform have brought about a relaxed artistic atmosphere, architects have been damaged by the many years in which they were shackled ideologically and prohibited form blazing new trails."[10]

Under Mao, the nation even adopted an anti-urbanism policy and pursued measures to restrain urban growth, placing an emphasis on the "rustication" of its populace from the 1950s to the end of the Cultural Revolution.[11] As such, China's current urbanization—demographically the fastest and largest in recorded history—and the sudden boom of its real estate market—fueled by legislative reform in the late 1980s legalizing the ownership of private property—have caught the nation unprepared. China's urban population more than doubled between 1985 and 2008, from approximately 250 million (or 33 percent of the total population) to 607 million (or 46 percent of the population).[12] Shenzhen alone, whose population increased from around sixty-eight thousand in 1978 to over 8 million by 2006, effectively grew from a city the size of Temple, Texas, to one comparable in size to New York City in under a generation.[13] At the same time that cities have been expanding, so too have homes: the average per capita housing space for the urban Chinese has increased threefold in the past three decades.[14] The move has occurred on a phenomenal scale and at a startling pace;

statisticians estimate that during the past two decades, 90 percent of the population of Shanghai has moved or been relocated to new, more spacious residences.[15]

This breakneck speed of urbanization has made the inexperience of Chinese urban planners and architects painfully glaring. In part, the simulacra cityscapes have been the result of a Chinese effort to use Western know-how to bridge the gap between an outmoded construction technology and the burgeoning demand for housing fed by a migratory and economically upwardly mobile labor force. AS&P architect Timo Nerger notes the following from his experience working in China over many years:

> Since the opening, for the last twenty years or so, China has been very keen on getting fresh ideas into the country about architecture, technology— everything—because China doesn't have it. This is especially true if you think about building technology, urban spaces, and design because there was a big lack of development from the Communist era, which is still ongoing. For fifteen to twenty years, it wasn't possible to study urban planning or architecture because everything related to urban themes, such as planning, was bad. Mao Zedong put intellectuals in farms . . . so there was a real lack of study on how cities develop. The Chinese want to get knowledge on how cities work and what they look like . . . and it's a problem for Chinese architects to find their own identity. They are pretty much reliant on a Western architectural point of view because, from my understanding, they do not know how they can define themselves and their work.[16]

Nerger takes the stance that the themed communities are, in part, by-products of China's attempt to study and replicate a model they view as being tried and true in the West. Wang Daoquan, an entrepreneur from Shaoxing living in the Blue Cambridge community, argues that Western architectural approaches can benefit China's architects. "Europe is more advanced, so in China, we try to learn from more advanced countries by copying their superior styles," he explains.[17] The link between the simulacrascapes and China's effort to learn from developed nations helps account for the type of architecture that is being imported. "People are always looking up to advanced cultures. They will not follow disadvantaged cultures but advanced ones. If people in New York were to follow Chinese styles [of building], it would seem strange, but it's normal that the Chinese would follow the Italian or Baroque styles, quite normal," says Tong Ming.[18] That China's developers are attempting to learn by replication explains their choice of national architectural and urbanistic models. One looks in vain among the theme-towns for examples of Third World prototypes—Brazilian *favelas*, Mexican *barrios*, or the *quartiers* of Algiers or Casablanca—whereas Bavarian palaces, the U.S. Pentagon, and the U.S. Capitol Building have each been replicated in cities as diverse as Shenzhen, Chongqing, Wuxi, and Wenling.[19] The logic of the "normal" to which Tong appeals, however, is

A rendering of the Venice-inspired Kowloon Mountain Resort in Pinghu. The development is targeted to cover ten square kilometers and include a hotel, villas, apartment buildings, wedding chapel, yacht club, golf course, and horse-racing track. Image by France K&M Architecture Sight Design.

tenuous when applied to antiquarian architecture and begs the question of why the Chinese might consider it normal to import a European or American architectural past as opposed to cutting-edge Western technology and design.

One explanation—that still, however, does not fully resolve the issue—is provided by officials involved in the support and sponsorship of the simulacrascapes. Their stance is that by copying Western models, they gain experience and expertise in Western construction and design and can advance more quickly by imitation than they can by innovation. In providing the rationale for the European style of the One City, Nine Towns plan and Tianducheng development, the Shanghai Urban Planning Bureau and Guangsha Development Company both stress the opportunity to learn from international experience and use it to China's advantage in much the same way that Western intellectual property is being appropriated as it relates to manufacturing watches, computers, or pharmaceuticals.[20] The planning memorandum on the development of Shanghai notes, "As we enter the twenty-first century, we must draw on the successful expertise of foreign nations to achieve a high-quality planning model, high-quality construction, and a high level of efficiency, constructing several types of towns, each in a unique style."[21] The bureau even proposes offering financial subsidies to lure foreign architects and planners into the building and design processes, although it does not specify exactly how such a system would work.[22] Likewise, the Guangsha

Development Company describes its Tianducheng project as "extensively drawing on the construction experience of advanced countries, such as Europe and the United States, in order to use their knowledge as instruction and as a foundation [for growth]."[23]

Chinese architects receive training that is based on Western principles. Chinese architect Liu Yichun, co-founder of Atelier Deshaus, notes that Western architectural theories and practices have played a major role in shaping the designs and outlook of Chinese architects today. "The whole system of architecture education in China is based on the Western style, so we are learning from the West all the time. Once we enter university, we begin learning all the theories of Western architecture," he observes. "It's a natural process for Chinese architects and college students to learn theories of Western [architectural] education."[24] Writing in *Urban China* magazine, architecture critic Kuang Xiaoming sees this attitude of "borrowing from the best" as fundamental to the Chinese approach to urbanization. By contrast with America or Europe, Kuang explains,

> China has its own style of urbanization, suburbanization, and urban revitalization, which is a more flexible alternate path to follow [different from the strategy pursued by the United States and Europe]. The strategy that is being adopted is what we could call the "mixing method" mode used to solve the challenges of city expansion brought about by rapid urbanization. In this "mixing method" mode of development, knowledge is drawn from the experience of others, whether [by] adopting Western influences from Europe and the United States or learning from Japan or Southeast Asia's own ideology. Still, at the heart of this approach is China's own, indigenous cultural philosophy of incorporating diverse ideas.[25]

In essence, Kuang highlights that China's methodology for city building has been to incorporate Western methods, among other influences.

This strategy of seeking out the best achievements of alien cultures and applying them, through selective adaptation, to meet domestic needs and to solve uniquely domestic problems has characterized China's approach to technological change for millennia. The Chinese have "eagerly acquired all the technical discoveries of the foreigners," observed Johan Gunnar Andersson during his travels to China in 1928.[26] Xing Ruan points out that the tendency to embrace the skills of outsiders when they stand to benefit China runs deep in the nation's history and forms a part of its cultural character. "The Chinese basically have no problem with accepting something 'alien,' 'exotic,' or 'Western' if these things are considered to be at the 'center of the cosmos.' These days, we're talking about Western civilization and the Western image as being the representation of that," Ruan says.[27] The architecture and engineering of the developed world are seen as promising solutions to China's rapid urbanization and thus have

The San Carlos development brands its residences, shown here, as "platinum palace villas" that are "tasteful," "quiet," and "sumptuous," while its slogan trumpets the community as being "Baroque Romantic since 1715." San Carlos's yellow townhouses have purple tiled roofs and façades decorated with white plaster bas reliefs, carvings, and columns. Shanghai. Photograph by author.

been both studied and emulated by local developers and architects. By importing the "hard skills" of Western urban planners, designers, business people, and engineers, the Chinese are betting that the tutelage of foreign experts and the replication of globally acknowledged jewels of urban design will bring about the nation's rapid transformation into a global leader and will ensure the continuation of its "peaceful rise." In other words, the simulacrascapes may not be driven only by the individual Chinese consumer's desire to learn the "soft skills" of the West, but also by the hope of the Chinese state that it can teach itself the "hard skills" of the foreign developed nations. This is learning by doing at its most massive.

The Competitive Edge: Euro-Branding

There is a puzzling inconsistency between the professed Chinese intention to learn from the technologies of "advanced" countries, on the one hand, and the choice to replicate historical European and American architectural prototypes, on the other. Western architects and engineers operating in China are able to offer more sustainable, progressive building designs than the environmentally unsound, low-density tracts of suburban housing embraced by Chinese developers. But this newer, more modern approach, from the appearance of the nation's simulacrascapes, is not what the Chinese appear to want. In fact, they do not seem to see—or care—that, by Western standards, many of their historicist developments are unsustainable and inefficient.

The image shows two Grecian statues on an arched entrance with Chinese characters 西林花园.

Grecian statues of two figures flanked by a lion, deer, and other creatures overlook the entrance to Blue Cambridge, a housing development outside of Shanghai. Photograph by author.

The "learn by imitation" rationale does not go far enough in explaining why the Chinese would opt for outmoded styles, technologies, and planning paradigms as the idiom for their modernization. After all, other East Asian cultures have responded to the challenge of assimilating the icons and conventions of the First World by pioneering innovative urban solutions. Witness South Korea's New Songdo City, a "ubiquitous city" that is hardwired with the most advanced computer technologies capable of linking human activity to urban infrastructure.[28]

To account for the historical styles selected for China's replica residences, it is helpful to examine China's real estate market and how it is influenced by government policies. China's ownership laws and political system put pressure on developers to realize construction projects quickly. The antiquated, European "skins" of China's themed communities are a rapid and inexpensive response to the urgent need for housing and ensure a quick return on investment. Under Chinese property law, all land belongs to the state, although it may be "leased" from the government by private individuals for a period of up to fifty or even seventy years. Because real estate companies do not own outright the land that they develop, they are under heavy pressure to realize profits from their investment as quickly as possible, rather than bank on the long-term success of a property by developing it over a period of several years. Architect Neville Mars, chairman of the Dynamic City Foundation, explains, "The current

These illustrations present three examples of the villas available at Chateau Comte de Sunac in Chongqing, a development that spans 1,800 acres and has embraced a "four countries, one town" design ethos. According to the developer, the homes for sale in the community have been inspired by Tuscan architecture, Spanish-style homes, "Santa Barbara" residences in California, and the French manor style. Images by Sunac China Holdings Limited.

land value system requires paying an extraordinary amount of money up front, even more than in the United States. This means that you're almost financially forced to get your money back immediately, or at least as quickly as possible."[29] In addition, local government officials are judged, in part, on the construction and urbanization efforts they are able to realize during their tenure. For this reason, bureaucrats, who often lend financial support to real estate ventures, are eager to see new properties completed as quickly as possible to ensure that their performance is favorably rated by their superiors in Beijing. "The government exudes an enormous amount of pressure on developers to realize projects," says Mars. "Even in China, politics is a four-year business. If officials are building a city, as it concerns their careers, the only results that matter are the number of buildings they've put on the ground."[30] Importing Queen Anne or Mediterranean styles wholesale from the West allows developers to save time in the design phase, as well as to reduce expenditures on architects' fees.

Moreover, Western-branded communities are seen as having an established track record in providing a competitive edge in the crowded real estate market. In the early 1990s Euro-style gated communities pulled ahead of other types of housing in terms of both higher prices and record-fast sales to China's early entrepreneurs and "overseas Chinese" returning to the PRC. On the premise that what worked in the past will work even better in the future, real estate investors and developers view themed communities as promising virtually fail-safe, quick, and profitable returns on their investment.

These developers frankly acknowledge that the most compelling motive for building themed suburbs is to secure a competitive edge in the glutted Chinese real estate market. Thematic branding is used to distinguish what might otherwise be just another interchangeable gated community. Thames Town developer James Ho confirmed that the advantage of building a British enclave lay in the revenue to be earned from its aesthetics and distinctiveness: "Beautiful buildings are always welcomed by customers. . . . If the building's style is different from others, it will have its own market. It will be easy

to make money, to add profit."[31] Lin Hai, an architect with the Alibaba Group, notes that Western theming, "from a functional standpoint, doesn't matter, but from a commercial point of view is very useful."[32]

Well-trimmed hedges, tall columns, and a wrought-iron gate ornamented with gold flowers distinguish the entrance to a stately home in Vienna Gardens, Shanghai. Photograph by author.

Asked to account for the popularity of Western designs, developers, architects, brokers, and investors always stress their selling advantage. According to Hu Yiding, a manager at Citta Di Pujiang, the Italian theme of the development, promising "Fine living in Venice," was a way to compensate for the double marketing disadvantage of an undesirable location and a builder with low name recognition. "When we were selling properties in this place, it was important to have this Italian identity. . . . We needed gimmicks to sell this place because this is far away from Shanghai, and the developer is not so well known," Hu explains.[33] Xie Shixiong had the same experience in the case of a German-themed community he helped to build: "This [Western-style] design was obviously an added value for development because the houses sold much faster than others around it, and the price has gone up faster than those around it." Xie reports that even small flourishes such as Italianate columns, friezes, and domes or replacing "Sunshine" with "Guttenberg" as the name of the development could increase profits by an average of 500 RMB per square meter.[34]

Even though the targets of replication are historical and look as if they might have been built using outmoded building techniques, in most cases they are actually engineered and constructed according to conventional, or even innovative, methods.

Anting Town, for example, used the most up-to-date construction. State-of-the-art sustainable waste treatment plants, energy efficient façades, and other "green" building practices were standard. Indeed, a handful of theme-towns—from Luodian Town to Palais de Fortune to Canadian Maple Town—exhibit this split-identity of anachronistic "skins" on hyper-modern bodies. The disconnect between form and function only serves to signal that the fundamental motives driving the creation of simulacra colonies are less pragmatic than they are symbolic and have to do with reflecting and shaping attitudes toward what it means to be Chinese in a world in which China is competing with the West for economic dominance.

Giving Up on Chinese

Real estate developers may build the Euro-style forms because they sell well, but why have these replica communities been so successful in the marketplace? What underlies the appeal of an anachronistic West? What can the Western theme provide that a Chinese style cannot? A closer examination of the contemporary Chinese sociocultural landscape helps to reveal why the Western style was chosen for these residential enclaves, as well as the significance and connotations of foreign architecture.

Eco writes in *Travels in Hyperreality*, "Baroque rhetoric, eclectic frenzy, and compulsive imitation prevail where wealth has no history."[35] To be sure, with a past of several thousand years, no one would argue that China lacks history. Yet it is true that wealth is perceived as having neither a history nor a place in China's most recent national architectural idioms, defined as those dating back to the early nineteenth century through the pre-Reform era in the twentieth century. This outlook helps to explain why autochthonous building forms have not been exploited for the construction of new residential developments.

During the Mao era, the nation developed a signature indigenous architectural style based on the idea of design with a "national form, socialist content."[36] New construction was Soviet-inspired socialist neoclassicism at best, and at worst it was plain, stark, and cramped. The mis-industrialization of the country under Mao left the nation short on both building materials and funds. Having to scrimp on shelter, the nation perforce opted to have function precede form. A government slogan adopted in the 1970s both sums up the official policy on housing construction and highlights the scarcity of the nation's resources at this time: "Functional, economical; delightful if conditions permit."[37]

Chinese architects do not look to this recent past for design inspiration. This type of building is no longer desirable, and the crowded apartment complexes and concrete structures that were the product of this design credo have become inextricably linked with China's grim socialist past. While today the West may symbolize "rich, comfortable, and advanced," the Chinese socialist style connotes "poor, uncomfortable, regressive."[38]

The Chinese "do not want to replicate the styles of architecture that represent their most recent past," notes Paul Rice, an architect with Atkins, the firm that designed Thames Town. "People are not quite comfortable with the recent past in terms of the quality of the architecture and of the urban planning that existed in the 1950s and 1960s."[39] Indeed, this past form of Chinese architecture fails to provide the proper trappings for a class of Chinese hoping to signal their ascent. Instead, it has fallen by the wayside, deemed unfit as a model to be replicated in the new residential communities.

An earlier stratum of indigenous architecture from the late nineteenth and early twentieth centuries, predating the socialist period, could conceivably have served as a reservoir of "native" historicist templates. Yet successful Chinese who make up the nation's new globally minded and ambitious middle and upper classes have exhibited limited interest in its revival. Perhaps this is the case because the deco-meets-*siheyuan*-meets-neoclassical structures of this period are also symbolic of a China in an age of decline, not glory. These styles are linked to a time in Chinese history when the nation was caught in uncomfortable growing pains, struggling to modernize and adapt long-standing traditions in light of new demands. During the half-century preceding Mao's rise, the nation was not only haunted by China's humiliating defeat in the Sino-Japanese and Opium Wars, but was also traumatized by the Japanese invasion before and during World War II. Moreover, under Mao, many of the single-family homes in these styles, particularly in China's major metropolises, were repurposed to serve as residential units

Three views of *shikumen* lane houses in Shanghai's city center. The homes, previously built as single-family residences, now house multiple families under one roof, a situation that has led to crowded interiors, courtyards, and front yards. Photographs by author.

Apartments in Eaton Town, a development in Suzhou covering over one hundred thousand square meters. The marketing materials for Eaton Town highlight the community's British architectural elements, specifically its dormer windows, brick façades, black tiles, stonework, and iron lamps. "The British lifestyle and modern urban living blend together perfectly," one description notes. Photograph courtesy of Zhang Jun.

for multiple families and fell into disrepair due to overcrowding and financial distress, which may have contributed to their rejection. Alan Balfour, dean of the College of Architecture at the Georgia Institute of Technology, observes, "It is much safer and palatable for [the Chinese] to build their fantasies based on European and American imaginations than on Chinese imaginations because the history of China over the last five hundred years has been so corrupt and abusive. All of the failures at the end of the empires resided in the buildings, so they've torn them down."[40] Starting fresh, with a new style of architecture, thus seems preferable to the forms associated with darker days.

Additionally, until very recently, contemporary designers have not been inclined to draw on China's more distant premodern architectural traditions, such as the timber-frame courtyard dwellings; multi-story, brick-wall Ming dynasty homes; or low-rise waterside canal houses. These forms, too, appear to be deemed inappropriate for housing the successful, ascendant Chinese. "There was this unspoken belief, especially when it came to these sorts of high-end developments, that if it's Chinese, it can't possibly be nice," says freelance design journalist Andrew Yang.[41] This idea persists in numerous other situations. Yang notes the belief among the Chinese that "If you buy a Chinese brand, there is not a chance in hell that it is better than a foreign brand," adding, "There is sort of an automatic belief that they do not want something that is local, as it is much more prestigious to have something that is foreign."[42] Meanwhile, for many consumers, the West, which "exudes luxury," holds a very particular allure. These home buyers "take it for granted that the architecture of a Western style is more advanced than the Chinese style."[43]

It is interesting that producers in sectors including electronics, retail, and fashion have, like real estate developers, attempted to associate their products with the West and disassociate them from China. *Newsweek* reports that when the iPhone launched in China, the model was tweaked slightly from its U.S.-distributed counterpart. Whereas phones sold in the United States bore the inscription "Designed by Apple in California and assembled in China," the Apple phones on sale in China removed the reference to China to read "Designed by Apple in California."[44] Likewise, members of the fashion and luxury goods industries admit to shipping all-but-assembled garments and accessories that are manufactured in China to Europe for final stitching and additions so that these items can legally bear labels claiming the garments have European origins. These anecdotes speak to the strength of the Chinese preference for Western products over domestic consumer goods, and it extends over the entire gamut of shopping options, from real estate to clothing, accessories to gadgets.

There is a pragmatic dimension at play here as well that should not be overlooked. Their negative cultural connotations aside, traditional Chinese homes are not as easy to adapt to the specifications of the new, high-density developments that are made to hold as many properties as possible so as to maximize a return on investment. Even the most extravagant gated enclaves, with single-family villas of 800 square meters or more and each with a private garden, are denser than their counterparts in American and European suburbs. For example, at Palais de Fortune, each of the 172 villas is approximately 1,500 square meters in size, and together these occupy a total of eighty-one acres. That averages out to little over one-third of an acre per three-story mansion.[45] Such high-density construction poses significant problems for some types of traditional Chinese residential forms. Zhu Xuan, chief architect with the Excellence Real Estate Group, contrasts the Western-type housing of "multilevel, high-density buildings" to traditional Chinese single-family detached homes, such as the *siheyuan*, which are low density and therefore "hard to adjust to the high density of China's urban population."[46] The adoption of European architecture, says Zhu, is thus "partly functional because the European style is better equipped to increase land use than traditional Chinese architecture of the past."[47] Western villa models allow developers to pack more units onto smaller lots.

Ornate Louis XV furniture, a Victorian painting in a gilded frame (not shown here), delicate teacups, and a glittering chandelier decorate the interior of a model home in the Chateau Comte de Sunac development. Chongqing. Photograph from SouFun.com.

The English County development has replicated the gates at Buckingham Palace, including even a copy of the official gilded coat of arms of the British monarch. Kunshan. Photograph from SouFun.com.

Architects and developers also point out that the "villa" is a distinctly European form that has no equivalent in Chinese culture. It should be noted that what they understand by the term "villa" is a far cry from the original country residence of Roman antiquity or the Italian Renaissance compounds. The historical villa was a sprawling enclave—part residence, part production unit, part stable and granary—surrounded by vegetable gardens and orchards and enclosed with a defensible wall in cases of attack by marauding bands. The contemporary version merely appropriates the name and uses it to denote a substantial European-styled detached residence. Among the full range of premodern Chinese houses, "free standing villas were quite rare," Ruan notes.[48] Zhu adds, "In the past, in China, we have not really had what would be referred to as a 'villa' concept."[49] Chinese consumers seem to prefer the idea of an "authentic" replica of a villa to the indigenous single-family dwellings found in their own tradition. Size alone is not the deciding factor; size plus brand is.

Many Chinese homeowners say European and American-inspired homes make a better public statement than their Chinese counterparts. That is, they project an instantly legible, forceful message about the owner's achievements and worth. For one, Western houses face outward not inward, and provide a street-facing "stage" on which to broadcast status. By contrast, premodern Chinese homes were inward-looking, surrounded by high walls and gates. The interiors of Western villas offer ample opportunity for display, featuring grandiose entrances and supersized public areas, in contrast to the more segregated living spaces of traditional homes that relegated specific, confined rooms to the function of receiving guests. "Generally speaking, the villas in China have very oversized public rooms, which has very much to do with entertainment," explains Rice. "Your home is used to entertain your colleagues or your relatives and should appear to be something very grand and formal, so there is an emphasis on the living room and reception room."[50] The layout of the Chinese residences lends itself less well to the cultural displays sought out by today's upper and middle classes.

Dreamscapes

Beneath the key practical reasons for the spread of these themed communities—a strategic interest in acquiring Western technology and style and the need for expediency and profit—lie deeper, less tangible motives and motivators. The symbolism and the cultural connotations of these stylistic "brands" play a critical role in determining the specific choices and preferences, the preeminence of Western paradigms among the simulacrascapes suggesting an impulse to manifest parity with the developed world in which these originated.

In an accounting of these communities, it must be remembered that the initiative for constructing these themed landscapes does not originate with private developers alone. Many of them were the result of directives issued by the Chinese government—an actor with a considerable holding of currency reserves and even more power. For example, the creation of a replica of Dorchester in Chengdu was conceived entirely by government officials who reportedly "fell in love" with the likeness of the British county town after seeing photographs of it on the cover of a Christmas card they had received.[51] In Anhui Province, Zhang Zhian, the former party secretary of Yingquan district in Fuyang, spent approximately 300 million RMB—or nearly a third of the district's annual revenue—to build an "extravagant" and "gargantuan" complex that replicates the U.S. Capitol and has been nicknamed the "White House."[52]

Given their size, scale, and complexity, the themed communities also require the financial and legal support of the government to assist in procuring land, obtaining financing, and resettling the residents displaced by the new construction. Moreover,

White picket fences, slate roofs, stone building façades, and a sculpture of a woman tending to a ram give an English feel to a street in British Town. Chengdu. Photograph by Zhu Zhao.

The "New York, New York" skyscraper in Chongqing evokes Manhattan's Chrysler building. Photograph by Central Business District of Chongqing Jiefangbei.

in trying to secure a peaceful transition to a new economy and a new social order, the government has a deeply vested interest in providing far more than the proverbial "iron rice bowl" to its citizens. Recognizing its people's newly awakened appetite for consumer goods, the government seems ready to feed it—though not at the expense of its ideological orthodoxy. This is why teasing out the tangle of explanations for the existence of China's Western theme-towns also requires considering these projects from a government perspective and recognizing that the motivations are both more complex and more interesting than market demand alone.

Just as many Chinese consumers aspire to owning these themed residences as personal status symbols, their government endorses them as benchmarks of the progress of the "New China" and the country's parity with the West at a countywide, provincial, and even national level. The state is set on modernizing and on staking its claim on global preeminence, and the European and American towns represent its bid to do so on the residential front.[53]

New Symbols of New China

Many commentators view the simulacrascapes as a form of "self-colonization," reading China's replication of the West as both a sign of the body politic's self-loathing and its glorification of the West.[54] A more careful, nuanced look at these projects suggests otherwise. Instead, the themed townscapes are able to serve as a symbol of the country's progress in the post-Reform era and of the successes of the Communist

Party's leadership. In replicating Westerners' homes, city plans, and lifestyles in the context of these suburban micro-territories, the Chinese are exhibiting two of their most important accomplishments: their accumulated wealth and their technical prowess. In this way, the replication of alien landscapes may be a product of China's desire to assert, for domestic and international onlookers, its ascent and entry into the ranks of global, developed nations.

These simulacra cityscapes are thus symbols of the country's recent economic miracle; they would not be possible without the government's deep pockets, nor the country's growing banks and expanding economy. In part, the answer to the question "Why has China gone West?" is "Because it can." China scrimped on building materials during the late years of the Cultural Revolution, making do with sparse ornamentation and even window screens in place of glass, but now its developers, politicians, and elite feel able to afford excesses like marble staircases in government office complexes, imported roof tiles from France, or life-size Gothic cathedrals.[55] Kuang observes that China's improved economic status has been writ large on the nation through its skyscrapers and feverish pace of construction: "China's position within the world economy is fundamentally a factor of the macroeconomic development of the nation, as well as the driving force behind urban development, which is both the result and expression of China's augmented position."[56]

The Western themed developments, with all of their extravagant expenditures on imported materials and extra-architectural flourishes, are monuments to the nation's boom. Howard French, a former *New York Times* China correspondent, highlights this stance, noting, "There is a very important symbolic value to this [simulacra-building] architectural movement. It is a statement of having arrived, of being rich and successful. It says, 'We can pick and choose whatever we want, including owning a piece of the West. In fact, we're so rich we can own the West without even having to go there.'"[57] Indeed, the foreign character of these towns—so completely recreated and such a superfluous luxury—offers evidence of just how rich China has become.

Moreover, the replication of Western cityscapes acts as a signifier of the nation's advanced state of development, made manifest through its ability to replicate Western landscapes, technology, and forms. The knowledge and familiarity with the West implied in the construction of historical architectural types offers testament to China's erudition and thorough understanding of the "other." In this ability to master the technology, design, and order of the West, the architecture serves a symbolic function as a sign of parity (economic, cultural, and social) with the top Western competitors. As one of the main characters in Jia Zhangke's film *The World* brags to his acquaintance, showing off the thorough, complete replication of the world in a Beijing theme park, "New York doesn't have the Twin Towers anymore. But we still

Upper left: A view of "Shanghai's Little White House," the Shanghai Arts and Crafts Museum, which was built in 1905 to house the director of the French Concession's Chamber of Industry. Photograph by Marlene Wilson. *Upper right:* A "White House" located in a suburb outside of Shenzhen, designed by the owner to resemble the Washington, D.C., original. Photograph by author. *Lower left:* A Tianjin concert hall built in a Palladian style has a prominent portico, row of columns, and dome. Photograph by Yue Yuewei. *Lower right:* Wuxi's "White House," pictured in front of several fish farms and adjacent to undeveloped plots of land. Photograph by Adam Minter.

have them."[58] Surpassing the West is linked with emulating the accomplishments of the West. French explains: "There is a deeply embedded ideology of progress in China that has obsessed the Chinese for the last century: to catch up to the West and, more recently, to surpass the West. Because the West is the target and object of this obsession, it also becomes the model of the obsession. Overtaking the West very often boils down to copying the West."[59] Less an architectural homage to the West, the simulacra cityscapes are a celebration of China's financial success, progress, and "ownership" of Western cultural and technical expressions.

Kuang identifies the construction of "symbolic" urban forms as one of the top ten characteristics of Chinese city building, indicating, perhaps, that the age of monumental and ideology-inflected architecture is not behind us. He compares contemporary Chinese structures to "commercial advertising" in the way that these forms often have "symbolic or metaphorical connotations" or are showy and built to impress.[60] Some architects and onlookers have criticized certain among these theme-towns as being both fiascos in their failure to attract residents and pathetic "fakes" in their "slavish imitation" of architectural "clichés."[61] But consider an alternative view: from the perspective of the planners and conceivers of these communities, the very fact of being able to master these foreign templates is sufficient for their success. What is at stake is the production of a monument rather than a city, an exhibit more than a functional object. This experiment in mythologizing the state through its skyline can be witnessed elsewhere throughout China. From the Herzog and de Meuron National Stadium to Paul Andreu's National Theater in Beijing to Rem Koolhaas's CCTV tower or the World Financial Center in Shanghai, the incredible skyscrapers rising up throughout the country may be the taller counterparts of the simulacrascapes—all projects that aim to show the nation's having achieved global status.

The instinct to use replication as a means of displaying China's sophistication is not limited to the simulacra-building movement but was also manifest in the nation's preparation for and hosting of the 2008 Olympic Games. In this case, the People's Republic was proving its ability to faithfully recreate not a constructed landscape but a cultural and athletic event of global prominence. The massive sums spent in preparation for the event—over $40 billion—not only set a record for the greatest amount ever spent on a sports tournament, but also highlighted the importance of this public propaganda effort.[62] An article in the *Wall Street Journal* explains that in the eyes of Chinese leaders and scholars, the Beijing games would "mark the country's arrival as a modern, industrialized nation" and would be a "celebration of what they [China's 1.3 billion people] see as their country's enormous economic, political, and social progress."[63] The monumental effort coincided with the country's ambitions to play a greater role on the world stage, and China's hosting of the Olympic Games, itself a tradition with roots in the West, might have been intended as a signal of China's capacity to realize the same accomplishments as the West—be it in sports, capitalism, or city building.

Imperial Theme Parks Revived

Viewing the themed government projects in the context of China's long-standing tradition of landscape construction, we recall that to the Chinese, replication has never been an entirely neutral act. Drawing this parallel between past and present offers additional evidence to indicate how on a symbolic level, these themed environs could be seen as stemming from a desire to show China's mastery over—or at the very least parity with—the West.

For many centuries Chinese emperors and commoners alike employed the flora, fauna, topography, and architecture of alien places to create true-to-scale or miniaturized duplications of real-world spaces. The emperors used their parks and paradise gardens to illustrate their own grandeur to their subjects. The natural gardens of the literati, which grew out of these imperial parks, were likewise idealized landscapes that showed elites' ability to domesticate nature and bring it under the regime of refined Chinese culture.[64] Subscribing to a worldview that posits the authentic and the copy as fluid and interchangeable, the image and its referent equally capable of harnessing the "life force" or *qi*, the Chinese may see these transplanted foreign-style cityscapes in a more literal manner than the Western viewer. As Stein notes, classical Chinese belief structures have maintained that in controlling the replica of something, one equally controls and exerts power over the real.[65] Viewed through this lens, the simulacra-building movement might be intended as a projection of China's power: its ability to control and rearrange the cosmos by metaphorically transplanting Europe and the United States into China's domain. In the act of replicating an alien referent, not only does the creator exhibit his power through the act of building a legitimate copy that captures the same "essence" as the original, but power and status are also derived from the act of possessing this replica. By underscoring a similarity between the contemporary theme-towns and traditional Chinese imperial parks, we observe that the development of these Western-style enclaves may well serve a social and symbolic purpose for the modern-day Chinese, just as they did in the past.

This explanation helps account for why the Chinese would have chosen the West—and particularly the assortment of foreign places, landmarks, and referents on display—to replicate. The European and American locales duplicated on Chinese soil represent China's conquerors and competitors from both the past and present. Given traditional Chinese conceptions of landscape replication, noted by Stein, we might observe that constructing the Western landscape on Chinese soil is a way of symbolically conquering both the former conqueror and the current competitor.[66]

Parts of China were once ruled by Western "imperialists," whose presence was at one point a grave humiliation for the nation. Early Communist revolutionaries, for example, saw Shanghai, even then a highly internationalized treaty port, as a "bitch-goddess who gnawed at their souls, scarring them brutally and indelibly."[67] China's insecurity vis-à-vis the West, a holdover feeling from the country's colonial and Communist past, may factor into the decision to replicate foreign spaces. City planners may also be appropriating and transcending the colonial past. By "imitating some of the very architectural styles that would have been offensive if imposed on them by European colonialists and Americans, we may be observing a re-appropriation or inversion of meaning, as these styles become to the Chinese something 'we can do,' rather than something that is being 'done to us,'" explains Phillip Kennicott.[68] China's simulacrascapes are Chinese-made substitutes for the original French concessions, British settlements, and German outposts; these foreign theme-towns of indigenous origins replace the European constructions built and imposed by others.

These replicated communities may not be about exerting mastery only over a past competitor, but also over current ones as well. China's rapid growth has increased its status on the world stage and resulted in a stunning increase in its influence, wealth, and capabilities. In the midst of this "peaceful rise," it appears to have set its sights on overtaking the world's richest and most powerful nation: the United States. "Based on these architectural projects, one has the feeling that China has no other ambition than to be a bigger and better America," argues Kenneth Frampton, a professor of architecture at Columbia University.[69]

Just as the landmarks of their enemies were transposed by China's premodern rulers, the American architectural icons replicated by contemporary Chinese are most often symbols of power, such as the White House, the Capitol, and even the Chrysler Building. These structures have been carefully selected for their cachet and cultural connotations: "If you build a White House, it is much more about building a symbol of power than it is about building an . . . artifact of the Renaissance," notes Mars.[70] Indeed, the Chinese have transplanted the most revered American buildings—architectural manifestations of the prized U.S. tenets of democracy, freedom, and equality—and made them their own. Yung Ho Chang, a Chinese architect and the head of the Massachusetts Institute of Technology's architecture department, notes that the U.S. White House is the "most copied building in China," serving as the model for everything from seafood restaurants to single-family homes to government offices in locales such as Guangzhou, Wuxi, Shanghai, Wenling, and Nanjing.[71] The tourism tycoon Huang Qiaoling spent $10 million on a replica of the White House and scaled-down versions of the Washington Monument and Mount Rushmore outside Hangzhou.[72] Billionaire Li Qinfu, chairman and CEO of Shanghai Matsuoka Group, built his headquarters in a canola field outside of Shanghai in the image of the U.S. Capitol Building, topping it with an eighteen-foot, three-ton bronze of himself, right hand raised as if beckoning to the future.[73] Transposing the home of the "leader of the free world" can be interpreted as a figurative appropriation of American stature and accomplishment.

The Palace of Versailles has also inspired countless private homes and even office buildings. A state-owned pharmaceutical company modeled its headquarters after Louis XIV's château and appears to have spared no expense in mimicking the original appointments. The interior is festooned with gilded bas-relief scrollwork, and the railings, ceilings, walls, and columns gleam with gold. Flowers and curlicues animate the marble flooring, chandeliers drip from the ceilings, and the long hallways are hung with paintings showing Christian themes. The windows in the conference rooms are fitted with stained glass, and the exterior of the colossal six-story edifice has been outfitted with statues, columns, and ornate carvings. All these trappings of the *ancien régime* suggest an intentional effort to inflate the status of the Harbin Pharmaceutical

Group and to embellish its reputation by association with imperial majesty, power, and wealth.

The Western-themed landscapes manifest the traditional trophy taking of alien models by ingesting, appropriating, and recreating foreign signs of prestige in a perhaps untraditional iteration. Viewing these simulacra developments in light of Chinese architectural history both complicates and elucidates the modern "theme park" developments. The simulacrascape movement becomes both new and old; something both highly Westernized and yet fundamentally Chinese; an act of insecurity and self-aggrandizement; a showing of strength and of weakness. In building the quaint, out-of-date architectural styles of developed nations, this act of duplicating the West may actually accomplish the opposite of what China intends—that is, betray the country's weakness or lack of modernity, rather than impress the world with its advanced state of development. Is it more impressive to copy the West or invent a new, better process, one that is perhaps more Chinese?[74] It is crucial to recognize that new technology, new political systems, and new information shaping the nation may not have resulted in completely new, unprecedented types of behavior but rather have given the Chinese the tools with which to continue traditional architectural legacies.

In his Pritzker Prize acceptance speech, Dutch architect and Harvard University professor Rem Koolhaas declared the age of "ideological architecture" over. He claimed that architectural undertakings were no longer dictated by the whims of a larger state apparatus. As Koolhaas explained, a new order has emerged: "The system is final. The market economy. We work in a post-ideological era. . . . The themes we invent and sustain are our private mythologies."[75] Koolhaas may have spoken too soon. As these themed residential projects attest, in nations like China, where top officials still have the final say, the laws of supply and demand do not hold as much sway. Checks and balances do not keep the more irrational impulses—feelings of cultural insecurity, unbridled ambition, or delusions of grandeur—from choking out considerations of practicality or even profit. The simulacrascape movement goes to show that in China, the market mechanism is imperfect, and it is still possible to construct not just private but also public mythologies on a grand scale.

5 RESIDENTIAL REVOLUTION

Inside the Twenty-first Century Chinese Dream

The way to live best is to eat Chinese food, drive an American car, and live in a British house. That's the ideal life.[1]

In the over three decades since the beginning of China's "Opening and Reform," the Chinese government has instituted a series of policy changes that set into motion a residential revolution that is shaping the face of the "New China." The scope of centralized planning has been judiciously reduced. Barriers to foreign investment have been lowered and in some instances dismantled. Legislation has been passed that encourages the formation and autonomy of private enterprise. A tremendous effort has gone into expanding the infrastructure and the technology that undergird urban and suburban development. And, not least, laws governing the purchase, sale, and ownership of private property have been fundamentally redrafted to relieve the state of the onus of guaranteeing and providing housing for all citizens.

Chandeliers, leather couches, and silk curtains create an ambiance of luxury at the Forest Manor sales office. Shanghai. Photograph by author.

In the midst of these reforms, China's top-down, "build-it-and-they-will-come" approach to planning is being energetically challenged in the field of residential development. The family home has emerged as the intimate arena in which socialist centralized planning is colliding with consumer resistance, and the growing success of thematic suburban communities attests to the vigor of the demand for customized lifestyles. Here, the impact of reforms that have empowered consumers to imagine and give shape to their individual identities, aspirations, and preferences is palpable and on display in the décor of the home and the decorum of daily life.

The replication of these alien residential communities and the shifts in the social order that they appear to be triggering recall philosopher Michel Foucault's seminal insight into the ways in which specific types of spaces—or "emplacements"—are amalgamated to produce new arrangements that foster cultural heterogeneity. Foucault calls these kinds of spaces "heterotopias," literally "different spaces" or "spaces of otherness." As he explains in his 1967 text "Of Other Spaces," they are "different" with respect to the dominant space of society, and they are "other" in that their very existence sets up disruptive, destabilizing juxtapositions of incompatible entities within the social order. Spatially isolated, these "other spaces" bring together dissimilar objects, practices, places, and discontinuous times that open up into "heterochronisms."[2] Disorderly by relation to the social body, they themselves propose an order that is incommensurate with that outside itself. These "real, effective places," Foucault proposes, are "are a sort of counter-emplacements . . . in which the real emplacements, all the other real emplacements that can be found within culture, are simultaneously represented, contested and inverted; a kind of places [sic] that are outside all places, even though they are actually localizable."[3] Foucault sees these places in dynamic terms, as catalysts for change within the larger social framework. "The heterotopia has the power to juxtapose in a single real place several spaces, several emplacements that are in themselves incompatible," Foucault notes.[4]

It is by thinking of the themed communities in this sense of the heterotopia as an "other"—an alternative, altered, and alternating space that interrupts the linear continuities of time and space—that their potential to mediate between opposed and opposing power positions, ideologies, and practices comes into sharper relief. These enclaves of civilizational "otherness" rupture the historical and territorial continuity of China's residential and urban traditions. Within their usually gated confines, the Chinese residents stage notions of European or American or Australian modes of life that are prompted by the architecture; the landscaping; the urban plan; the marketing program; the covenants; and the amenities of shopping, recreation, and celebration. In recreating alien models, the Chinese are introducing alien manners and mores that are inoculating the population with the habit of making lifestyle choices. As such, these residential communities stand among the most subversive forces operating on the quotidian level of Chinese life.

Within a social order that severely restricts opportunities for immersion in the alien through travel, the themed architectural landscapes provide the most expansive reference point of other spaces and through them, of non-indigenous cultural "realities." Put another way, the heterotopic communities represent an escape from a top-down imposition of ideologically viable life plots. They open up a space that permits options— in this instance, residential options—that had not typically been available or had not heretofore existed in the built landscape. In a society in which opportunities to exercise freedom of choice are limited politically and, until recently, materially, architecture allows for the exercise of certain quotidian choices. The freedom to choose between an Iberian and a British enclave gives the "New Chinese" an anodyne to mitigate the frustrations and tensions that build up within a difficult political climate. Packaged as triumphantly literal copies of iconic Western sites, cities such as Thames Town and micro-communities such as Upper East Side in Beijing seduce the body politic, specifically the new salaried and entrepreneurial classes, with a creeping heterodoxy that encourages appropriation of the token benchmarks of the Euro and American bourgeoisie.

Just as it spatializes an idea of social dynamics, so too does architecture force communities to organize in very specific ways. The Balinese *jero*, or traditional dwelling compound of the nobility, for example, translates cosmology into topography; materializes the cultural symbolism of space; and within its thick walls and central open yard precisely defines the movements, positions, and activities of its residents.[5] What it lacks in formal sleeping and eating areas it makes up for with a multiplicity of shrines to deified ancestors and other deities and ceremonial sections set apart for various sorts of rites of passage. The architecture of the home here tends to transform quotidian life into religious ritual and ceremony. In a similar way, the Chinese themed enclaves are potent shapers of relationships among the people within the communities. Moreover, their residents' lifestyles also serve as signposts to outsiders who are looking into the community of what kinds of aspirations and expectations are possible and available. These literal insights into alien spaces on domestic soil offer inspiration that is a salutatory departure from the model template of community organization that had been available to the masses in China. The heterotopic residential community in China has the potential for becoming a potent agent of a kind of pluralism that could sow the seeds for significant societal shifts. This chapter will examine the political and economic implications of an empowered consumer society exercising an unprecedented freedom to choose and will investigate the lifestyle embraced by homeowners within these themed communities, a lifestyle that offers suggestions for the future composition of the contemporary "Chinese dream."

The State in Flux

With the government reforms of the post-1979 era, such as a relaxation of restrictions on private property ownership and new economic policies that fueled wealth creation, the Chinese cast off the pragmatic and ideological straightjacket of the Mao years. As recently as four decades ago, all property in urban China, including housing, was still owned, developed, and allocated by the state. Brook Larmer writes, "Communist bureaucrats dictated where every person worked and lived, sometimes assigning family members to different cities and forbidding travel outside the 'work unit' without explicit authorization. . . . Most urban families ended up crammed into a single room,

In the Tianducheng sales office, a model of the apartments and townhouses for sale highlights their proximity to the community's replica of the Eiffel Tower. Hangzhou. Photograph by author.

surrendering privacy to neighbors with whom they shared communal bathrooms and kitchens."[6] Then, finding housing was a matter of making one's way through a cumbersome state bureaucracy that led to being assigned a unit in a concrete apartment block, crowded *siheyuan* courtyard dwelling, or repurposed *shikumen* lane house. Today the rules of the game have been completely revised. An entirely new cadre of investors, real estate developers, sales agents, and PR spinners has materialized to cater to—and shape—the tastes of buyers. China has emerged from the period of rationing, allocation, and communal living to a new era marked by discretionary income, consumer goods, and the ideal of the autonomous, individualized home.

The nation's burgeoning real estate market, which serves up almost every conceivable fantasy and competes relentlessly for new consumers, has thrown into relief the altered relationship between the government and the individual. Able to choose between Tudor townhouses and Spanish apartments, prospective buyers are in the novel position of pushing the (albeit small) levers of power that hitherto were beyond their reach. For its part, the hierarchical bureaucracy of the state has had to learn to attend to the voices of the citizens, at least when it comes to housing preferences, and to cater to their desires. Economic reform has not only thrown open the gates to involvement in the global economy and let a flood of global brands into China. By increasing the spending power of Chinese consumers, the Chinese state has also de facto given license to its citizens to experiment with freedom of expression by introducing a relative freedom of consumption. The more heterogeneous Chinese Red Guards and *tongzhi* (comrades) of yesteryear have morphed into the fashion avant-garde of today who have the financial clout and, increasingly, the marketplace savvy to define and individuate themselves through the consumer choices they make, from fashion to food. In the

process, they also subtly shape the contours and customs of a new, fluid, and multi-layered society of consumers.

Advertisements for luxury goods cover the windows of still empty storefronts in Luodian Town. Shanghai. Photograph by author.

Missing (and Making) the Mark

The mixed success of residential developments sponsored, conceived, and built by the government illustrates the dangers of proceeding without consideration for the demands of the consumer. Many of the simulacrascapes that resulted from top-down decisions by bureaucrats and officials who did not adequately consult consumer preferences or demographic trends have turned into desolate ghost towns. On the other hand, developments that were built with a more thorough understanding of the consumer have more consistently blossomed into vibrant communities.

These two different processes, one top-down and the other market-driven, have netted sharply divergent results. Two communities, one initiated by the government and another by a private firm, help illustrate this point. Spearheaded by the Shanghai government as part of the city's 2001 Master Plan, the One City, Nine Towns scheme was, for all intents and purposes, railroaded through by then mayor and secretary of the CPC Shanghai Municipal Committee Chen Liangyu, who has since been expelled from the Communist Party on corruption charges.[7] A member of the municipal advisory committee asked to evaluate Chen's plan recalls, "None of us supported the idea, but we weren't called in to criticize. We were called in to make the proposal work."[8]

Several years after completion, the majority of the ten communities built under the One City, Nine Towns plan remain ghost towns, the lavish homes unoccupied.

Completed in 2007, Luodian Town, one of the ten government-constructed towns, stands all but empty. Although nearly all of the Swedish-style residential properties had been sold, by October 2008 only twelve families had moved into a compound of 225 houses, and the town's commercial center had a mere 10 percent occupancy rate for its two hundred shop units.[9] Speculators had bought many of the properties, but a great many other units were purchased by families who were later discouraged from setting up residence by the lack of amenities and commercial tenants in the community. Even late in 2008, store fronts in Luodian Town's center were filled with refuse, imitation designer advertisements, and used cooking equipment stacked to the ceiling. Similarly, Anting Town, also constructed under the One City, Nine Towns initiative and completed in 2005, still showed an inventory of between 10 and 15 percent of total units unsold as of December 2007; a year later, in the fall of 2008, fewer than 10 percent of the residences had been occupied by homeowners.[10] Some of the residences in the One City, Nine Towns communities, such as in Canada-themed Fengjing Town, Spanish-themed Fengcheng Town, and Italian-themed Citta di Pujiang, were so difficult to sell that they were converted from commercial to government-allocated housing. Following the lackluster success of these developments, the Shanghai government, loathe to lose its investment, dedicated a portion of units to housing individuals who had been forcibly dislocated from their residences due to the state's reallocation of land.

These government-sponsored communities have been plagued by several features that a market-driven approach might have forestalled. First, the choice of location has frequently been problematic. Central planners have not always taken into account the difficulties posed by the need to commute in the absence of trains, buses, and (for some) private vehicles. Chinese have been deterred from buying into these communities given their location in remote suburbs that are cut off from established urban centers and lack public transportation. Hu Yiding explains that the Citta di Pujiang theme-town is much too far away from the city center to be appealing to home buyers: "We have trouble selling this place because the transit to the city is so far. This location is not very desirable."[11]

Second, people in the real estate industry complain of the government's lack of follow-through in supporting the projects that it initiates. Flagging communities languish unoccupied as they often fail to receive the investment in marketing efforts, transportation infrastructure, or incentives to tenants (both enterprises and individuals) necessary to grow these towns into flourishing hubs of residential and commercial life. Instead, the government-run enclaves seem to be managed with the "build-it-and-they-will-come" mentality that overlooks the need to make concerted efforts to attract tenants following the completion of the towns. According to reports from agents and managers at government-built properties, local officials are mostly concerned with selling the properties rather than filling them with families because their personal success is measured by the number of units they sell. They are less concerned with increasing land values and developing a genuine, multi-dimensional, and vibrant community. "They sold most of the apartments, and the prices went up, so they're happy," says Xing Lei of local bureaucrats. "The developer is state-owned, but if this were a private company, they would have put money into this place to try to get businesses going, so that people would be happy to move in. A private developer would make an investment in this property. The government has not."[12] This failure to follow up with developing businesses or spearheading community-promoting initiatives is attributable to some combination of bureaucratic ignorance, indifference, and inertia and evidences an instance of Maoist "old think" in the new clothing of European residential construction.

Inside the vacant shopping mall in the Spanish-themed Fengcheng Town. Shanghai. Photograph by author.

Third, the local bureaucrats who oversaw the One City, Nine Towns project did not adequately anticipate the demands of their potential consumers. Anting, Luodian, and other new towns contain high-priced luxury residences unattainable by all but the ultra-rich, many of whom have bought not one, but even several properties on a speculative basis. "This place is a waste," laments Gu Jianmin, a resident of "old Luodian," the community that borders on the new Luodian Town. "The government didn't build houses for the people who [were displaced from this land when Luodian was built], just villas, which are far too expensive for them."[13] Consumers have complained not only about the price of these homes, but also about their manner of construction. For example, some residential communities, such as Anting, included a large number of east-west facing apartments, an orientation that is considered unlucky according to the Chinese principles of *fengshui*. The inauspicious orientation of many homes means that developers have had difficulty selling anything but north-south facing residences. Chen Jiang, a native of Wenzhou now living in Thames Town, complains that the poor orientation of the house's staircase, front door, and bedrooms is "mainly what bothered me about the house. . . . The developers should have thought about this, about *fengshui* and Chinese people's way of living. That the architects didn't take that into consideration bothers me a little bit."[14] Government-initiated projects such as the One City, Nine Towns plan highlight the danger of creating massive communities and towns built according to the specifications of senior officials rather than to suit the demands of the target consumers.

By contrast, China Vanke, which counts a government-controlled conglomerate among its shareholders but is not wholly government-owned, has pursued a more consumer-focused approach that has helped it become the largest real estate developer in China, with a presence in more than thirty Chinese cities and revenues that increased 2,000 percent between 2000 and 2008.[15] China Vanke has embraced head-on the Euro-theming movement, with an ample stable of Western-branded developments to suit a range of buyer budgets and tastes, such as Galaxy Dante, Dream Town, Rancho Santa Fe, Stratford, and Holiday Landscape. China Vanke's edge, as Larmer explains, is "its ability to anticipate the needs of China's burgeoning middle class," as well as to offer properties at varying price points to encourage the burgeoning middle class to "trade up" as their financial situations improve.[16] Indeed, Li Yan outlines the rigorous market research that is conducted before the company chooses the theme, brand, and scale of its development: "We investigate the type of developments that are nearby; what schools, such as international schools, are nearby; the population of the area; the income of our target demographic; their educational background; the number of kids they have and where they go to school; whether they are foreigners, overseas Chinese, or local; and generally, their lifestyle."[17]

Before China Vanke built the Rancho Santa Fe community, modeled after the architecture found in southern California, Li says the company examined the area it intended to develop and took note of the American school, Singaporean school, and tennis club located nearby. "From that we saw that senior managers and foreigners might go there, so we figured that Rancho Santa Fe would probably be catering to people who would send their kids to these schools," Li explains. "We researched the people who were sending their kids to these schools, looking into their income, which is very important, their family structure—like how many kids they have—and also at the housing developments that had already been built nearby."[18] China Vanke's Stratford development, located not far from Rancho Santa Fe, boasted a 90 percent occupancy rate in the winter of 2008, two years after its completion.[19] Seventy percent of the villas at Rancho Santa Fe were occupied in the fall of 2008, and the homes have, according to the management, tripled in value from 10,000 to 30,000 RMB per square meter.[20] Although it is only one example, China Vanke's success in building a real estate empire highlights the power that consumers, more than ever before, can claim, as well as the benefit of creating homes that meet their demands.

It appears, at least based on an interim report, that the One City, Nine Towns Shanghai simulacrum—one of many dubiously developed government projects—failed to replicate what may have been the single most important code of the Western operating system: the checks and balances of the market economy and a democratic government, unfettered by political corruption. Perhaps a more responsive, responsible urban

Flower pots line a bridge in China Vanke's southern California–style Rancho Santa Fe development. Shanghai. Photograph by author.

design project that addressed the fundamental, functional needs for housing (affordable, sustainable, accessible, and of higher quality) would have produced a better result for a society in a state of demographic upheaval and blistering social change.

The cool reception of government-sponsored simulacra cities such as Luodian Town and Anting Town highlights the shrinking of government control over the private sector and expansion of the individual freedoms of Chinese consumers, who have new wealth, new rights, and new expectations. The tempered success of the One City, Nine Towns project, as well as other communities of its kind, suggests that the Chinese state is losing its sway over its citizenry and that the Chinese are once again reclaiming their homes as the real and symbolic centers of identity and self-realization.

The New Chinese Dream

What do these themed developments mean for the people who purchase residences in them, decorate them, cook in them, sleep in them, and raise children in them? What motivates people to take up residence in foreign abodes? And what influence will these self-contained enclaves have on the world around them? Just as they evidence political and ideological shifts on the state level, the Occidental antiquarian homes illuminate key changes in the private sphere. Anecdotal evidence and interviews with residents suggest three themes: first, that the home has reemerged as an important status symbol for the Chinese; second, that Chinese consumers are eager to acquire and adapt to foreign

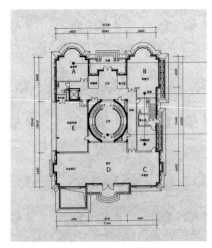

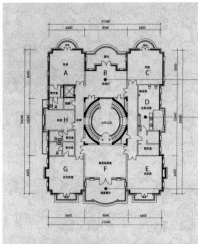

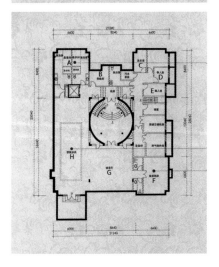

goods and customs, greeting the flood of global goods with open arms; and third, that even as the Chinese embrace aspects of foreign lifestyles, they have maintained local traditions and adapted them to their Western surroundings.

Becoming Bourgeois

The success of these landscapes speaks to a desire among wealthy Chinese to turn money into an expression of self-cultivation and self-civilization. In the midst of this new aspiration, the home has become one of the most important elements defining status and class identity. Even in the wake of communism, which brought reforms that not only abolished private property, but also demonized the landholders, the Chinese have once again embraced the mindset that property equals prestige. "If you own property, it's status," says James McGregor, a Beijing-based senior counselor for APCO Worldwide and the author of *One Billion Customers*. "Who were the wealthiest people in China before the revolution? The landlords. Mao may have killed them all, but now everybody wants to be a landlord."[21] While the form of the homes has evolved, from traditional courtyard dwellings to Italianate villas, the contemporary attitude toward the homestead seems to have reverted to the perspective prominent in premodern China, where a family's compound conveyed its social standing, the number of walls, rooms, and courtyards corresponding to the prestige of the owners.

The villas at Palais de Fortune, where each model is named after an icon of French culture, offer a glimpse at how luxurious and outsized China's Western-style mansions can be. The enormous homes, each between 1,400 and 1,600 square meters in size, offer a seemingly endless number of bathrooms, sitting rooms, bedrooms, balconies, and lounges. In the "Versailles" villa model, a grandiose curving staircase at the entrance to the home, capped by an oversized crystal chandelier, is meant to awe visitors. The ground floor alone, an expanse of marble and gold-covered fixtures, offers a plethora of public areas in which to socialize, including several dining rooms, multiple living rooms, and a drawing room. A level lower, residents have access to an indoor pool, multiple showers, and two saunas, as well as enough room for two live-in help. These mansions go far beyond providing a basic level of comfort and space, instead aiming to satisfy a deeper ambition to affirm status through residential display.

Villas fill a need that "is not material but psychological and ideological," writes architectural historian James Ackerman in his analysis of villas, and indeed China's simulacrascape inhabitants affirm that the home is the "most important" expression of identity.[22] Xie Shixiong, who is building a custom-made "palace" for his private use, observes, "Your home represents everything: your status, your taste, your style. It represents your dream. Your dream is a building. Your home symbolizes you."[23] The residents of China's simulacrascapes explain that their houses help to distinguish the class to which they belong and showcase their accomplishments. They describe in specific terms the type of image they believe their Western-inspired homes are able to convey: wealth, sophistication, modernity, and upward mobility. Zhang Xiaohong says that living at Galaxy Dante in what she describes as a "Western" house affects her identity, as well as the way she is perceived: "Galaxy Dante is a legend in its own right, so living here means we have a social identity at the upper level. When I mention that I live here, people notice. They're impressed. That's definitely part of the appeal: it shows status. That was a big thing for my husband. At middle age, my husband needs a brand or label to show his established identity in society." She observes that in a country of China's size, it is difficult, and all the more important, to find ways to distinguish and define oneself. "I would say that in contemporary China, with such a large population, you need to stand out from the crowd, which means you must show your identity in your house, or maybe in your car's brand. All that matters very much," she explains.[24] Stanley Rosen, a China specialist and professor of political science at the University of Southern California, reaffirms Zhang's explanation: "China is so big and crowded that separating yourself from the unwashed masses has always been a sign that you've made it."[25] In addition to appreciating the security and environment of their Euro-style gated communities, as will be discussed, the residents of China's themescapes are drawn to them as architectural prostheses of the self that signal their owners' distinctive and privileged identity.

As China's upper and middle classes search for the home that will best convey their achievements, developers have stepped in to help define to what they should aspire. In the absence of a vision of what the Communist Party will deliver, "these real estate projects based on European architecture have set up the new dream," says Zhou Rong. "It is not a Chinese dream but a dream that has come from abroad, from Western countries."[26]

The real estate rhetoric and fantasy of the themescapes seem to have worked: both the Chinese living in the simulacrascapes and those merely familiar with them affirm this link between "West" and "luxe." Qian Deling, a twenty-year-old interior decorator living in the outskirts of Shanghai, describes European architecture and design as "advanced," "cultured," and "beautiful."[27] Having settled in Blue Cambridge,

The floor plans for Palais de Fortune's "Versailles" line of villas. The ground floor (top) includes a drawing room (A); a dining room connected to a "Western" kitchen (B); a second dining area, adjacent to a "Chinese"-style kitchen (C); a second drawing room that is connected to a third (D); and a garage (E). The second floor (middle) amenities include four bedrooms (A, E, G, H), two of which are master bedrooms (E, G), one of which opens onto a master bath (D); a lounge with a balcony (B); a study that has a small private porch (C); and a sitting room connected to a terrace (F). The basement (bottom) offers two twin bathrooms, each with space for a sauna, shower, and lockers (A); a vault (B); a laundry room (C); two small rooms for live-in help (D, E); a home theater (F); a fitness center (G); a swimming pool (H); and several rooms dedicated to maintenance and utilities, such as the boiler, air conditioning, and plumbing systems. Beijing. Image by Fortune Real Estate Group.

Zhang Xiaohong poses in the master bedroom of her home in Shenzhen's Galaxy Dante development. Photograph by author.

Wang Daoquan says he prefers Western themed communities because he believes European culture "stands for pleasure and a more artistic, refined lifestyle."[28] His wife, Lin Hai, agrees that the style "represents wealth, advancement, and beauty," while she calls Western forms "better" and "more high-class."[29] Xie sums up his view of Western things in a single word: "Terrific."[30]

However, the Chinese preference for foreign architecture is highly selective. Only styles suggesting privilege and evoking upper-class living are chosen for replication. Developers have eagerly imported France's Haussmannian apartments and châteauesque villas while exhibiting little or no interest in the buildings of Paris's *banlieues* or Naples's fascist-era high-rises. And while China's Western simulacrascapes largely look to the past for design inspiration, not all historical styles have been equally welcomed. Architects have limited themselves to copying a distinct subset of Western architecture that stems from prosperous periods of history during which the upper classes and bourgeoisie were at their zenith—celebrated, secure, wealthy, and admired—and when aesthetics took precedence over asceticism. Rational Bauhaus, anti-bourgeois Brutalist, technological Futurist, and the radically simple International style are all ignored in favor of the more lavish, opulent, and playful designs of Greek revival, Rococo, Victorian, and Beaux Arts architecture. The florid ornamentation (animals, figures, flowers) of these styles "shows that you have status, taste, and a lot of money," explains Xie.[31] Drawing parallels between the Baroque period and post-Reform China, he notes that the newly minted middle and upper classes feel a closer kinship with the ethos embodied by the more "indulgent" architectural styles: "During both the Baroque period and China's 'Open Door' policy, people were able to break through restrictions, do away with the old class systems, and enjoy a liberation of their thoughts and politics. This new liberation brings with it economic prosperity, and after this, people demand more on a spiritual level: culture, art, and pleasure."[32]

Notably, the "antique" architectural styles embraced by the Chinese in these theme-towns can generally be traced to historical periods during which Europe was defined by the ascension and dominance of the aristocracy and bourgeoisie. This preference presents a striking evolution: the Chinese have emerged from a period under Mao that sought to eliminate class distinctions, only to embrace cultural symbols and styles linked to eras when social hierarchies and class distinctions were at their most formal and institutionalized. The imitations of Versailles, Château Maisons-Laffitte, and

Italian Renaissance villas, among other forms, hark back to an age of sumptuary laws, strenuously reinforced class hierarchies, and a powerful, privileged aristocracy.

Yet it is not only the style that makes these communities appealing, but also their separation. The rigid boundaries setting these compounds apart from the people and places beyond their tightly controlled, guarded perimeters help underscore the advantaged status of the homeowners within the elite and unattainable territories. Visitors face severe scrutiny by scores of security personnel, as well as examination by the dozens of security cameras mounted throughout the properties. These selectively penetrable borders have a more practical appeal for residents as well: safety. Along with wealth and the desire to display it, the residents of these enclaves have acquired paranoia and anxiety about threats to that wealth, such as theft from the poor or persecution by the "have-nots." It is interesting that gating, once an essential feature of the Maoist *danwei*, or work unit, has been adapted by the post-socialist middle class to cordon off their communities. China's more capitalist economic policies have helped a few get very rich quickly, sometimes through means of dubious legality, and the state is frequently ambiguous on whether the rich should be celebrated or censured. A new insecurity has arisen from the emergence of divergent views on how life should and can be lived in twenty-first-century China. Those who "have" fear threats from those who do not. Inequality, competition, and jealousy have been fostered by the rapid rise enjoyed by some and the lack suffered by many. Such anxieties are evident in the domestic architecture.

A guard wearing a red coat and white gloves at Palais de Fortune mans a gate, one of several that visitors must pass through to gain entrance to the carefully guarded development. Beijing. Photograph by author.

Just beyond this imposing, Neoclassical archway at the entrance to the Fontainebleau Villas development awaits a second set of gates, tended to by a team of security guards. Shanghai. Photograph by author.

To those who are excluded from them, these communities function as spectacles and, depending on one's ideological slant, objects of repugnance or desire. Outsiders recognize the themed landscapes as desirable and admit that they are something to which they aspire even as they criticize the waste and indulgence they observe within. The ethos of conspicuous consumption seems to have replaced, and stands in direct contrast to, the Mao-era ethic of conspicuous asceticism. Groundskeepers at the Fontainebleau Villas development in Shanghai complain that the wealthy homeowners are wasting the land. Yet the workers say they would treat themselves to the very same if they could afford to. "People are starving in China, and yet every year, these people here redo their lawns. It's a real waste of money, but they don't care how others live. They don't care if they waste 1,000 yuan on their grass [while] others are starving; they'll just throw money around to redo their lawn," Liu Junsheng, a security guard at Fontainebleau Villas, grumbles. Asked if he would want to live in the development, Liu looks surprised at the question. "Of course I'd move in and enjoy myself," he answers. "When you have so much money, you can waste it. I'd definitely waste it on all that, on enjoying myself."[33] A resident of "old Luodian" touring the newer Luodian Town says the Sigtuna look-alike, though currently far beyond his means, is a community to which he aspires. "I like everything about this place. There's nothing I dislike," Xing Yao affirms.[34]

In so closely linking identity with their homes, the Chinese seem to be embracing a mindset characteristic of suburbanites and members of the middle class. In *Visions of*

Suburbia, sociologist Roger Silverstone argues that suburban spaces provide a hospitable environment for the expression of social status:

> Suburban culture is a consuming culture. Fueled by the increasing commoditization of everyday life, suburbia has become the crucible of a shopping economy. It is a culture of, and for, display. The shopping mall, all glass and glitter, all climate and quality control, is the latest manifestation of the dialectic of suburban consumption. The hybridity displayed in the shopping mall is a representation, a reflection and a revelation of the hybridity of suburbia. Suburbs are places for transforming class identities. The differences grounded in the differences of position in the system of production have gradually, as Bourdieu states, been overlaid and replaced by the differences grounded in the system of consumption.[35]

Like the Americans in Levittown before them, the Chinese seem to have evolved their Californian, French, and German gated communities into habitats that express class anxieties and aspirations. The Chinese simulacra-spaces, like other suburban milieus, have been "redesigned, reformed into expressions of personal taste and identity."[36] What remains to be seen, however, is whether the Chinese will continue to view property as the foremost indicator of status, as well as what form will be viewed as the most "high profile" and desirable. As will be discussed, with time, it is possible that neotraditional Chinese architecture, or a yet-to-be defined breed of contemporary Chinese design, may supplant replicas of Paris and the White House as the coveted architectural status symbols.

Get Away in a Day

The appeal of the simulacrascapes is also conditioned by the very industrialization and accelerated development that put money in the workers' and managers' pockets. As the pollution, grime, crowding, and conflicts of the inner cities increase, wealthy Chinese are turning to safer, healthier havens for their private lives. Thus, in addition to providing wealthy Chinese with a way of showing off their financial and, more important, cultural accomplishments, these simulacrascapes also offer a place "away from it all," just as the suburbs received middle-class Americans fleeing cities in the 1950s.

Residents affirm that the fine atmosphere of the townscape is a great draw. A Tianducheng homeowner notes that one of his favorite parts of living there is that it is clean, airy, and spacious: "The environment here is very good," he explains.[37] Many Chinese have bought country homes in China's themed developments to use as a kind of rural retreat, a "get away" from the city to visit on weekends. A Tongji University survey of Anting Town residents conducted in 2008 found that over 40 percent had decided to buy homes in the German-style development because they enjoyed its "agreeable environment."[38]

A view of a main street in Holland Village, which attracts tourists from Shanghai and other nearby cities during the weekend. Photograph by author.

While those who are wealthy enough to afford the Western-style villas can travel abroad with ease, the majority of Chinese cannot, and for them, these simulacra-spaces, which they can visit on weekends or holidays, are the next best thing. In the present communities, the private living space seems at least partially transformed into a tourist environment. This prompts the question: why would the upper classes want to put their lives on public display? China's wealthy may, perhaps unwittingly but perhaps intentionally, have turned themselves into a tourist attraction for China's 1.3 billion citizens.

The duplicated Western forms also help satisfy the general populace's interest in experiencing the comforts and trademark sights of the Western world. The Chinese government has strict guidelines on foreign travel. Unless individuals are able to obtain a visa—a difficult process—Chinese are able to visit only countries officially given "approved destination status," and even then they must travel by group and leave large deposits, refundable upon return, to ensure they come back to China. Rather than relax travel policies or risk aggravating eager would-be travelers, the government may have deemed it wise to bring the world to China since so many Chinese cannot themselves go to the world.

In *The World*, a film set in a theme park, one character tells another, "And for you, too, a new world every day. . . . I see the world without leaving Beijing."[39] In China, thanks to the construction of the nation's myriad simulacrascapes, it is also now possible to "see the world" without leaving the PRC. Several articles about Thames Town, which describe with breathless enthusiasm the authentic architecture, authentic British essence, and feeling of total immersion in a foreign world, have highlighted that a great part of the appeal is the escapism the town provides.[40] Journalist Lei Min laments in an article for *Shanghai and Hong Kong Economy* that it is hard to find a place to "set yourself free and daydream" but that Thames Town provides the perfect destination.[41] "This is completely a fairy tale world," she writes. "Even though the town is less than fifty minutes from the People's Square [in the center of Shanghai], from the very first glance you would think that you are in a completely different world."[42] Indeed, except for the guarded gated communities, China's themed residential developments have been taken over by tourists, day-trippers eager for a slice of Europe. One visitor to Thames Town remarked that she had come to the *faux*-English village because "it's a good way to get the feeling of being somewhere foreign without going abroad. I feel very relaxed here, the atmosphere is so fresh and different."[43] An agent at one theme-town notes that many groups of tourists, especially retired people, come for day or weekend visits, explaining, "People who live in China cannot really go abroad, but they like the exotic, and they want to feel like they're in a different place, so they come here."[44]

The communities that have been selected for replication are those that over the centuries have evolved an instantly readable, tourist-destination identity, complete with iconic buildings and building styles. Many of these enclaves are not generic suburban tract homes but "slices of an alien world" that reproduce the distinctive features of the original "travel destination" experience—Paris, Venice, London, Orange County, New York, Madrid, Amsterdam. As such, the construction of these simulacrascapes would seem to speak to a hunch—on the part of the originators of the idea, the developers, and the consumers alike—that by broadening the stock of templates for experiences, these theme-towns satisfy the desire for an escape from the restrictions of a China walled in by centuries of subsistence economy, the iron rice bowl, and Maoist isolationism.

Moreover, in addition to satisfying Chinese people's curiosity regarding the "outside" Western world, these themed communities also provide a means of keeping China's wealthy entrepreneurs, innovators, and educated individuals from emigrating abroad. These European- and American-style enclaves provide China's wealthy and educated classes—from the factory owners in Blue Cambridge to the financiers in Thames Town or the museum directors in Vienna Gardens—with the opportunity to remain in China while living as the Western elite, with the best comforts the developed

The owners of a villa in a small Shenzhen neighborhood have relied heavily on European designs in decorating their home. This particular view of the living room shows a grandfather clock, a landscape painting evoking the Hudson River School, and leather sitting chairs on display in the public areas on the ground floor. Photograph by author.

world has to offer and that money can buy. Frequently, the people living in these communities have traveled abroad and even lived abroad. Li observes, "Most of the people who buy European-style villas to live in will either have been abroad to study or have lived abroad for several years. They are used to living in a very Western environment, and their lifestyle is more Western, and they would like Western-style things."[45] Having grown accustomed to a certain amount of space, fresh air, and comfort, China's elite seem to require a lifestyle different from the current Chinese norm. These communities satisfy their demands while also benefiting the PRC, as China is able to retain high-value human capital—the educated, aspiring engineers, educators, scientists, and business elite who have the potential to help grow the country's GDP.

In Pursuit of the "Good Life"

As noted in chapter 3, Deng Xiaoping is credited with having affirmed that to "get rich is glorious," and these themed locales offer a specific model for what "glorious" means, communicating the definition of this refined lifestyle through promotional materials, architectural and extra-architectural elements within the landscapes, as well as sponsored leisure activities. But beyond the branding, just what is the "good life" that these theme-towns offer to their residents—daily, monthly, yearly?

The experiences of families living in China's Euro-burbs reveal how an ascendant class of "New Chinese" is embracing the material comforts and cultural practices of the West, all the while maintaining a Chinese lifestyle. "The hardware may be all Western," Thames Town resident Chai Yehua explains, "but the software is all Chinese."[46] In their form, decoration, and use, the Western-style homes reveal that a new generation of Chinese is seeking the best of all worlds: they want the ultimate comfort, luxury, and status that they see the Western forms as best suited to provide, while they also demand the familiar customs of Chinese culture. They want the privacy and individual space of the West, the technological advances of the developed world, and the material comforts of the foreign, but they seek to maintain the familiar habits native to China—the social customs with which they are familiar. They are able to choose from the best of the world, and they borrow liberally from a global buffet of possessions and practices.

This new attitude is best conveyed by Wang Daoquan's personal slogan: "The way to live best is to eat Chinese food, drive an American car, and live in a British house. That's the ideal life," he advises.[47] It is interesting that this lifestyle motto seems to have been embraced by a great many homeowners living in Western themed communities; it was mentioned on several disparate occasions during my research in China. Like Wang, Xie Shixiong observes, "There are three things that are the best in the world: the first is European buildings, the second is Chinese food, and the third is a traditional Japanese wife."[48]

Hei Hong highlights a pair of imported lamps hanging in the living room of his home in Venice Gardens. Beijing. Photograph by author.

The themed homes are a potpourri of mixed cultural influences, and the décor of the homes reflects the desire to accommodate both foreign and Chinese lifestyles. Hei Hong, a former professional ping-pong player living in the Italianate Venice Gardens development in Beijing, has positioned a white marble statue of a woman wearing a toga and a crown of leaves at the entrance to his home. A self-taught decorator and co-founder of the interior design firm HYDC, he shows off with great pride the Spanish lamps he has imported—"Most Chinese wouldn't buy these because they're uneven, and Chinese like symmetrical things, but I know European culture"—the Empire-style table and chairs he features in his dining room, and a light cornice modeled after Roman pottery, as well as portraits of his wife dancing the flamenco—"She's been to Spain," he notes. Hei is encouraging his offspring to be equally versed in Western consumer culture: he has given his five-year-old son a deck of luxury car flashcards featuring pictures of upmarket automobiles that must be matched with their maker, such as BMW, Bentley, or Lexus—and Hei reviews them with him daily.[49]

Even as Hei takes pride in his knowledge of Western culture—"Through old films and books like *Casablanca* or Victor Hugo's *Hunchback of Notre Dame*, as well as my love of ancient Greece and Rome, I've developed my sense of art and design"—the floor above his stately living room houses a traditional Chinese tearoom, decorated with calligraphy, Chinese teapots, and ornate replicas of Ming dynasty furniture. The walls are covered in gray stonework, the windows ornamented with wooden latticework, and the entrance to the room framed by a wooden curving archway. Hei emphasizes the authenticity of this Chinese enclave with the same fervor he highlights the European accents of his home. "The stone walls are made using a traditional material," Hei notes. "What people have done for thousands of years, we continue to follow. However it was done before, we now follow those rules."[50] Like Hei, Fang Fang in the Spanish-themed Goya residence in Hangzhou has decorated her home to have a decidedly modern appearance, save for a single room within the apartment that she has made into a traditional Chinese tearoom.[51]

In taking what they view as the best from all cultures, the Chinese have maintained their own lifestyles and traditions intact. Although thrilled with her British-style abode,

Inside the traditional Chinese tea room in Hei Hong's home in Venice Gardens. Beijing. Photograph by author.

Chai has maintained a Chinese way of life within her English "dream home."[52] The décor liberally combines traditional Chinese and Western elements: a replica of a Tang dynasty ceramic horse dominates the center of an ornately carved coffee table; blue and white porcelain vases hug the Queen Anne style sofa; a chandelier, imitation Botticelli painting, and silk brocade curtains frame the room. Yet returning from a trip to the market, Chai arrives with live fish in a long, flat basin of water, revealing an adherence to the Chinese preference to kill fish just before they are eaten to ensure its freshness. "The most important thing is to combine the Western and the Chinese. Now, the world is a global village, and it's good to have a combination," she observes—a maxim she is living out daily, as she drives her Audi sedan, prepares her Chinese dinner, and admires her wedding portrait, all white lace and frills.[53] Fang agrees: "People might choose to decorate in a Spanish way, but they still live in Chinese way and still cook Chinese food."[54] China's twenty-first-century consumers are now, for the first time in decades, equipped with the means, knowledge, and freedom to pick and choose from an array of cultures the comforts, habits, and goods they most desire. And this they do, combining what they view as the best of both East and West.

Status Skills

What are the implications—and potential outcomes—of the hybrid culture that is being fostered in these communities? Although the residents of these theme-towns have thus far wedded a combination of indigenous and foreign habits, striking a balance between the two, these micro-territories lure with the promise of both architectural and cultural immersion. Status symbols are not enough; status *skills* are also in high demand. That is, the Chinese inhabiting these landscapes seem to be willing to adopt, learn, and mimic the habits associated with the alien places replicated in these simulacra cityscapes and the citizens in the developed nations these environs recreate. Witness the extensive instructions on French food, art, and music given to Chinese attendees of Tianducheng's French culture festival. The development's guide to French cuisine goes beyond broad descriptions of national dishes into such minutiae as what type of fork to use; at what time the French typically take their meals ("Most French restaurants offer lunch between 12:00 and 14:00"); a taxonomy of French restaurants ("Bistros offer traditional, home-style cooking") and the appropriate dress code for each ("The men should be wearing a suit jacket and tie; ladies should in be a tailored suit or something comparable"); recommended wine pairings; the order in which dishes should be served; and even step-by-step instructions on how to savor French delicacies ("As for how to eat caviar, first lightly spread it onto the surface of the tongue, then use the tip of the tongue to slowly crush each individual grain one by one").[55] These Chinese citizens seem eager to join the ranks of the global elite, and since the cultural model of modernity is, at least for now, Western in origin, the Chinese are employing this model.

Furthermore, the churches that are standard fare in many of the Western-style enclaves have fostered the development of industries alien to China and enabled Chinese citizens to adopt certain cultural practices of their Western peers.[56] Chinese residents and visitors have adapted these cathedrals, which do not go a day without use, to serve a nonspiritual end: they are used as backdrops for bridal portraits of newlywed Chinese couples, who come in droves to pose in Western wedding gear against these *faux*-chapels. At Thames Town, the site in front of the church is so frequently used that a prop table adorned with a fake wedding cake, bottle of champagne, and basket of baguettes remains standing in front of it at all times.

An entire industry has grown around the strong desire of "New Chinese" to act out Western weddings. Over a quarter of the businesses in Thames Town are wedding service shops specializing in portraits, ceremonies, and wedding dress rentals. At Tianducheng, young Chinese brides and grooms, on a special day trip to the Hangzhou "Paris," can pay to rent Western wedding garb, take a horse-drawn carriage throughout the property, enjoy a mock wedding ceremony (priest and all), and have a professional photographer take pictures of them against the French backdrop. The practice seems to be highly popular: a Tianducheng security guard recalls that during a single October weekend, eighty-nine couples came to be "married" at the property. In this site, we can observe the replication of Western culture accompanying the replication of Western

Several couples pose for wedding portraits in front of the cathedral in Thames Town. Shanghai. Photograph by author.

cityscapes. The slogan of one town's bridal shop, Paris Dresses, even cheers, "Fall in love with a British lover!"[57]

This inclusion of Western town amenities suggests an interest in the duplication of the cultural content of foreign cities as well as their urban form. The churches not only accentuate the European character of the towns, but also help propagate Western customs. There are signs that this has already been the case. Portraits of married couples in Western bridal gear—tuxedos for the men, veils and white lace for the women—were nearly ubiquitous in the Euro-style homes. Moreover, these churches are significant because they put the Western elite lifestyle fantasy, evidently in high demand, within reach of those not able to afford a piece of the real estate. For the price of a rented wedding gown and professional portraits, young, ambitious Chinese can act out their desire to be a part of the "worldly," "cultured" Chinese global elite.

As noted, in several key ways, these Western spaces are a way for the upper and middle classes to set themselves off from the other socioeconomic groups: through

A bride and groom walk down the aisle at a chapel in Tianducheng as their re-creation of a Western wedding ceremony draws to a close. A Tianducheng employee dressed as a pastor leads the ceremony at the makeshift altar. Hangzhou. Photograph by author.

spatial sequestering, as they isolate themselves in gated communities enclosed in suburban garden cities; through conspicuous consumption, purchasing and displaying extravagant, expensive, highly distinctive private properties that others cannot afford; and also through cultural differentiation, as these micro-territories offer the opportunity to experience, practice, and adopt new cultural norms. In these simulacrascapes, the members of the Chinese upper and middle classes can become "citizens of the First World" without having to endure the solitude, marginalization, and shuffling to the bottom of the heap that is typical of the immigrant experience.

Whence comes this desire for cultural emulation? The affect of Western mannerisms may itself be a kind of status symbol—a signal of having joined the ranks of the First World global citizenry—but it could also stem from other factors. Perhaps it results from a sense of cultural insecurity? Or might it be China's desire to learn from and exploit not just the West's IP—intellectual property—but CP—cultural property?

Schooling in international etiquette has also been part of the preparation of citizenry in the elite cadres of a global culture. Like Russian nobility in the reign of Peter the Great and the Empress Catherine, who built replicas of French châteaux and English manor houses and imported French hair stylists, dressmakers, dance masters, and speech coaches so they could manifest their cultural supremacy in the coin of the realm (i.e., by mastering French elite and prestige manners), the replication of alien mannerisms and customs occurring in these residential "theme parks" is part of a larger trend going on in China today, where we see the adoption of Western practices, norms, standards of decorum, and lifestyle patterns. For example, in preparation for the Olympics, the Chinese government launched a nationwide "etiquette initiative" to do away with certain longstanding "bad habits." The rallying cry was, "Welcome the Olympics, become civilized, plant new customs."[58]

"Create a civilized and harmonious human environment for the Beijing Olympic Games!" the Communist Party urged its constituents.[59] Such measures seemed to reflect an effort to "civilize" Chinese citizens by instilling in them certain internationally recognized elements of decorum. The effort included an anti-spitting campaign, as well as the inauguration of "Seat-Offering Day."[60] The Spiritual Civilization Steering Committee of the Communist Party created a travel etiquette guidebook, offering Chinese tourists advice, such as "no spitting," "no littering," and "do not speak loudly in public," in an aim to "help correct some embarrassing habits of Chinese tourists at home and abroad."[61] Unlike their Western counterparts, the Chinese are not accustomed to waiting in line; to combat "queue hopping," the government mandated that the eleventh of every month must be "Wait in Line Day."[62] A Communist Party official, Zi Huayun, declared in a 2007 party meeting regarding the planning of the Olympic Games, "Spitting, cutting in line, smoking at will, and criticizing the nation: these are what I see as the four 'evils.' . . . These uncivilized action behaviors all may seem like small things, but they have a grave influence on the spirit and ethos of the capital."[63]

While it is far-fetched to suggest that cultivating good manners is akin to a government effort at Westernizing the Chinese population, it is worth noting that through these campaigns the government does seem to be aiming to do away with certain local behavioral predilections and cultural habits. This government-backed "makeover" appears to be an effort to teach Chinese to replicate behaviors common abroad and typical of Western countries. In an article for *Vanity Fair*, journalist William Langewiesche observes that stewardesses on the state-owned Air China

> have taken it upon themselves to teach their passengers about the international norms of behavior. Don't shove strangers from behind when boarding the airplane, or spit on the floor, or climb over your neighbor's lap to take your seat, or stand up and start pushing for the exit immediately after the airplane has landed. An airplane is not a train, you see, and there is no chance you'll miss your stop. . . . The Chinese are said to be individualists, and a culture of self-centeredness is often on display, but at this point in their history they seem to be mostly just imitative.[64]

The simulacra cityscapes are not finishing schools for China's elite—residents do not go to these places explicitly in order to lose their "Chineseness" and be "retrained" as Western citizens. But these towns are culturally significant as they seem to be part of a larger national trend toward not only incorporating the technology and intellectual property of foreign nations, but also adopting the lifestyle and mannerisms of the Western "bourgeoisie." Furthermore, the effort suggests Chinese leaders perceive the nation's domestic citizens as suffering from cultural backwardness; the government's efforts imply the populace, like unruly schoolchildren or country-bumpkin relatives on their first trip to the big city, needs lessons on how to behave so as not to detract from the prestige of the modern, international, successful "New China."

Just as there seems to be an identity crisis in Chinese architecture, this effort to foster foreign norms may provoke an identity crisis regarding what it means to be Chinese. With communism having fallen by the wayside, what is the nation meant to strive for, dream of, hope for, and believe in? Is "glorious" enough?

Democra-scapes

It should be noted that the Western "ideology" or "lifestyle" being fostered in these "theme park" towns is not political but capitalistic and materialistic. Aristocratic, noble, and aesthetically rich lifestyles filled with luxury and fortune are relentlessly foregrounded and celebrated through a variety of mechanisms, from marketing to architecture, but nothing is said of other Western traditions, such as free speech, suffrage, and judicial limits. These towns do not yet seem to be loci for planting the seeds of democracy or fomenting the demand for a revised legislative system. Yet over time, this could very well be the end result. Property rights, which were written into the Chinese constitution only in 2007, have the potential to bring with them the call for more representation and an equal say in decision making. For example, former Shanghai bureau chief for *Newsweek* Brook Larmer reports in the *New York Times* that gated communities have led to the rise of homeowners' associations, where residents have a chance to "debate—and vote on—issues affecting their communities."[65] In January 2008, middle-class homeowners in Minhang "banded together . . . to protest the extension of a high-speed train through their neighborhoods."[66]

Even if the theme-towns do not lead to such extremes, they suggest that the residents are engaged in an ambiguous kind of cooperation with the mandates of the state. These upper- and middle-class Chinese agree with Deng's dictum that "to get rich is glorious," but having done so, they are now dramatically setting themselves apart from the rest of the country. Given that the wealthy are diverging from the norms, this may not be the kind of conformity the Chinese state had anticipated or cares to tolerate. It will be interesting to observe, over time, whether these simulacrascapes act as incubators of democracy and whether the residents will embrace the political relations characteristic of the cultures from which the architecture has been borrowed.

CONCLUSION

From Imitation to Innovation?

A Chinese proverb tells about a man who disliked his own way of walking and decided to learn how it was done in the city of Handan, whose cultural cachet was among the highest in the land. He went to the city and tried to copy the Handan walk. But instead of learning it, he only managed to forget how he had walked originally. Now incapable of walking at all, he could only crawl home, to the universal mockery of all who met him. The moral of "Learning how the Handan residents walk" (handan xue bu) is to copy only what one needs, and not everything one likes.[1]

From the perspective of the future, will the simulacra communities of the last two decades prove to be just another expensive, expansive instance of "learning how the Handan residents walk"? Or will they take root and become part of China's residential landscape? If these simulacra are to endure as anything but a passing fad in China's dynamic evolution, they must strike the proper balance between indigenous cultural attitudes and novel accommodations to the changing position of China in the global arena.

At various moments in its past, as conditions dictated, China has productively copied and internalized the alien, though never exactly as it has been doing in the present. Within the last two decades, a conjunction of political, economic, and personal catalysts has transformed China from a nation focused on satisfying basic survival needs into a major purveyor and consumer of cultural commodities.[2] Motivated by symbolic and pragmatic goals, the state and a freshly minted private market in real estate have invested vast resources into housing that offers native Chinese the experience of living abroad without leaving home and the comforts of the developed world within an emerging nation. Within their living rooms, kitchens, bedrooms, and public spaces, the residents of China's Western-style homes are—consciously or not—participating in an unprecedented experiment in culture shift that moves both from the inside out—from the walls of the communities into society at large—and from the outside in—from the residential spaces to the psychological and social constituents of the self.

The stories told by these homeowners, in their own words as well as through the mediation of the décor and the habits they have chosen, suggest that the appeal of Western antiquarian styles taps deeply into traditional beliefs, national anxieties, and a newly awakened confidence and ability to appropriate the "biggest hits" and best of Western civilization. They also clarify the algorithms of desire by which upwardly mobile Chinese calculate the vision of their ideal life.

The type of Western architecture replicated in these residential communities helps illuminate the importance of mythical connotations and their resonance with the rising middle class of Chinese. Investment-worthy cachet for Chinese home buyers goes with architectural styles that are associated with mythical images or fantasies of the source nation. New York's SoHo and Upper East Side, and California's Beverly Hills and Orange County, for example, are popular templates in the recurring Americana "heritage series" of housing developments. New York, with its aura of cosmopolitanism, sophistication, and modernity, represents one benchmark of urbanism that China aspires to surpass. California, with its legendary Hollywood glamour, theatrical wealth, luxury lifestyles, and envy-inspiring celebrity, is perceived as another pole in the oneiric self-image China projects of its new position. The choice of architectural Western paradigms says a great deal about what China wants to avoid. Tellingly, there are no Texas-themed developments, no Chicago Town, Eugene Town, or New Orleans Town. Only cities with a tourist "personality" and a distinct connection to fine living have succeeded in capturing the Chinese imagination.

Given China's tradition of embracing a more permissive attitude toward duplication and architectural imitation, there is an element to these simulacrascapes that is deeply conservative and consistent with distinctive, traditional Chinese cultural practices. Yet in this historical moment of political flux in the early twenty-first century, the simulacra landscapes are also markers of change and shift, as they foreground the new power of the people to choose and individualize their life situations. As this phenomenon moves into its third decade, it continues not only to grow at a robust rate, but also to spawn two new directions of development. Specifically, the gated-community market offers, beyond its currently widespread "Western antiquarian" stock, a growing body of newly "gentrified" homes and neighborhoods of refurbished traditional structures and new construction based on indigenous historical styles. Developers are also beginning to invest in experimental "green" architecture that is engineered according to the most advanced standards of sustainability and minimal environmental impact.

Mediterranean-style villas are crowded close together in Shanghai's Palm Springs development, which offers residents access to a sizable clubhouse and is located minutes away from a man-made beach. Photograph by author.

Sustaining the Simulacra

The extent to which the simulacra cities might represent China's best bet for achieving "onward and upward" mobility for its residential population is difficult to project. Several major factors might instead easily land them in the "hall of shame" of China's failed national improvement schemes. By and large, the success of these properties, particularly the villa communities, is contingent on China's continued economic growth. They will be viable only so long as the coffers of the upper and middle classes continue to swell. Until now, China's real estate market has been booming. Even as the United States has experienced the burst of its housing bubble and is struggling to work itself out from under a catastrophic collapse in home values, China has been riding the crest of real estate growth. Government statistics indicate that in 2009, $560 billion of residential property was sold in China, an 8 percent increase over the preceding year and a new record for the nation.[3] According to official data, home prices nationwide increased by 5.7 percent in 2009, while in cities like Shanghai housing prices have risen 150 percent since 2003.[4] Although new controls aimed at cooling the property market require any Chinese family purchasing a second house to provide at least a 40 percent down payment, speculation remains common in cities from Hangzhou to Ordos (Inner Mongolia), and many investors are content to sit on empty properties and watch their value grow. Millionaire speculators have been known to buy over fifty properties in a single sitting or to own so many hundreds of homes that they are unable to name exactly how many they have purchased.[5]

The current real estate boom in China may fuel the proliferation of and purchases in China's theme-towns, but this trend does not guarantee the development of healthy, active residential communities—or the security of their future. The almost insatiable demand for properties bodes well for the commercial success of China's Western-style estates, yet the skyrocketing prices, flood of investment, and loose credit may portend a looming real estate bubble. "Many China watchers fear the economy is running on a 'sugar high' from government stimulus funds and free-flowing credit that simply can't be sustained," warned Andy Hoffman in the *Globe and Mail* in February 2010.[6] Moreover, in September of the same year, statistics provided by Chinese media outlets indicated that approximately 64 million homes and apartments—enough property to accommodate 200 million people—had stood vacant over the past six months.[7] What will become of these townhouses, luxury apartments, and villas over time? Are they sustainable or merely additional supply for a market hungry to make a quick profit on property?

Unless the wealthy keep earning money and investing it in real estate, these residences will not only stay empty, but, worse still, could become part of the fallout from a massive real estate implosion. If China's political or economic climate shifts, these themed micro-territories could also come under fire. Isolated, distinctive, and ostentatious, the simulacra cities are easy targets for the aggression of the nation's disgruntled poor, many of whom have been left behind in China's economic miracle. Moreover, China's relationship with the West has been unpredictable; any changes in international dealings with the nations that inspired the residential communities could spell doom for these simulacrascapes.

From an ecological perspective, too, these gated communities already look like trouble. Most of them are still conceived and operationally functioning at a pre-sustainability-movement level. They are outrageously reliant on the automobile, guzzle water, and devour crucially needed farmland. Many are located miles outside the urban core and require energy-intensive long-distance commutes. In my visits to these suburban communities, I found there was at least one car per household. A personal vehicle is a necessity; most of the developments are inaccessible by public transportation owing to their having been constructed outside of urban centers and the government's failure, thus far, to connect them to a mass transit infrastructure. While China's suburbs do not replicate whole cloth America's ex-urban landscapes, they do appear to have embraced their car-dependent lifestyle.

The landscaping schemes, construction materials, and nearly ubiquitous artificial lake and canal systems in these developments necessitate large volumes of water, putting these simulacrascapes on track to exacerbate China's already dire water supply issues. Pollution from untreated waste and toxic chemicals has made 70 percent of China's rivers "not suitable for human contact."[8] Already, over 600 million people

Creeks, lakes, and small ponds crisscross the landscape in the Mediterranean Villas gated community. Shanghai. Photograph by author.

drink contaminated water every day, and the World Bank has warned that "if the current unsustainable situation is not changed, then by 2020 China will suffer the worst consequences of water scarcity: some 30 million people will become environmental refugees."[9] Sand, unobtainable from either deserts or salt water dredging, is necessary to produce the very backbone of China's growing construction campaigns: concrete. The material must be dredged from China's lake beds, frequently with disastrous environmental consequences. In *Outside In*, Jerome Silbergeld, Cary Liu, and Dora C. Y. Ching describe how such dredging has destroyed local habitats, such as Lake Poyang in Jiangxi Province, where "on average, one large dredging boat is said to pass through the mouth of the lake every thirty seconds." The lake, originally 3,700 square kilometers in size, has seen its area diminished to less than 500 square kilometers.[10]

The on-ground footprint of these communities also represents an inefficient use of land. With their driveways, manicured lawns, and acres of pavement, these expansive communities have displaced farmers from acres of arable agricultural land. An estimated forty-four thousand square miles of farmland was lost to development between 1980 and 2004.[11] Hong Kong University professor Charlie Q. L. Xue observes, "The land around big cities is usually very arable agricultural land, and now it has been eaten [up] by the unlimited development."[12] Gu Shunjun, a driver and former factory worker, has watched the farmland surrounding his home in Nanhui, a district outside of Shanghai, give way to Fontainebleau Villas, Original Mediterranean Villas, and other gated communities.

Whereas every square foot of property surrounding Gu's modest home has been cultivated with a mosaic of crops—a patch, three feet square, of eggplant; a slightly larger rectangle of rice; two apple trees; a mattress-sized crop of tomatoes, cabbage, red beans, and corn—the stately homes at Fontainebleau Villas sit on approximately four hundred hectares (nearly one thousand acres) of land.[13] "That land is wasted—they should be planting rice," Gu comments when he sees the estates, adding that farmers had lived on and cultivated that land before real estate developers took it over.[14]

A home in the Fontainebleau Villas development sits on a vast yard. Shanghai. Photograph by author.

As recently as 2006, the Chinese government imposed new land restrictions in order to curb sprawl and increase the population density of new developments. One policy, for example, required that at least 70 percent of homes in a development be smaller than ninety square meters.[15] Yet the damage has already been done: as a result of the land grabs that have transformed farmland into residential properties and factories, for the first time in the country's history, China has become a net importer of food.[16] Given the environmental fallout from these real estate ventures, the "Great Leap Forward" the Chinese government may have hoped these replicated landscapes would deliver could very well prove to be a "Massive Stumble."

The entrance to a model home in the modern, Chinese-style development Jiu Jian Tang. Shanghai. Photograph by author.

Evolving Architecture

Eco-conscious architecture and contemporary building styles are gaining ground and suggest China's evolving interest in moving beyond historicist Western designs. Already some of China's most expensive and exclusive new enclaves have embraced a design ethos more reminiscent of Frank Lloyd Wright than Louis Le Vau, Louis XIV's pet architect. For example, OCT Properties has hired architects the likes of Richard Meier to build a mere fifteen sleek cubist homes in what will be one of Shenzhen's priciest properties, nestled high in the leafy hills overlooking the coastline. Designed by Japanese architect Arata Isozaki, Jiu Jian Tang, a standout among Shanghai's most coveted and most expensive developments, combines clean, ultra-modern lines with the traditional layout of Chinese courtyard homes, labeling itself as "an endeavor to explore the modernization of China's architecture."[17] Future City, a One City, Nine Towns development located in Shanghai's Lingang district, was built several years later than its Euro-style counterparts and has abandoned the antiquated Western style for a more modern look, as its name suggests. Just as Rococo, Baroque, and Beaux Arts villas were once accessible to the elite only, China's middle classes may be quick to develop an appetite for these more modern-style homes, which may enjoy a cachet because of their as yet limited number. Over time, the consumers of the current copycat communities may even come to view the European and American simulacrascapes as critically as many Western and Chinese intellectuals do today.

A row of townhouses in Future City, a development in a suburb of Shanghai that was part of the government's One City, Nine Towns plan. Photograph by author.

Architects and developers are also beginning to experiment with "green" architecture. Beijing's Modern MOMA (also called the Linked Hybrid), designed by Steven Holl, is one of the nation's most famous examples. The high-end residential complex emphasizes "green" design and includes "geothermal heating, a wastewater recycling plant (to partially feed the site's sprawling garden), and an elaborate indoor ventilation system that pipes in clean air."[18] A score of new developments boast names evoking "harmony with nature" and eco-friendly living, such as Eco-Town, Garden Villa, Green World Garden, Greenery Villas, and Beautiful Garden, to name but a few. However, the trend toward ecological architecture appears to be less about saving the environment and more about helping developers' bottom lines. Like "French," "German," or "Swiss," "green" has emerged as yet another distinctive and desirable brand used to attract potential buyers. "Green design is still seen by developers not as smart and economical, but as a mark of luxury," journalist Alex Pasternack writes in *China Dialogue*.[19] "It is a way to sell real estate in a competitive market," adds Wang Hong, head of the Beijing branch of the environmental consultant EMSI.[20]

Even as the Chinese embrace modern forms, they are also turning toward more traditional, indigenous architectural styles, a direction that suggests potential outcomes for the Western-style enclaves. The prestige of Western symbols has helped fuel the proliferation of China's European- and North American-themed communities, culturally loaded landscapes built to project China's modernity and progress. In his analysis of

A walkway in the MOMA (Linked Hybrid) residential complex. The architect boasts that the towers' geothermal wells, as well as other eco-conscious features, make it one of the world's largest "green" residential projects. Beijing. Photograph by author.

these "transnational" suburban developments, University of Essex professor Anthony King argues that ascendant nations, including China, routinely import the cultural symbols of developed countries in order to demonstrate themselves equal to the more established states from which they borrow. He suggests this phase of replication and imitation is "inherent" in the process of "global modernity" and has been repeated in other contexts. "Every 'real' or aspiring world city strives to define itself in the context of other world cities," he writes, citing instances of Western-inspired developments in Indonesia, India, Malaysia, and Egypt, among other nations, where the aim is to "create an equivalence between these two different sets of places"—the Western and the local/domestic.[21] China's replication of Western architecture may stem from the PRC's having entered a certain "phase," one that is not unique to China, in which aspiring nations in the midst of rapid growth, urbanization, and wealth accumulation cling to architectural symbols from an established Western order, believing them to offer the aspirant the appearance of being modern and of having "arrived." Rowe echoes King's claim, linking China's "stunningly literal" architectural replicas to "similar moments in other places where you have a rapid boom and people have a sense of having arrived in the market system."[22] The transposition of Western cities and architecture into China aims to demonstrate the nation's transformation from "developing nation" to "developed," from "Third World" to "First."

If the driving force behind these communities is, in no small part, the aim to prove China's parity with the "superior" West that it imitates, what happens if and when the Chinese no longer view Western symbols as more desirable than Chinese ones but equal—or even inferior? The desirability and appeal of foreign cultures seems to be predicated in part on national wealth, making this question especially relevant in light of the global financial crisis that reached its climax in 2008. The economic woes, set off by a U.S. housing bubble, plunged the United States and Europe, among other nations, into serious recessions from which they are only beginning to recover—and even when these nations have emerged from their economic plight, they will be saddled with some of the most burdensome national debts in their histories. Although the global financial troubles have taken a toll on China, the nation's economy not only grew during the same time period in which others' faltered, but China's economic growth even outpaced economists' predictions in the second quarter of 2009.[23] It has been hailed as the first country to emerge from the global financial crisis; it overtook Germany as the world's top exporter in 2009 and in 2010 overtook Japan as the world's second-biggest economy.[24]

For China's architectural duplicators, a nation's wealth seems to be among the determinants of the value of replicating a given country's cultural symbols. If the nouveaux riches are searching for ways to showcase their wealth, sophistication, and modernity, the strategy of appropriating the culture of the most developed nations seems justifiable on the grounds that a particular package of "high-status nation" elements connotes an individual's high level of prestige. The simplistic equation—high national income equals high cultural value—suggests China could easily turn its back on the West as soon as financial troubles and reversals arise. As China becomes more developed, amasses greater wealth, and comes to see itself as the equal of its foreign competitors, will its cultural idioms and expressions be viewed as being on par with the more advanced West? And if so, what will become of these Western-style micro-territories?

Already early signals are emerging to suggest that Chinese consumers may be turning away from Western architecture in favor of their own traditional building forms. Although still a minority when compared to the Western-style residential developments, neotraditional Chinese and Chinese-themed residential communities are gaining in popularity, especially in Beijing, Chengdu, and other more conservative inland markets. Beijing's Cathay View and Yi Jun Villas, for example, are based on Beijing's traditional siheyuan courtyard houses, while other Chinese-style villa projects across China are

A home in the Cathay View development sits behind a white wall and red gate inspired by traditional Chinese residential architecture. Beijing. Photograph by author.

modeled on the vernacular architecture of other locales. Tsinghua House in Chengdu and Guangzhou or Tianlun Suiyuan in Suzhou have drawn their inspiration from the white-and-black canal-crossed communities of Suzhou, while Xuanyi Jiayuan in Beijing is modeled on building traditions native to the capital.

China Vanke's Fifth Garden community in Shenzhen, which has met with such success that it will be expanded into one of the largest developments in the area, replicates the residential architecture of Anhui, with the addition of some contemporary flourishes. The neotraditional development is built on a series of man-made canals, interlaced with intimate pathways inlaid with stone and lined with bamboo. In imitation of the regional vernacular style, each house is set behind a perimeter of tall brick walls covered, in places, with white plaster and is capped by a slate gray roof that is interrupted by a sky well (*tianjing*) within. The two-story homes also diverge from tradition to embrace more modern flourishes: they are asymmetrically composed with white exteriors, clean geometrical lines, and a scattering of different-sized windows.

Homes and a small man-made lake in the Chinese-themed Fifth Garden development. Shenzhen. Photograph by author.

Despite these updates, according to the brochure for Fifth Garden, these "old-style houses . . . shout out a feeling of being Chinese to their core," and the community's slogan boasts it is "Chinese to the bone."[25] To enhance and add authenticity to the neotraditional theme, China Vanke even renovated an old house from Anhui, transported it to the Fifth Garden site, and rebuilt it inside of a glass-walled museum showcasing traditional architecture, building methods, and illustrations and models of traditional homes. Wang Dan, a journalist who purchased a home in the development says, "My husband feels that he's regaining his childhood life when he enters the place. It's like picking up his old childhood life, only better."[26]

China's architectural critics believe this renewed appreciation for Chinese architecture has been driven by the increasing cultural "self-confidence" of the Chinese, as well as their nation's economic success. Zhou Rong observes, "China got to host the Olympic Games and took part in the WTO, and these made Chinese people think, 'We're accepted by the international family.' Chinese people also realize now, 'We have money. We have a lot of money. We're even richer than our Western rivals,' so this is part of the reason they have turned away."[27] Architect Liu Xiaoping with Shanghai's SIADR, points out that as China has become wealthier and more developed, some people have found their local architectural idioms more appealing: "Now, people are getting rich, and they are building up confidence in their own culture."[28] Campanella predicts China's interest in Western architectural accessories will only decrease as the nation's status

In Suzhou's Tianlun Suiyan, sixty-three villas are nestled behind curving walls and next to intimate gardens that attempt to re-create traditional Chinese forms. Photograph by Zhang Jun.

grows: "As this rising middle class becomes more self-confident, they're not going to need these aids or accessories pilfered from other elite cultures. Instead, they'll look to their own culture more and more."[29] Although still too early to predict the outcome of China's European and North American simulacrascapes, the rising esteem of things Chinese could potentially put an end to the nation's replication of the West and might usher in a new era in which the Pearl Tower replaces the Eiffel Tower and the Forbidden Palace replaces Versailles as the coveted status symbols.

Moreover, what is to stop the Western architectural forms from being not just left behind but actively rejected? Given China's fickle relationship with the West in the past, we should be wary of the vulnerability of these Western prototypes. As the history of Western-style architecture in China suggests, the Chinese have welcomed, turned their backs on, and embraced foreign architectural influences with equal vehemence at various points in twentieth-century history. Nationalist Chinese have shown they have little loyalty to Western nations that cross China: In the months preceding the 2008 Olympic Games, some Chinese reacted to pro-Tibetan protests in Western cities by boycotting foreign goods produced by those nations.[30] Such an outcry raises the question: Is the popularity and longevity of this simulacra-cityscape trend vulnerable to the diplomatic relations and foreign policy of the state? If so, the developers may be in trouble. Might these properties become unmarketable if anti-Western rhetoric were to get far worse?

Already China seems poised to begin exporting not only its consumer products, but also its innovations, engineering feats, and technical know-how to the developed nations for whom it has served as principal manufacturer. For example, the United States has turned to China to supply the engineers, technology, financing, and equipment to construct high-speed rail lines in California.[31] Meanwhile, even in the midst of concerns over China's environmental degradation, the nation has emerged as a leader in "green" technology, with countries eager to import its "clean coal" alternatives, solar panel cells, and wind turbine expertise. The gap may continue to widen, with China in the lead: in 2010, the PRC overtook the United States in spending on clean energy.[32] Indeed, the "culture of the copy" may represent a stage in the development of China from imitative to generative, from "apprentice" to "master" of new paradigms, from retrograde to innovative in architectural design and urban planning. China's view of the West, as well as its incorporation of Western culture into residential communities, could change drastically as the nation's position evolves.

Contradictions and Continuity

The messages these simulacra send are profoundly equivocal. Even as they evidence China's accomplishments in the economic explosion since Deng Xiaoping's Opening and Reform, they speak of a nation's preference for foreign rather than autochthonous architectural vocabularies, a want of confidence in indigenous idioms, and a lack of checks and balances on the government's legislative and executive powers. While they celebrate the triumphs and capabilities of a new class of upwardly mobile and ambitious Chinese, they also betray a nagging sense of cultural uncertainty that plagues a population grasping for appropriate symbols of modernity and achievement. To show they're "making it big," the Chinese have turned to "faking it big." And though the ability to own their own dream homes testifies to the efficacy of recent economic and political reforms, the sparsely populated status of many simulacrascapes attests to the failure of market mechanisms in a country where a single party still reigns supreme and where feasibility and function are fettered by political corruption and greed.

One of the most puzzling contradictions percolating through the simulacrascape phenomenon is also one that drills directly to its core. China may be emulating the West, but this very instinct for replication emerges from somewhere deep in the Chinese economic, political, philosophical, and social matrix.

Historical attitudes toward replication, particularly China's openness to copyworks, have provided a hospitable medium for China's contemporary ventures into place duplication. And in the decades after exiting the "dark ages" of the Cultural Revolution, flush with cash and ready to flaunt it, many in the New China found themselves casting about for a language of achievement and modernity. The vacuum left by outdated and unpalatable indigenous markers of prestige has been filled by goods, lifestyles, and building forms from the West that are viewed as exemplary of modernity, progress, and fine living. Although borrowing the methodologies of the Western world to create landscapes that harness both the spirit and "body" of the "other," it is precisely the act of borrowing these alien templates and reconstructing them on such an extensive scale that could only have emerged out of China, where a combination of power, philosophy, ambition, wealth, need, and desire came together to provide a uniquely hospitable environment in which these livable "theme park" enclaves could thrive.

The complex project of constructing simulacra cityscapes was born out of a twenty-first-century union among multiple endogenous elements: the permissive "replication of the alien" impulse that predated the Han dynasty; the openness to Western architectural innovation; the position and authority of a single-party state; and the economic empowerment of a populace chasing a Western-influenced "Chinese dream." While Tiananmen Square was a symbol of Communist China, an architectural shrine to a Socialist People's Republic, these simulacra spaces—the Venice Towns, "Oriental Paris-es," White Houses, and Versailles copies—may become the most enduring monuments to the "New China."

NOTES

Chapter 1: Into "the Land of Courtly Enjoyments"

1 Alan Balfour, interview with the author, August 27, 2008; Lin Hai, interview with the author, October 14, 2008; Quang Nguyen, interview with the author, April 17, 2010.

2 See Ronald Knapp, *China's Living Houses: Folk Beliefs, Symbols, and Household Ornamentation* (Honolulu: University of Hawai'i Press, 1999).

3 Jonathan D. Spence, *The Search for Modern China* (New York: W. W. Norton, 1991), 683–738; Fulong Wu, ed., *Globalization and the Chinese City* (New York: Routledge, 2006); Zhou Rong, interview with the author, October 16, 2008.

4 See Thomas J. Campanella, *The Concrete Dragon: China's Urban Revolution and What It Means for the World* (New York: Princeton Architectural Press, 2008).

5 Robert Fogel, "$123,000,000,000,000*," *Foreign Policy*, July 14, 2010; http://www.foreignpolicy .com/articles/2010/01/04/123000000000000.

6 Campanella, *The Concrete Dragon*, 15.

7 J. P. Morgan, "China Property Monthly Wrap," *Asia Pacific Equity Research*, March 11, 2010.

8 Wang Qian, "Short-Lived Buildings Create Huge Waste," *China Daily*, March 6, 2010; http:// www.chinadaily.com.cn/china/2010–04/06/content_9687545.htm.

9 Campanella, *The Concrete Dragon*, 15; Zhuang He, "China Real-Estate Investment Rose 16.1% in 2009, Ministry Says," *Bloomberg*, March 8, 2010; http://www.businessweek.com/news/2010–03 –08/china-s-2009-housing-investments-rise-16-1-percent-update2-.html.

10 John Ng, "Privatized Housing Impedes Cooling Efforts," *Asia Times*, July 6, 2006; http://www .atimes.com/atimes/China_Business/HG06Cb06.html.

11 "Chinese Per Capita Housing Space Triples in 20 Years," *China Daily*, March 17, 2008; http:// www.chinadaily.com.cn/bizchina/2008–03/17/content_6542889.htm.

12 David Barboza, "Skyrocketing Prices May Point to a Real Estate Bubble in China," *New York Times*, March 4, 2010; http://www.nytimes.com/2010/03/05/business/global/05yuan.html.

13 Chia-Peck Wong, "China Property Sales Rise 75.5% to 4.4 Trillion Yuan," *Businessweek*, January 18, 2010; http://www.businessweek.com/news/2010–01–18/china-s-2009-property-sales-rise -75-5-to-4–4-trillion-yuan.html; "China's Home Mortgage Lending Up 48% in 2009," *China Daily*, January 21, 2010; http://www.chinadaily.com.cn/bizchina/2010–01/21/content_9354507.htm.

14 "China's Local Governments Strive to House Average People," *People's Daily*, January 29, 2010; http://english.peopledaily.com.cn/90001/90776/90882/6882281.html; J. P. Morgan, "China Property Monthly Wrap."

15 Elizabeth Rosenthal, "North of Beijing, California Dreams Come True," *New York Times*, February 3, 2003; http://www.nytimes.com/2003/02/03/international/asia/03CHIN .html?pagewanted=1.

16 Li Yan, interview with the author, October 9, 2008.

17 "Beverly Hills," Beverly Hills; http://www.beverlyhills.com.cn; Campanella, *The Concrete Dragon*, 212.

18 "New Investors Sought for Japanese Theme Park Huis ten Bosch," GoDutch.com, April 7, 2003; http://www.godutch.com/newspaper/index.php?id=109.

19 Tom Lewis, *The Hudson: A History* (New Haven, CT: Yale University Press, 2005), 193.

20 Ibid. See also Kathleen Eagen Johnson, *Washington Irving's Sunnyside* (Tarrytown, NY: Historic Hudson Valley Press, 1995); Benson J. Lossing, *The Hudson: From the Wilderness to the Sea* (Hensonville, NY: Black Dome Press, 2000), 341–349.

21 "The Rise of Collegiate Gothic 1888–1899," Princeton Campus: An Interactive Computer History 1746–1996; http://etcweb.princeton.edu/Campus/chap5.html.

22 Robbie Brown, "In Hard Times, White House Replica Goes Up for Sale," *New York Times*, January 8, 2009; http://www.nytimes.com/2009/01/08/world/americas/08iht-08atlanta.19175714 .html.

23 "Origins of Classical Place Names in Upstate New York," York Staters; http://yorkstaters .blogspot.com/2006/01/whats-in-name-no2-origins-of-classical.html.

24 Thomas Campanella, interview with the author, September 17, 2008.

25 Xin Zhigang, "Dissecting China's 'Middle Class,'" *China Daily*, October 27, 2004; http://www .chinadaily.com.cn/english/doc/2004–10/27/content_386060.htm; "Report: China Has World's Fifth Largest Number of High Net Worth Households," *People's Daily*, October 31, 2007; http:// english.peopledaily.com.cn/90001/90776/90882/6293645.html; "Who Are China's Middle Class?" *China.org.cn*, January 23, 2010; http://www.china.org.cn/china/2010–01/23/content_19293900 .htm.

26 Angela Wiederhecker, "China: Retailers Tap into Hierarchy of the Nouveau Super-Riche," *Financial Times*, June 4, 2007; http://www.ft.com/intl/cms/s/0/0825bf90-1238-11dc-b963 -000b5df10621.html#axzzIpWHYAPY8.

27 James Fallows, *Postcards from Tomorrow Square* (New York: Vintage, 2009), 66–105.

28 See Tong Jun, "Foreign Influence in Modern China," *T'ien Hsia Monthly*, May 1938.

29 Peter G. Rowe and Seng Kuan, *Architectural Encounters with Essence and Form in Modern China* (Cambridge, MA: MIT Press, 2002), 90–95; Charlie Q. L. Xue, *Building a Revolution: Chinese Architecture since 1980* (Hong Kong: Hong Kong University Press, 2006), 85–103.

30 Rowe and Kuan, *Architectural Encounters*, 90, 92.

31 Ibid., 90.

32 Tong Ming, interview with the author, December 20, 2007.

33 Zhou Jian, "Zhongguoshi zaocheng de gainian renshi" (Understanding the Concept of Constructing the Chinese City), *Chengshi zhongguo* (Urban China), September 19, 2005; http:// www.urbanchina.com.cn/Magstall/mag050915_WMC.html.

34 "Fangzao" (Copying), *Chengshi zhonguo* (Urban China) 4 (2005): 115.

35 Lei Min, "Taiwushi xiaozhen: Yi ge chongman zhengyi de Shanghai xin dibiao" (Thames Town: A Controversial New Shanghai Landmark), *Hugang jingji* (Shanghai and Hong Kong Economy), no. 135 (2006): 18–21.

36 Tong Ming, interview with the author, December 20, 2007.

37 Charlie Q. L. Xue and Zhou Minghao, "Haiwai jianzhushi zai Shanghai 'yi cheng jiu zhen' de shijian" (Overseas Architects in Shanghai's "One City, Nine Towns" Plan), *Jianzhu xuebao* (Architectural Journal), March 2007: 24–29; Bo Hongtao, "Ouzhou chuantong chengshi kongjian zai zhongguo de fuhe yizhi" (Transplanting Traditional European Urban Spaces into China), *Jianzhu xuebao* (Architectural Journal) 20, no. 442 (2005): 76–78.

38 Rossana Hu, interview with the author, October 8, 2008.

39 Alex Chu, interview with the author, July 17, 2008; K. M. Tan, interview with the author, October 8, 2008.

40 Phillip Kennicott, interview with the author, July 31, 2008.

41 Zhou, "Zhongguoshi zaocheng de gainian renshi"; Alex Chu, interview with the author, July 17, 2008.

42 S. Anton Clavé, *The Global Theme Park Industry*, translated by Andrew Clarke (Cambridge: CAB International, 2007), 28.

Chapter 2: The Fascination with *Faux*

1 Couplet appearing on the Fulung Kuan in the Chinese temple at Er Lang miao. Quoted in Rolf A. Stein, *The World in Miniature: Container Gardens and Dwellings in Far Eastern Religious Thought*, translated by Phyllis Brooks (Stanford, CA: Stanford University Press, 1990), 53.

2 Lionel Trilling, *Sincerity and Authenticity* (Cambridge, MA: Harvard University Press, 1972).

3 Wen Fong, "The Problem of Forgeries in Chinese Painting, Part One," *Artibus Asiae* 2/3 (1962): 103.

4 Ibid.

5 Ibid., 113.

6 Yue Ko, *Da Qian Zong Lu* (*Pei Wen Zhai*, VII, 4r); quoted in Wen Fong, "The Problem of Forgeries in Chinese Painting, Part One," *Artibus Asiae*, no. 2/3 (1962): 113.

7 Fong, "The Problem of Forgeries," 115, 117.

8 See Jean Baudrillard, *Simulacra and Simulation*, translated by Sheila Faria Glaser (Ann Arbor: University of Michigan Press, 1994); Umberto Eco, *Travels in Hyperreality*, translated by William Weaver (San Diego: Harcourt, 1986); Frederic Jameson, "Postmodernism, or the Cultural Logic of Late Capitalism," *New Left Review* 1, no. 146 (July–August 1984): 53–92; Brian Massumi, "Realer than Real: The Simulacrum according to Deleuze and Guattari," *Copyright* 1, no. 1 (1987); www .anu.edu.au/hrc/first_and_last/works/realer/htm.

9 Hay writes, "China's history, in comparison [with European history], seems far more homogeneous. Even though historical study is constantly revealing a far more complex edifice than that allowed by the conventional account, there indubitably was a more significant homogeneity over a far greater stretch of time and place than was ever the case in Europe. Besides, in the way to which we have repeatedly referred, the Chinese tradition was constantly 'reprocessing' itself so that there was a generally elastic quality to its historical change" ("Values and History in Chinese Painting, II," *Res* 7/8 [Spring/Autumn 1983]: 134).

10 Ibid.

11 Jameson, "Postmodernism," 58.

12 *Notebook on Cities and Clothes*, edited by Ulrich Felsberg and Wim Wenders (Berlin: Road Movies Filmproduktion, 1989), DVD.

13 Baudrillard, *Simulacra and Simulation*, 168.

14 Massumi, "Realer than Real," 6.

15 Baudrillard, *Simulacra and Simulation*, 177.

16 Eco, *Travels in Hyperreality*, 12.

17 See Walter Benjamin, *The Work of Art in the Age of Mechanical Reproduction* (New York: Classic Books America, 2009).

18 Fong, "The Problem of Forgeries," 99.

19 Sky Canaves and Juliet Ye, "Imitation Is the Sincerest Form of Rebellion in China," *Wall Street Journal*, January 22, 2009; http://online.wsj.com/article/SB123257138952903561.html.

20 Quoted in Patti Waldmeir, "China's Mandarin Mamma Mia!" *Financial Times*, September 16, 2011; http://www.ft.com/intl/cms/s/2/0b05d818-de75-11e0-a2c0-00144feabdc0.html#axzz1oAkuBaLv.

21 Alexander Stille, *The Future of the Past* (New York: Picador, 2002), 42.

22 Michael Sullivan, *The Arts of China* (Berkeley: University of California Press, 1984), 97.

23 See Lothar Ledderose, "The Earthly Paradise: Religious Elements in Chinese Landscape Art," in *Theories of the Arts in China*, edited by Susan Bush and Christian Murck (Princeton, NJ: Princeton University Press, 1983), 165–183.

24 Quoted in Jerome Silbergeld, "Re-reading Zong Bing's Fifth-Century Essay on Landscape Painting: A Few Critical Notes," in Michael Sullivan *festschrift* volume, edited by Li Gongming (Shanghai: Shanghai shudian and Guangzhou Academy of Fine Art, forthcoming).

25 Ibid.

26 Stein, *The World in Miniature*, 51.

27 Ledderose, "The Earthly Paradise," 178.

28 Jacques Gernet, "Chinese and Christian Visions of the World in the Seventeenth Century," *Chinese Science* 4 (September 1980): 14–132.

29 Jonathan Hay, "Values and History in Chinese Painting, I," *Res* 6 (Fall 1983): 99.

30 Hay, "Values and History in Chinese Painting, I," 99–100. Zhuangzi's text reads as follows: "There is a beginning. There is not yet beginning to be a beginning. There is not yet beginning to be a not yet beginning to be beginning. There is being. There is nonbeing. There is a not yet beginning to be nonbeing. There is a not yet beginning to be a not beginning to be nonbeing. Suddenly there is being. But I do not know, when it comes to nonbeing, which is really being and which is nonbeing. Now I have just said something. But I don't know whether what I have said has really said something or whether it hasn't said something" (Zhuangzi, *The Complete Works of Zhuangzi*, translated by Burton Watson [New York: Columbia University Press, 1968], 42–43).

31 Hay, "Values and History in Chinese Painting, II," 135.

32 Laozi, *Dao de jing* (Mawangdui text, 197); quoted in Wang Pi, *Commentary on the Lao Tzu*, translated by Ariane Rump (Honolulu: University of Hawai'i Press, 1979), 128.

33 See Liu Dunzhen, *Chinese Classical Gardens of Suzhou* (*Suzhou gudian yuanlin*), translated by Chen Lixian and edited by Joseph C. Wang (Beijing: Zhongguo jianzhu gongye chubanshe, 1979).

34 See Ledderose, "The Earthly Paradise."

35 Ibid., 172.

36 Jerome Silbergeld, "Beyond Suzhou: Region and Memory in the Gardens of Sichuan," *Art Bulletin*, June 2004: 208.

37 Ban Mengjian, "Western Capital Rhapsody," in Xiao Tong, *Wen Xuan: Selections of Refined Literature*, vol. 1, *Rhapsodies on Metropolises and Capitals*, translated by David R. Knechtges (Princeton, NJ: Princeton University Press, 1987), 115.

38 Ledderose, "The Earthly Paradise," 166.

39 Ibid., 169.

40 Ledderose, "The Earthly Paradise," 169; *Xijing zaji* (I: 3a–b), quoted in Sugimura Yuzo, *Chugoku no niwa* (Tokyo: Kyuryudo, 1966), 24.

41 Ledderose describes how Emperor Wu, who had "long harbored a plan to conquer the kingdom of Kunming," finally conquered his nemesis in 107 BC. Before this victory, the emperor had constructed an artificial lake, named Kunming Lake, in his imperial park in 120 BC. Ledderose observes, "By building a Kunming lake in his park beforehand he [Emperor Wu] had symbolically anticipated this conquest" ("The Earthly Paradise," 166).

42 Commentary on Xiao Tong, *Rhapsodies on Sacrifices, Hunting, Travel, Sightseeing, Palaces and Halls, Rivers and Seas*, vol. 2 of *Wen Xuan*, 137.

43 Yang Ziyun, "Rhapsody on the Tall Poplars Palace," in Xiao Tong, *Wen Xuan*, vol. 2, *Rhapsodies on Sacrifices, Hunting, Travel, Sightseeing, Palaces and Halls, Rivers and Seas*, 149.

44 Ibid., 151.

45 Cary Liu, "Chinese Architectural Aesthetics," in Knapp and Lo, *House, Home, Family: Living and Being Chinese* (Honolulu: University of Hawai'i Press, 2005), 148.

46 Ledderose, "The Earthly Paradise," 166.

47 Stein, *The World in Miniature*, 52.

48 Liu Dunzhen, *Chinese Classical Gardens of Suzhou*, 6.

49 Ibid., 3–9.

50 Ledderose, "The Earthly Paradise," 172.

51 Ibid. See Yali Yu, *Gardens in Suzhou* (Stuttgart: Edition Axel Menges, 2003), 6–12.

52 Ledderose, "The Earthly Paradise," 172.

53 Liu Dunzhen, *Chinese Classical Gardens of Suzhou*, 6.

54 See Edward H. Schafer, "Hunting Parks and Animal Enclosures in Ancient China," *Journal of the Economic and Social History of the Orient* 11, no. 3 (October 1968): 328.

55 See Jonathan Hay, *Kernels of Energy, Bones of Earth: The Rock in Chinese Art* (New York: China House Gallery, China Institute in America, 1985), 40–68.

56 Ledderose, "The Earthly Paradise," 166.

Chapter 3: Manifestations of Westernization

1 Thames Town advertisement, Dreams Come True Realty, Shanghai, December 2007.

2 Song Yucai, interview with the author, December 16, 2007; Faith Hung and Roger Tung, "China Vanke Aims To Double Market Share to 5 Pct in Next Decade," *Reuters*, April 15, 2009; http://www.reuters.com/article/idUSTP4417920090415.

3 Chen Xin, "Yiliao zhi wai qingli zhi zhong" (Out of Expectation within Common Sense), *Xin Pujiang chengshi shenghuo* (New Pujiang City Life), June 2007, 45–53.

4 Wang Xian, interview with the author, October 2, 2008.

5 Roy Gluckman, "China Wants Growth to Go West," *Urban Land Institute*, January 2006; http://www.gluckman.com/ChongqingRealEstate.html; Mick Brown, "Chongqing, the World's Fastest Growing City," *The Telegraph*, July 12, 2009; http://www.telegraph.co.uk/news/worldnews/northamerica/usa/6207204/Chongqing-the-worlds-fastest-growing-city.html.

6 Hannah Beech, "Wretched Excess," *Time Asia Magazine*, September 23, 2002; http://www.time.com/time/asia/covers/1101020923/story.html.

7 Thomas J. Campanella, *The Concrete Dragon: China's Urban Revolution and What It Means for the World* (New York: Princeton Architectural Press, 2008), 211.

8 Peter Rowe, interview with the author, October 2, 2008.

9 "China's Local Governments Strive to House Average People," *People's Daily*, January 29, 2010; http://english.peopledaily.com.cn/90001/90776/90882/6882281.html.

10 Shen Jian, interview with the author, October 10, 2008; Yang Lijuan, interview with the author, October 13, 2008.

11 This list of architectural and design elements is similar to a set of criteria used by Guillaume Giroir in his study of gated communities in China; see Guillaume Giroir, "A Globalized Golden Ghetto in a Chinese Garden: The Fontainebleau Villas in Shanghai," in *Globalization and the Chinese City*, edited by Fulong Wu (New York: Routledge, 2005), 208–226.

12 Gu Beifang, interview with the author, October 1, 2008.

13 Wu Lingjun, interview with the author, October 10, 2008.

14 Wang Xian, interview with the author, October 2, 2008.

15 "Beverly Hills," Beverly Hills; http://www.beverlyhills.com.cn/.

16 Elizabeth Rosenthal, "North of Beijing, California Dreams Come True," *New York Times*, February 3, 2003; http://www.nytimes.com/2003/02/03/international/asia/03CHIN.html?pagewanted=1.

17 Quoted in Anthony D. King, *Spaces of Global Cultures: Architecture, Urbanism, Identity* (New York: Routledge, 2004), 120.

18 Johannes Dell, "Anting New Town: 'German Town,' a Case Study," speech delivered at UIA conference "City Edge," Anting, Shanghai, April 22, 2005; Zhang Fan, "Chengshi zhi lishi xingtai bijiao yanjiu—Yi ge lishi chengshi leixing zaisheng" (Comparative Study of Historical City Form—The Regeneration of a Type of Historical City), in *Jiedu Anting xinzhen* (Reading of Anting New Town), edited by Xu Gu (Shanghai: Tongji daxue chubanshe, 2004), 75–83.

19 Shiuan-Wen Chu and Ruurd Gietema, "Dutchness at Your Service," *Archis*, October 9, 2002; http://swchuarchitect.blogspot.com/2002_10_01_archive.html.

20 Ibid.

21 See Ronald Knapp and Kai-yin Lo, eds., *House, Home, Family*.

22 Sky Canaves, "Goodbye Holland Village: A Development Mired in Corruption Goes Down," *Wall Street Journal*, April 7, 2009; http://blogs.wsj.com/chinarealtime/2009/04/07/goodbye -holland-village-a-development-mired-in-corruption-goes-down/tab/article/.

23 Dieter Hassenpflug, "European Urban Fictions in China," *EspacesTemps.net*, October 11, 2008; http://www.espacestemps.net/document6653.htm; "Holland Village in China: Dream in Ruins," June 22, 2006; http://scorpsportal.spaces.live.com/blog/cns!DC7D6B58190D4C3D!1036.entry.

24 AP, "Chinese Copy of Austrian Village Stirs Emotions," *USA Today*, June 18, 2011; http://content .usatoday.net/dist/custom/gci/InsidePage.aspx?cId=poughkeepsiejournal&sParam=48565854 .story#.

25 Quoted in Wendy Urquhart, "Chinese Replica Plans Concerns Villagers," *BBC News*, June 18, 2011; http://www.bbc.co.uk/news/world-europe-13820048.

26 Zhou Rong, interview with the author, October 16, 2008.

27 Xie Shixiong, interview with the author, October 12, 2008.

28 Lisa Bate, interview with the author, October 1, 2008.

29 Quoted in AFP, "Les Chinois visitent Paris dans l'est de la Chine," *Atlas Vista*, November 26, 2007; http://www.avmaroc.com/actualite/chinois-visitent-a110215.html.

30 Rosenthal, "North of Beijing."

31 Fu Min, interview with the author, October 13, 2008.

32 Zhou Rong, interview with the author, October 16, 2008.

33 Cai Li, interview with the author, September 30, 2008.

34 Wen Fong, "The Problem of Forgeries in Chinese Painting, Part One," *Artibus Asiae* 2/3 (1962): 108.

35 Xing Yu, interview with the author, October 2, 2008; Dai Yin, interview with the author, October 2, 2008.

36 Guangsha Tiandu City Group, "Aili shanzhuang" (Aili Villas), *Guangsha Tianducheng*; http://www .tianducheng.net/alsz.asp.

37 Xing Ruan, interview with the author, September 15, 2008.

38 "Tianjin Tuanbo New Town, China," Halcrow: Development, Planning and Design; http://www. halcrow.com/dpd/projects/?id=0000000026; "Jiujiu bieshu (feichang dizhonghai)" (Jiujiu Villas [Very Mediterranean Style]), *Shanghai Nanhuiqu fangwu chushou* (Shanghai Nanhui District Houses for Sale); GO007.com; http://www.go007.com/Detail/108_1110246212.htm.

39 Dai Yin, interview with the author, October 2, 2008.

40 Ibid.

41 Xing Lei, interview with the author, October 1, 2008.

42 Rosenthal, "North of Beijing."

43 Wang Daoquan, interview with the author, October 1, 2008.

44 Similar methods, it should be noted, are used in theme parks. See S. Anton Clavé, *The Global Theme Park Industry*, translated by Andrew Clarke (Cambridge: CAB International, 2007).

45 Guangsha Tiandu City Group, *Guangsha Tianducheng*, sales brochure on private residential properties in Tianducheng. Retrieved from China Guangsha Real Estate offices, Hangzhou, October 2008.

46 James Tourgout, "High East Street in the Far East," *This Is Dorset*, July 27, 2007; http://www .thisisdorset.net/news/1577194.high_east_street_in_the_far_east/#.

47 "Wuhan Changdao yangbanjian" (Wuhan Long Island Showroom), *Wuhan Changdao* (Wuhan Long Island), Sina.com; http://data.house.sina.com.cn/wh32823/yangban/0_1/.

48 Er Xiaohong, interview with the author, December 18, 2007.

49 Ibid.

50 Ibid.

51 M. Brown, "Chongqing."

52 Shanghai Henghe Real Estate Co., *Taiwushi xiaozhen* (Thames Town), sales brochure on private residence properties in Thames Town. Retrieved from Dreams Come True Real Estate, Shanghai, December 2007.

53 Guangsha Tiandu City Group, "Aili shanzhuang."

54 "Façade of the Architecture," Beijing Palm Beach; http://www.bjpalmbeach.com.cn/english/main .htm.

55 Quoted in M. Brown, "Chongqing."

56 Fan Ruishu, interview with the author, December 18, 2007; Song Yucai, interview with the author, December 16, 2007.

57 "Shanghai hongjun" (Stratford), China Vanke; http://sh.vanke.com/shanghai/stratford/.

58 See Shanghai Henghe Real Estate Co., Taiwushi xiaozhen guoji yishu qu (Thames Town International Art District); http://www.thamestown.com.

59 Shanghai Henghe Real Estate Co.: "Mingren pinwei" (Celebrities' Tastes), Taiwushi xiaozhen guoji yishu qu (Thames Town International Art District); http://www.thamestown.com/people1 .htm; and "Xiaozhen xinwen" (Town News), Taiwushi xiaozhen guoji yishu qu (Thames Town International Art District); http://www.thamestown.com/culture1.htm.

60 "Chengdushi qingyangpu shangwuju guanyu 2009 Chengdu pijiujie Yingguo xiaozhen zhuti huichang huodongde zongjie baogao" (Report by Qingyang District, Chengdu Bureau of Commerce on the Organization of the 2009 British Town Oktoberfest Festival), Qingyang District Bureau of Commerce; http://www.chengdu.gov.cn/GovInfoOpens2/detail_allpurpose .jsp?id=ZH2CrCnIIZ8rP6kPoF8I.

61 Shanghai Henghe Real Estate Co., "Shanghai yuanshi yinyue jiuba" (Shanghai's Nrock Music Bar), Taiwushi xiaozhen guoji yishu qu (Thames Town International Art District); http://www .thamestown.com/business2_14.htm.

62 Shanghai Henghe Real Estate Co. "Xiaozhen shangjia" (Town Businesses), Taiwushi xiaozhen guoji yishu qu (Thames Town International Art District); http://www.thamestown.com/ business2.htm.

63 Li Xiaowei, "German Lifestyle Festival," *Shanghai Star*, May 12, 2005; http://app1.chinadaily.com .cn/star/2005/0512/ls32-1.html.

64 Ibid.

65 Ibid.

66 "Hangzhou Faguo wenhuazhou" (Hangzhou French Culture Week), Tianducity; http://www .tianducity.com/En_kjys.asp.

67 Gu Beifeng, interview with the author, October 1, 2008.

68 Zhang Xiaohong, interview with the author, October 18, 2008.

Chapter 4: Simulacra and the Sino-Psyche

1 Umberto Eco, *Travels in Hyperreality*, translated by William Weaver (San Diego: Harcourt, 1986), 26.

2 Xiaozu Wang, "State-Owned Enterprise Reform and Corporate Governance of China" (School of Management, Fudan University, 2003); http://coe21-policy.sfc.keio.ac.jp/ja/event/file/s1-6.pdf.

3 Shanghai Henghe Real Estate Co., "Guanyu xiaozhen: Songjiang xincheng jianshe fazhan youxian gongsi" (About Us: Songjiang New Town Development and Construction Company), Taiwushi xiaozhen guoji yishu qu (Thames Town International Art District); http://www.thamestown.com/ culture3_2.htm.

4 Guangsha Tiandu City Group, "Qiye wenhua" (Corporate Culture), *Guangsha Tianducheng*; http://www.tianducheng.net/qywh.asp; Fu Min, interview with author, October 13, 2008.

5 Andrew Jacobs, "Trial in Chongqing, China, Reveals Vast Web of Corruption," *New York Times*, November 3, 2009; http://www.nytimes.com/2009/11/04/world/asia/04crimewave.html ?_r=1&pagewanted=2.

6   David Barboza, "Morgan Stanley's Chinese Land Scandal," *New York Times*, March 1, 2009; http://www.nytimes.com/2009/03/02/business/worldbusiness/02morgan.html?fta=y.

7   Joe McDonald, "China Cracks Down on Stimulus-Linked Graft," *ABC News*, May 20, 2010; http://abcnews.go.com/Business/wireStory?id=10696224.

8   Peter Rowe and Seng Kuan, *Architectural Encounters with Essence and Form in Modern China* (Cambridge, MA: MIT Press, 2002), 95.

9   Ibid., 128.

10 Zheng Shiling, "Contemporary Architecture and Urbanism," in Balfour and Zheng, *Shanghai*, 130.

11 R. J. R. Kirkby, *Urbanization in China: Town and Country in a Developing Economy 1949–2000 AD* (New York: Columbia University Press, 1985).

12 "Urban and Rural Population in China, 1952–1997," *China Statistical Yearbook* (Beijing: 1998), 105; http://www.iiasa.ac.at/Research/SRD/ChinaFood/data/urban/urban_5.htm; "Population," *China Yearbook 2004*; http://english.gov.cn/2005–08/08/content_27315.htm; "China's Population Exceeds 600 Million," *China Daily*, June 16, 2009; http://www.chinadaily.com.cn/china/2009–06/16/content_8288412.htm.

13 Thomas J. Campanella, *The Concrete Dragon: China's Urban Revolution and What It Means for the World* (New York: Princeton Architectural Press, 2008), 35.

14 "Chinese Per Capita Housing Space Triples in 20 Years," *China Daily*, March 17, 2008; http://www.chinadaily.com.cn/bizchina/2008–03/17/content_6542889.htm.

15 Barbara Munch, "Orange County China, or the Genius Loci of Suburbia in the Age of Global Capitalism," *Architectural Design* 74, no. 4 (July/August 2004): 21.

16 Timo Nerger, interview with the author, December 20, 2007.

17 Wang Daoquan, interview with the author, October 1, 2008.

18 Tong Ming, interview with the author, December 20, 2007.

19 Fei Wang and Yan Wang, "Simulacra," Chinese Archimage Phenomena; http://caipcaip.blogspot.com/search/label/Simulacra.

20 "Guanyu Shanghaishi cujin chengzhen fazhan de shidian yijian" (Concerning Shanghai's Plan to Promote the Development of Towns and Cities), Falu tushuguan (Law Library); http://www.law-lib.com/lawhtm/2001/38881.htm.

21 Ibid.

22 Ibid.

23 Guangsha Tiandu City Group, "Qiye wenhua."

24 Liu Yichun, interview with the author, December 20, 2007.

25 Kuang Xiaoming, "Zhongguoshi zao cheng" (Constructing the Chinese City), *Chengshi Zhongguo* (Urban China), no. 4 (2005); http://www.urbanchina.com.cn/Magstall/mag050915_WMC.html.

26 Johann Gunnar Andersson, *The Dragon and the Foreign Devils* (Boston: Little, Brown, 1928), 242–243.

27 Xing Ruan, interview with the author, September 15, 2008.

28 Pamela Licalzi O'Connell, "Korea's High-Tech Utopia, Where Everything Is Observed," *New York Times*, October 5, 2005; http://www.nytimes.com/2005/10/05/technology/techspecial/05oconnell.html?_r=1&scp=1&sq=korea+u-city&st=nyt&oref=slogin.

29 Neville Mars, interview with the author, July 24, 2008.

30 Ibid.

31 Quoted by Louisa Lim, "China Gets its Own Slice of English Countryside," *NPR*, December 12, 2006.

32 Lin Hai, interview with the author, October 14, 2008.

33 Hu Yiding, interview with the author, September 28, 2008.

34 Xie Shixiong, interview with the author, October 12, 2008.

35 Eco, *Travels in Hyperreality*, 26.

36 Charlie Q. L. Xue, *Building a Revolution: Chinese Architecture since 1980* (Hong Kong: Hong Kong University Press, 2006), 16.

37 Quoted in ibid., 17.

38 Liu Yichun, interview with the author, December 20, 2007.

39 Paul Rice, interview with the author, September 5, 2008.

40 Alan Balfour, interview with the author, August 27, 2008.

41 Andrew Yang, interview with the author, October 4, 2008.

42 Ibid.

43 Ibid.

44 Bruce Nussbaum, "iPhones in China Don't Say They Are Assembled in China," *Businessweek*, November 30, 2009; http://www.businessweek.com/innovate/NussbaumOnDesign/archives/2009/11/iphones_in_chin.html.

45 Geoffrey A. Fowler, "In China, the Wealthy Show off Wealth with Lavish Homes," *Wall Street Journal*, October 22, 2007; http://www.realestatejournal.com/buysell/regionalnews/20071022-fowler.html.

46 Zhu Xuan, interview with the author, October 18, 2008.

47 Ibid.

48 Xing Ruan, interview with the author, September 15, 2008.

49 Zhu Xuan, interview with the author, October 18, 2008.

50 Paul Rice, interview with the author, September 5, 2008.

51 James Tourgout, "High East Street in the Far East," *This Is Dorset*, July 27, 2007; http://www.thisisdorset.net/news/1577194.high_east_street_in_the_far_east/#.

52 Chen Zhong Xiaolu, "Anhui 'baigong shuji' bei qisu" (Anhui "White House Secretary" Charged), *Caijing*, December 29, 2008; http://www.caijing.com.cn/2008–12–29/110043276.html; "Anhui baigong shuji Zhang Zhian shezian haisi jubao ren bei qisu" (Anhui "White House" Secretary Zhang Zhian, Suspected of Killing Informer, Charged), *Renmin wang* (People Online), December 27, 2008; http://bla.nointrigue.com/blog/2008/12/28/the-land-of-the-supersized-government-office/.

53 Anthony D. King, *Spaces of Global Cultures: Architecture, Urbanism, Identity* (New York: Routledge, 2004), 114.

54 See Lim, "China Gets Its Own Slice of English Countryside"; Ariana Eunjung Cha, "West Rises in China's Back Yard," *Washington Post*, April 11, 2007; http://www.washingtonpost.com/wp-dyn/content/article/2007/04/10/AR2007041001656.html.

55 Xue, *Building a Revolution*, 91.

56 Kuang, "Zhongguoshi zao cheng."

57 Howard French, interview with the author, September 11, 2008.

58 *Shijie* (The World), directed by Jia Zhangke (New York: Zeitgeist Films, 2004); DVD.

59 Howard French, interview with the author, September 11, 2008.

60 Kuang, "Zhongguoshi zao cheng."

61 Joy Wang, interview with the author, October 13, 2008; Frances Y. P. Wang, interview with the author, October 8, 2008.

62 Evan Ramstad and Gordon Fairclough, "No Comparison," *Wall Street Journal*, April 12–13, 2008, sec. Journal Report.

63 Ibid.

64 Liu Dunzhen, *Chinese Classical Gardens of Suzhou* (Suzhou gudian yuanlin), translated by Chen Lixian and edited by Joseph C. Wang (Beijing: Zhongguo jianzhu gongye chubanshe, 1979), 3–9.

65 Lothar Ledderose, "The Earthly Paradise: Religious Elements in Chinese Landscape Art," in Bush and Murck, *Theories of the Arts in China*, 166.

66 See Rolf A. Stein, *The World in Miniature: Container Gardens and Dwellings in Far Eastern Religious Thought*, translated by Phyllis Brooks (Stanford, CA: Stanford University Press, 1990).

67 Herman Mast, "Tai Chi-t'ao, Sunism, and Marxism During the May Fourth Movement in Shanghai," *Modern Asian Studies*, no. 5 (1971): 229.

68 Phillip Kennicott, interview with the author, July 31, 2008.

69 Kenneth Frampton, interview with the author, August 4, 2008.

70 Neville Mars, interview with the author, July 24, 2008.

71 Yung Ho Chang, interview with the author, September 24, 2008.

72 Hannah Beech, "Wretched Excess," *Time Asia Magazine*, September 23, 2002; http://www.time.com/time/asia/covers/1101020923/story.html.

73 Rupert Hoogewerf, "Li Qinfu, Size XL," *Forbes.com*, November 11, 2002; http://www.forbes.com/global/2002/1111/062.html; Craig S. Smith, "For China's Wealthy, All but Fruited Plain," *New York Times*, May 15, 2002; http://www.nytimes.com/2002/05/15/world/for-china-s-wealthy-all-but-fruited-plain.html.

74 Jerome Silbergeld, e-mail correspondence with the author, January 14, 2008.

75 Rem Koolhaas, speech delivered at the Pritzker Architecture Prize Formal Presentation Ceremony, Jerusalem, May 29, 2000.

Chapter 5: Residential Revolution

1 Wang Daoquan, interview with the author, October 1, 2008.

2 Michel Foucault, "Of Other Spaces" (1967), in *Heterotopia and the City: Public Space in a Postcivil Society*, edited by Michiel Dehaene and Lieven De Cauter (New York: Routledge, 2008), 20.

3 Ibid., 17.

4 Ibid., 19.

5 See R. Tan, "The Domestic Architecture of South Bali," *Bijdragen tot de Taal-, Land- en Volkenkunde* 123, no. 4 (1967): 442–475; http://www.kitlv-journals.nl.

6 Brook Larmer, "Building Wonderland," *New York Times*, April 6, 2008; http://www.nytimes.com/2008/04/06/realestate/keymagazine/406china-t.html?_r=1&emc=eta1.

7 Zhonggongzhongyang jueding jiyu Cheng Liangyu kaichudangji kaichu gongzhi chufen," (Communist Party Revokes Cheng Liangyu's Party Membership, Expels Him from His Position) *Xinhua wang* (Xinhua Net), July 26, 2007; http://news.xinhuanet.com/2007–07/26/content_6435299.htm.

8 Hannah Beech, "Ye Olde Shanghai," *Time*, February 7, 2005; http://www.time.com/time/magazine/article/0,9171,501050214–1025219,00.html.

9 Xing Yu, interview with the author, October 2, 2008.

10 Xing Lei, interview with the author, October 1, 2008; Fan Ruishu, interview with the author, December 18, 2007.

11 Hu Yiding, interview with the author, September 28, 2008.

12 Xing Lei, interview with the author, October 1, 2008.

13 Gu Jianmin, interview with the author, October 3, 2008.

14 Chen Jiang, interview with the author, September 30, 2008.

15 Larmer, "Building Wonderland."

16 Ibid.

17 Li Yan, interview with the author, October 9, 2008.

18 Ibid.

19 Wu Lingjun, interview with the author, October 10, 2008.

20 Shen Jian, interview with the author, October 10, 2008.

21 Quoted in Larmer, "Building Wonderland."

22 James Ackerman, *The Villa: Form and Ideology of Country Houses* (Princeton, NJ: Princeton University Press, 1990), 9.

23 Xie Shixiong, interview with the author, October 12, 2008.

24 Zhang Xiaohong, interview with the author, October 18, 2008.

25 Quoted in Larmer, "Building Wonderland."

26 Zhou Rong, interview with the author, October 16, 2008.

27 Qian Deling, interview with the author, October 29, 2008.

28 Wang Daoquan, interview with the author, October 1, 2008.

29 Lin Hai, interview with the author, October 14, 2008.

30 Xie Shixiong, interview with the author, October 12, 2008.

31 Ibid.

32 Ibid.

33 Liu Junsheng, interview with the author, October 11, 2008.

34 Xing Yao, interview with the author, October 2, 2008.

35 Roger Silverstone, ed., *Visions of Suburbia* (New York: Routledge, 1997), 8–9.

36 Ibid., 6–8.

37 Mr. Chen, interview with the author, September 30, 2008.

38 Rose Sauerborn, e-mail message to the author, February 27, 2008.

39 *Shijie* (The World), directed by Jia Zhangke (New York: Zeitgeist Films, 2004); DVD.

40 Lei Min: "Taiwushi xiaozhen: 'Tonghua shijie' changxiang qu" (Thames Town: A "Fairytale" World), *Hugang jingji* (Shanghai and Hong Kong Economy), no. 3 (2007): 34–36; "Taiwushi xiaozhen: Yi ge chongman zhengyi de Shanghai xin dibiao" (Thames Town: A Controversial New Shanghai Landmark), *Hugang jingji* (Shanghai and Hong Kong Economy), no. 6 (2006): 18–21.

41 Lei, "Taiwushi xiaozhen: 'Tonghua shijie' changxiang qu," 34–36.

42 Ibid. 34.

43 Cai Li, interview with the author, September 30, 2008.

44 Wu Feng, interview with the author, October 14, 2008.

45 Li Yan, interview with the author, October 9, 2008.

46 Chai Yehua, interview with the author, September 30, 2008.

47 Wang Daoquan, interview with the author, October 1, 2008.

48 Xie Shixiong, interview with the author, October 12, 2008.

49 Hei Hong, interview with the author, October 16, 2008.

50 Ibid.

51 Fang Fang, interview with the author, October 14, 2008.

52 Chai Yehua, interview with the author, September 30, 2008.

53 Ibid.

54 Fang Fang, interview with the author, October 14, 2008.

55 "Hangzhou Faguo wenhuazhou" (Hangzhou French Culture Week), Tianducity; http://www.tianducity.com/En_kjys.asp.

56 According to the CIA World Factbook, the total number of Chinese who are Daoist, Buddhist, or Christian is only between 3 and 4 percent of the total population. See "China," CIA: The World Factbook; https://www.cia.gov/library/publications/the-world-factbook/geos/ch.html.

57 Shanghai Henghe Real Estate Co., "Bali hunsha" (Paris Dresses), Taiwushi xiaozhen guoji yishu qu (Thames Town International Art District); http://www.thamestown.com/business2_3.htm.

58 "Wen jiabao zhuchi guowuyuanhui tingqu Beijing aoyun chouban jinzhan huibao" (Wen Jiabao Briefed on Preparations for Beijing Olympic Games at State Council Meeting), *Sina.com*, February 22, 2006, http://news.sina.com.cn/c/2006–02–22/18158275699s.shtml.

59 Li Yamin, "Wei Beijing aoyunhui chuangzao wenming hexie renwen huanjing" (Working Together to Build a Harmonious Society for the Beijing Olympic Games), *Beijing ribao* (Beijing Daily), February 20, 2006, http://news.sina.com.cn/c/2006–02–20/11468254334s.shtml.

60 Tao Xinlei, "Wenming limao pian: Wenming zai shengji shimin zai xingdong" (Civilizing Manners: To Improve Decorum, People Must Take Action), *Jin yang wang* (*Jin Yang* Express), August 8, 2007; http://2008.163.com/07/0808/10/3LC96DF000742437.html.

61 "Guidebook Spells Out Etiquette for Tourists," *China Daily*, September 2, 2006; http://www.china.org.cn/english/travel/179938.htm.

62 Tao, "Wenming limao pian."

63 Quoted in ibid.

64 William Langewiesche, "Beijing's Olympic Makeover," *Vanity Fair*, April 2008, 136.

65 Larmer, "Building Wonderland."

66 Ibid.

Conclusion

1 See Haiwang Yuan, *The Magic Lantern and Other Tales from the Han Chinese* (Westport, CT: Libraries Unlimited, 2006).

2 Jeff D. Opdyke, "Tapping China's Consumer-Culture Revolution," *Wall Street Journal*, May 8, 2008; http://online.wsj.com/article/SB121021001034675803.htm.

3 David Barboza, "Skyrocketing Prices May Point to a Real Estate Bubble in China," *New York Times*, March 4, 2010; http://www.nytimes.com/2010/03/05/business/global/05yuan.html.

4 Steve Mufson, "In China, Fear of a Real Estate Bubble," *Washington Post*, January 11, 2010; http://www.washingtonpost.com/wp-dyn/content/article/2010/01/10/AR2010011002767_2.html?sid=ST2010011100876.

5 Barboza, "Skyrocketing Prices."

6 Andy Hoffman, "A Shiny New City Fuels Talk of a Bubble," *Globe and Mail*, February 22, 2010; http://www.theglobeandmail.com/report-on-business/economy/a-shiny-new-city-fuels-talk-of-a-bubble/article1477545/.

7 Lillian Liu, "A Question of Time," Finance Asia, September 8, 2010; http://www.financeasia.com/News/231364,a-question-of-time.aspx.

8 Elizabeth C. Economy, *The River Runs Black* (Ithaca, NY: Cornell University Press, 2004), 69.

9 Quoted in Jiayan Mi, "Framing Ambient *Unheimlich*," in *Chinese Ecocinema in the Age of Environmental Challenge*, edited by Jiayan Mi and Sheldon Lu (Hong Kong: Hong Kong University Press, 2009), 18.

10 Jerome Silbergeld, Cary Liu, and Dora C. Y. Ching, *Outside In* (New Haven, CT: Yale University Press, 2009).

11 Thomas J. Campanella, *The Concrete Dragon: China's Urban Revolution and What It Means for the World* (New York: Princeton Architectural Press, 2008), 17.

12 Charlie Q. L. Xue, interview with the author, October 23, 2008.

13 Fulong Wu, ed., *Globalization and the Chinese City* (New York: Routledge, 2006), 211.

14 Gu Shunjun, interview with the author, October 11, 2008.

15 Jiang Zhuqing, "Ban on Villas to Be Strictly Implemented," *China Daily*, June 1, 2006; http://www.chinadaily.com.cn/cndy/2006–06/01/content_605398.htm.

16 Campanella, *The Concrete Dragon*, 17.

17 "Shanghai Zendai Group Contributes to Raising Awareness of China's Developing Architecture through Architecture Forum," *PR Newswire*, June 23, 2004; http://www2.prnewswire.com/cgi-bin/stories.pl?ACCT=104&STORY=/www/story/06–23–2004/0002198333&EDATE=.

18 Alex Pasternack, "Beijing's Eco-Friendly Architecture," *China Dialogue*, December 20, 2006; http://www.chinadialogue.net/article/show/single/en/635-Beijing-s-eco-friendly-architecture.

19 Ibid.

20 Quoted in ibid.

21 Anthony D. King, *Spaces of Global Cultures: Architecture, Urbanism, Identity* (New York: Routledge, 2004), 117.

22 Peter Rowe, interview with the author, October 2, 2008.

23 Frederik Balfour, "China Surprisingly Strong GDP Growth 7.9%," *Businessweek*, July 16, 2009; http://www.businessweek.com/globalbiz/blog/eyeonasia/archives/2009/07/chinas_gdp_grow.html.

24 "China May Report 8.5% Growth for 2009," *Businessweek*, May 1, 2010; http://www .businessweek.com/news/2010–01–05/china-may-report-8–5-growth-for-2009-official-says -update1-.html; "China First Out of Global Financial Crisis, Says Leading Expert," *Physorg.com*, July 28, 2009; http://www.physorg.com/news168010919.html; Kevin Hamlin and Li Yanping, "China Overtakes Japan as World's Second-Biggest Economy," *Bloomberg*, August 16, 2010; http://www.bloomberg.com/news/2010–08–16/china-economy-passes-japan-s-in-second -quarter-capping-three-decade-rise.html.

25 "Wanke diwuyuan: Guzili de zhongguo" (Vanke's Fifth Garden: Chinese at Its Core), sales brochure on Fifth Garden published by Vanke. Retrieved from Fifth Garden realty office, Hangzhou, October 2008.

26 Wang Dan, interview with the author, October 18, 2008.

27 Zhou Rong, interview with the author, October 16, 2008.

28 Liu Xiaoping, interview with the author, July 25, 2008.

29 Thomas Campanella, interview with the author, September 17, 2008.

30 Andrew Jacobs and Jimmy Wang, "Chinese Urge Anti-West Boycott over Tibet Stance," *New York Times*, April 20, 2008; http://www.nytimes.com/2008/04/20/world/asia/20china.html?ex=136 6344000&en=9d5069768bc4b5a7&ei=5124&partner=digg&exprod=digg.

31 Keith Bradsher, "China Offers High Speed Rail to California," *New York Times*, April 7, 2010; http://www.nytimes.com/2010/04/08/business/global/08rail.html.

32 Shai Oster, "World's Top Polluter Emerges as Green-Technology Leader," *Wall Street Journal*, December 15, 2009; http://online.wsj.com/article/SB126082776435591089.html?mod=WSJ _hpp_LEFTTopStories; Julie Schmit, "China Tops USA in Spending on Clean Energy," *USA Today*, March 25, 2010; http://www.usatoday.com/money/industries/energy/environment/2010–03–25 -china-clean-energy-investing_N.htm.

BIBLIOGRAPHY

Ackerman, James. *The Villa: Form and Ideology of Country Houses.* Princeton, NJ: Princeton University Press, 1990.

AFP. "Les Chinois visitent Paris dans l'est de la Chine." *Atlas Vista*, November 26, 2007. http://www .avmaroc.com/actualite/chinois-visitent-a110215.html.

Andersson, Johann Gunnar. *The Dragon and the Foreign Devils.* Boston: Little, Brown, 1928.

"Anhui baigong shuji Zhang Zhian shezian haisi jubao ren bei qisu" (Anhui "White House" Secretary Zhang Zhian, Suspected of Killing Informer, Charged). *Renmin wang* (People Online), December 27, 2008. http://bla.nointrigue.com/blog/2008/12/28/the-land-of-the-supersized -government-office/.

Balfour, Alan, and Zheng Shiling, eds. *Shanghai: World Cities.* Chichester, West Sussex: Wiley-Academy, 2002.

Balfour, Frederik. "China Surprisingly Strong GDP Growth 7.9%." *Businessweek*, July 16, 2009. http:// www.businessweek.com/globalbiz/blog/eyeonasia/archives/2009/07/chinas_gdp_grow.html.

Barboza, David. "Morgan Stanley's Chinese Land Scandal." *New York Times*, March 1, 2009. http:// www.nytimes.com/2009/03/02/business/worldbusiness/02morgan.html?fta=y.

———. "Skyrocketing Prices May Point to a Real Estate Bubble in China." *New York Times*, March 4, 2010. http://www.nytimes.com/2010/03/05/business/global/05yuan.html.

Baudrillard, Jean. *Simulacra and Simulation.* Translated by Sheila Faria Glaser. Ann Arbor: University of Michigan Press, 1994.

Beech, Hannah. "Wretched Excess." *Time Asia Magazine*, September 23, 2002. http://www.time .com/time/asia/covers/1101020923/story.html.

———. "Ye Olde Shanghai." *Time*, February 7, 2005. http://www.time.com/time/magazine/article/ 0,9171,501050214–1025219,00.html.

Benjamin, Walter. *The Work of Art in the Age of Mechanical Reproduction.* New York: Classic Books America, 2009.

"Beverly Hills." Beverly Hills. http://www.beverlyhills.com.cn.

Bird, Isabella. *The Yangtze Valley and Beyond.* Edinburgh: John Murray, 1899.

Bo Hongtao. "Ouzhou chuantong chengshi kongjian zai Zhongguo de fuhe yizhi" (Transplanting Traditional European Urban Spaces into China). *Jianzhu xuebao* (Architectural Journal) 20, no. 442 (2005): 76–78.

Bradsher, Keith. "China Offers High Speed Rail to California." *New York Times*, April 7, 2010. http:// www.nytimes.com/2010/04/08/business/global/08rail.html.

Brown, Mick. "Chongqing, the World's Fastest Growing City." *The Telegraph*, July 12, 2009. http:// www.telegraph.co.uk/news/worldnews/northamerica/usa/6207204/Chongqing-the-worlds -fastest-growing-city.html.

Bush, Susan, and Christian Murck, eds. *Theories of the Arts in China.* Princeton, NJ: Princeton University Press, 1983.

Campanella, Thomas J. *The Concrete Dragon: China's Urban Revolution and What It Means for the World.* New York: Princeton Architectural Press, 2008.

Canaves, Sky. "Goodbye Holland Village: A Development Mired in Corruption Goes Down." *Wall Street Journal*, April 7, 2009. http://blogs.wsj.com/chinarealtime/2009/04/07/goodbye-holland -village-a-development-mired-in-corruption-goes-down/tab/article/.

Canaves, Sky, and Juliet Ye. "Imitation Is the Sincerest Form of Rebellion in China." *Wall Street Journal*, January 22, 2009. http://online.wsj.com/article/SB123257138952903561.html.

Cha, Ariana Eunjung. "West Rises in China's Back Yard." *Washington Post*, April 11, 2007. http://www.washingtonpost.com/wp-dyn/content/article/2007/04/10/AR2007041001656.html.

Chen Xin. "Yiliao zhi wai qingli zhi zhong" (Out of Expectation within Common Sense). *Xin Pujiang chengshi shenghuo* (New Pujiang City Life), June 2007: 45–53.

Chen Zhong Xiaolu. "Anhui 'baigong shuji' bei qisu" (Anhui's "White House Secretary" Charged). *Caijing*, December 29, 2008. http://www.caijing.com.cn/2008–12–29/110043276.html.

"China." CIA: The World Factbook. https://www.cia.gov/library/publications/the-world-factbook/geos/ch.html.

"China First out of Global Financial Crisis, Says Leading Expert." *Physorg.com*, July 28, 2009. http://www.physorg.com/news168010919.html.

"China May Report 8.5% Growth for 2009." *Businessweek*, May 1, 2010. http://www.businessweek .com/news/2010–01–05/china-may-report-8–5-growth-for-2009-official-says-update1-.html.

"China's Home Mortgage Lending Up 48% in 2009." *China Daily*, January 21, 2010. http://www .chinadaily.com.cn/bizchina/2010–01/21/content_9354507.htm.

"China's Local Governments Strive to House Average People." *People's Daily*, January 29, 2010. http://english.peopledaily.com.cn/90001/90776/90882/6882281.html.

"China's Population Exceeds 600 Million." *China Daily*, June 16, 2009. http://www.chinadaily.com.cn/china/2009–06/16/content_8288412.htm.

"Chinese Per Capita Housing Space Triples in 20 Years." *China Daily*, March 17, 2008. http://www .chinadaily.com.cn/bizchina/2008–03/17/content_6542889.htm.

Chu, Shiuan-Wen, and Ruurd Gietema. "Dutchness at Your Service." *Archis*, October 9, 2002. http://swchuarchitect.blogspot.com/2002_10_01_archive.html.

Clavé, S. Anton. *The Global Theme Park Industry*. Translated by Andrew Clarke. Cambridge: CAB International, 2007.

Dell, Johannes. "Anting New Town: 'German Town,' a Case Study." Speech delivered at the UIA Conference "City Edge," Anting, Shanghai, April 22, 2005.

Eco, Umberto. *Travels in Hyperreality*. Translated by William Weaver. San Diego: Harcourt, 1986.

"Façade of the Architecture." Beijing Palm Beach. http://www.bjpalmbeach.com.cn/english/main.htm.

Fallows, James. *Postcards from Tomorrow Square*. New York: Vintage, 2009.

"Fangzao" (Copying). *Chengshi zhonguo* (Urban China) 4 (2005): 115.

Fogel, Robert. "$123,000,000,000,000*." *Foreign Policy*, July 14, 2010. http://www.foreignpolicy.com/articles/2010/01/04/123000000000000.

Fong, Wen. "The Problem of Forgeries in Chinese Painting, Part One." *Artibus Asiae* 2/3 (1962): 95–119.

"Foreign Fashions in Chinese Houses." *New York Times*, September 29, 1915.

Foucault, Michel. "Of Other Spaces (1967)." In *Heterotopia and the City: Public Space in a Postcivil Society*, edited by Michiel Dehaene and Lieven De Cauter, 13–29. New York: Routledge, 2008.

Fowler, Geoffrey A. "In China, the Wealthy Show off Wealth with Lavish Homes." *Wall Street Journal*, October 22, 2007. http://www.realestatejournal.com/buysell/regionalnews/20071022 -fowler.html.

Gernet, Jacques. "Chinese and Christian Visions of the World in the Seventeenth Century." *Chinese Science* 4 (1980): 14–132.

Giroir, Guillaume. "A Globalized Golden Ghetto in a Chinese Garden: The Fontainebleau Villas in Shanghai." In Fulong Wu, *Globalization and the Chinese City*, 208–226.

Gluckman, Roy. "China Wants Growth to Go West." *Urban Land Institute*, January 2006. http://www.gluckman.com/ChongqingRealEstate.html.

Guangsha Tiandu City Group. "Aili shanzhuang" (*Aili Villas*). *Guangsha Tianducheng*. http://www.tianducheng.net/alsz.asp.

———. *Guangsha Tianducheng*. Sales brochure on private residential properties in Tianducheng. Retrieved from China Guangsha Real Estate offices, Hangzhou, October 2008.

———. "Qiye wenhua" (Corporate Culture). *Guangsha Tianducheng*. http://www.tianducheng.net/qywh.asp.

"Guanyu Shanghaishi cujin chengzhen fazhan de shidian yijian" (Concerning Shanghai's Plan to Promote the Development of Towns and Cities). Falu tushuguan (Law Library). http://www.law-lib.com/lawhtm/2001/38881.htm.

Hamlin, Kevin, and Li Yanping. "China Overtakes Japan as World's Second-Biggest Economy." *Bloomberg*, August 16, 2010. http://www.bloomberg.com/news/2010-08-16/china-economy-passes-japan-s-in-second-quarter-capping-three-decade-rise.html.

"Hangzhou Faguo wenhuazhou" (Hangzhou French Culture Week). Tianducity. http://www.tianducity.com/En_kjys.asp.

Hassenpflug, Dieter. "European Urban Fictions in China." *EspacesTemps.net*, October 11, 2008. http://www.espacestemps.net/document6653.htm.

Hay, Jonathan. *Kernels of Energy, Bones of Earth: The Rock in Chinese Art*. New York: China House Gallery, China Institute in America, 1985.

———. "Values and History in Chinese Painting, I." *Res 6* (Fall 1983): 72–111.

———. "Values and History in Chinese Painting, II." *Res 7/8* (Spring/Autumn 1983): 102–136.

Hoffman, Andy. "A Shiny New City Fuels Talk of a Bubble." *Globe and Mail*, February 22, 2010. http://www.theglobeandmail.com/report-on-business/economy/a-shiny-new-city-fuels-talk-of-a-bubble/article1477545/.

"Holland Village in China: Dream in Ruins." June 22, 2006. http://scorpsportal.spaces.live.com/blog/cns!DC7D6B58190D4C3D!1036.entry.

Hoogewerf, Rupert. "Li Qinfu, Size XL." *Forbes.com*, November 11, 2002. http://www.forbes.com/global/2002/1111/062.html.

Hung, Faith, and Roger Tung. "China Vanke Aims to Double Market Share to 5 Pct in Next Decade." *Reuters*, April 15, 2009. http://www.reuters.com/article/idUSTP4417920090415.

Jacobs, Andrew. "Trial in Chongqing, China, Reveals Vast Web of Corruption." *New York Times*, November 3, 2009. http://www.nytimes.com/2009/11/04/world/asia/04crimewave.html?_r=1&pagewanted=2.

Jacobs, Andrew, and Jimmy Wang. "Chinese Urge Anti-West Boycott over Tibet Stance." *New York Times*, April 20, 2008.

Jameson, Frederic. "Postmodernism, or the Cultural Logic of Late Capitalism." *New Left Review 1*, no. 146 (July–August 1984): 53–92.

Jiang Zhuqing. "Ban on Villas to Be Strictly Implemented." *China Daily*, June 1, 2006. http://www.chinadaily.com.cn/cndy/2006-06/01/content_605398.htm.

Johnson, Kathleen Eagen. *Washington Irving's Sunnyside*. Tarrytown, NY: Historic Hudson Valley Press, 1995.

J. P. Morgan. "China Property Monthly Wrap." *Asia Pacific Equity Research*, March 11, 2010.

King, Anthony D. *Spaces of Global Cultures: Architecture, Urbanism, Identity*. New York: Routledge, 2004.

Kirkby, R. J. R. *Urbanization in China: Town and Country in a Developing Economy 1949–2000 AD*. New York: Columbia University Press, 1985.

Knapp, Ronald. *China's Living Houses: Folk Beliefs, Symbols, and Household Ornamentation*. Honolulu: University of Hawai'i Press, 1999.

Knapp, Ronald, and Kai-yin Lo, eds. *House, Home, Family: Living and Being Chinese*. Honolulu: University of Hawai'i Press, 2005.

Koolhaas, Rem. "Ceremony Acceptance Speech." Speech delivered at the Pritzker Architecture Prize Formal Presentation Ceremony, Jerusalem, May 29, 2000.

Kuang Xiaoming. "Zhongguoshi zao cheng" (Constructing the Chinese City). *Chengshi Zhongguo* (Urban China), no. 4 (2005). http://www.urbanchina.com.cn/Magstall/mag050915_WMC.html.

Langewiesche, William. "Beijing's Olympic Makeover." *Vanity Fair*, April 2008.

Laozi. Dao de jing (Mawangdui text, 197). Quoted in Wang Pi, *Commentary on the Lao Tzu*, translated by Ariane Rump, 128. Honolulu: University of Hawai'i Press, 1979.

Larmer, Brook. "Building Wonderland." *New York Times*, April 6, 2008. http://www.nytimes.com/2008/04/06/realestate/keymagazine/406china-t.html?_r=1&emc=eta1.

Ledderose, Lothar. "The Earthly Paradise: Religious Elements in Chinese Landscape Art." In Bush and Murck, *Theories of the Arts in China*, 165–183.

Leheny, David. *The Rules of Play: National Identity and the Shaping of Japanese Leisure*. Ithaca, NY: Cornell University Press, 2003.

Lei Min. "Taiwushi xiaozhen: 'Tonghua shijie' changxiang qu" (Thames Town: A "Fairytale" World). *Hugang jingji* (Shanghai and Hong Kong Economy) 3 (2007): 34–36.

———. "Taiwushi xiaozhen: Yi ge chongman zhengyi de Shanghai xin dibiao" (Thames Town: A Controversial New Shanghai Landmark). *Hugang jingji* (Shanghai and Hong Kong Economy), no. 6 (2006): 18–21.

Lewis, Tom. *The Hudson: A History*. New Haven, CT: Yale University Press, 2005.

Li Xiaowei. "German Lifestyle Festival." *Shanghai Star*, May 12, 2005. http://app1.chinadaily.com.cn/star/2005/0512/ls32-1.html.

Li Yamin. "Wei Beijing aoyunhui chuangzao wenming hexie renwen huanjing" (Working Together to Build a Harmonious Society for the Beijing Olympic Games). *Beijing ribao* (Beijing Daily), February 20, 2006. http://news.sina.com.cn/c/2006-02-20/11468254334s.shtml.

Lim, Louisa. "China Gets Its Own Slice of English Countryside." *NPR*, December 12, 2006.

Liu, Cary. "Chinese Architectural Aesthetics." In Knapp and Lo, *House, Home, Family*.

Liu Dunzhen. *Chinese Classical Gardens of Suzhou* (Suzhou gudian yuanlin). Translated by Chen Lixian; edited by Joseph C. Wang. New York: McGraw-Hill, 1993.

Liu, Lillian. "A Question of Time." Finance Asia, September 8, 2010. http://www.financeasia.com/News/231364,a-question-of-time.aspx.

Lossing, Benson J. *The Hudson: From the Wilderness to the Sea*. Hensonville, NY: Black Dome Press, 2000.

Massumi, Brian. "Realer than Real: The Simulacrum according to Deleuze and Guattari." *Copyright* 1, no. 1 (1987): 90–97; www.anu.edu.au/hrc/first_and_last/works/realer/htm.

Mast, Herman. "Tai Chi-t'ao, Sunism, and Marxism during the May Fourth Movement in Shanghai." *Modern Asian Studies*, no. 5 (1971): 229.

McDonald, Joe. "China Cracks Down on Stimulus-Linked Graft." *ABC News*, May 20, 2010. http://abcnews.go.com/Business/wireStory?id=10696224.

Mi, Jiayan. "Framing Ambient *Unheimlich*." In *Chinese Ecocinema in the Age of Environmental Challenge*, edited by Jiayan Mi and Sheldon Lu. Hong Kong: Hong Kong University Press, 2009.

Mufson, Steve. "In China, Fear of a Real Estate Bubble." *Washington Post*, January 11, 2010. http://www.washingtonpost.com/wp-dyn/content/article/2010/01/10/AR2010011002767_2.html?sid=ST2010011100876.

Munch, Barbara. "Orange County China, or the Genius Loci of Suburbia in the Age of Global Capitalism." *Architectural Design* 74, no. 4 (July/August 2004): 18–27.

"New Investors Sought for Japanese Theme Park Huis ten Bosch." GoDutch.com, April 7, 2003. http://www.godutch.com/newspaper/index.php?id=109.

Ng, John. "Privatized Housing Impedes Cooling Efforts." *Asia Times*, July 6, 2006. http://www.atimes .com/atimes/China_Business/HG06Cb06.html.

Notebook on Cities and Clothes. Edited by Ulrich Felsberg and Wim Wenders. Berlin: Road Movies Filmproduktion, 1989. DVD.

Nussbaum, Bruce. "iPhones in China Don't Say They Are Assembled in China." *Businessweek*, November 30, 2009. http://www.businessweek.com/innovate/NussbaumOnDesign/ archives/2009/11/iphones_in_chin.html.

O'Connell, Pamela Licalzi. "Korea's High-Tech Utopia, Where Everything Is Observed." *New York Times*, October 5, 2005.

Opdyke, Jeff D. "Tapping China's Consumer-Culture Revolution." *Wall Street Journal*, May 8, 2008. http://online.wsj.com/article/SB121021001034675803.htm.

"Origins of Classical Place Names in Upstate New York." York Staters. http://yorkstaters.blogspot .com/2006/01/whats-in-name-no2-origins-of-classical.html.

Oster, Shai. "World's Top Polluter Emerges as Green-Technology Leader." *Wall Street Journal*, December 15, 2009. http://online.wsj.com/article/SB126082776435591089.html?mod=WSJ _hpp_LEFTTopStories.

Pasternack, Alex. "Beijing's Eco-Friendly Architecture." *China Dialogue*, December 20, 2006. http:// www.chinadialogue.net/article/show/single/en/635-Beijing-s-eco-friendly-architecture.

"Population." China Yearbook 2004. http://english.gov.cn/2005–08/08/content_27315.htm.

Ramstad, Evan, and Gordon Fairclough. "No Comparison." *Wall Street Journal*, April 12–13, 2008, sec. Journal Report.

"Report: China Has World's Fifth Largest Number of High Net Worth Households." *People's Daily*, October 31, 2007. http://english.peopledaily.com.cn/90001/90776/90882/6293645.html.

"The Rise of Collegiate Gothic 1888–1899." Princeton Campus: An Interactive Computer History 1746–1996. http://etcweb.princeton.edu/Campus/chap5.html.

Rosenthal, Elisabeth. "North of Beijing, California Dreams Come True." *New York Times*, February 3, 2003. http://www.nytimes.com/2003/02/03/international/asia/03CHIN.html?pagewanted=1.

Rowe, Peter, and Seng Kuan, eds. *Architectural Encounters with Essence and Form in Modern China.* Cambridge, MA: MIT Press, 2002.

Schafer, Edward H. "Hunting Parks and Animal Enclosures in Ancient China." *Journal of the Economic and Social History of the Orient* 11, no. 3 (1968): 318–343.

Schmit, Julie. "China Tops USA in Spending on Clean Energy." *USA Today*, March 25, 2010. http:// www.usatoday.com/money/industries/energy/environment/2010–03–25-china-clean-energy -investing_N.htm.

Shanghai Henghe Real Estate Co. "Bali hunsha" (Paris Dresses). Taiwushi xiaozhen guoji yishu qu (Thames Town International Art District). http://www.thamestown.com/business2_3.htm.

———. "Guanyu xiaozhen: Songjiang xincheng jianshe fazhan youxian gongsi" (About Us: Songjiang New Town Development and Construction Company). Taiwushi xiaozhen guoji yishu qu (Thames Town International Art District). http://www.thamestown.com/culture3_2.htm.

———. "Mingren pinwei" (Celebrities' Tastes). Taiwushi xiaozhen guoji yishu qu (Thames Town International Art District). http://www.thamestown.com/people1.htm.

———. "Shanghai yuanshi yinyue jiuba" (Shanghai's Nrock Music Bar), Taiwushi xiaozhen guoji yishu qu (Thames Town International Art District). http://www.thamestown.com/business2_14.htm.

———. *Taiwushi xiaozhen* (Thames Town). Sales brochure on private residence properties in Thames Town. Retrieved from Dreams Come True Real Estate offices, Shanghai, December 2007.

———. Taiwushi xiaozhen guoji yishu qu (Thames Town International Art District). http://www .thamestown.com.

———. "Xiaozhen shangjia" (Town Businesses). Taiwushi xiaozhen guoji yishu qu (Thames Town International Art District). http://www.thamestown.com/business2.htm.

———. "Xiaozhen xinwen" (Town News). Taiwushi xiaozhen guoji yishu qu (Thames Town International Art District). http://www.thamestown.com/culture1.htm.

"Shanghai hongjun" (Stratford). China Vanke. http://sh.vanke.com/shanghai/stratford/.

"Shanghai Zendai Group Contributes to Raising Awareness of China's Developing Architecture through Architecture Forum." *PR Newswire*, June 23, 2004. http://www2.prnewswire.com/cgi-bin/stories.pl?ACCT=104&STORY=/www/story/06-23-2004/0002198333&EDATE.

Shijie (The World). Directed by Jia Zhangke. New York: Zeitgeist Films, 2004. DVD.

Silbergeld, Jerome. "Beyond Suzhou: Region and Memory in the Gardens of Sichuan." *Art Bulletin*, June 2004.

———. "Re-reading Zong Bing's Fifth-Century Essay on Landscape Painting: A Few Critical Notes." In Michael Sullivan *festschrift* volume, edited by Li Gongming. Shanghai: Shanghai Shudian and Guangzhou Academy of Fine Art, forthcoming.

Silbergeld, Jerome, Cary Liu, and Dora C. Y. Ching. *Outside In*. New Haven, CT: Yale University Press, 2009.

Silverstone, Roger, ed. *Visions of Suburbia*. New York: Routledge, 1997.

Smith, Craig S. "For China's Wealthy, All but Fruited Plain." *New York Times*, May 15, 2002. http://www.nytimes.com/2002/05/15/world/for-china-s-wealthy-all-but-fruited-plain.html.

Spence, Jonathan D. *The Search for Modern China*. New York: W. W. Norton, 1991.

Stein, Rolf A. *The World in Miniature: Container Gardens and Dwellings in Far Eastern Religious Thought*. Translated by Phyllis Brooks. Stanford, CA: Stanford University Press, 1990.

Stille, Alexander. *The Future of the Past*. New York: Picador, 2002.

Sullivan, Michael. *The Arts of China*. Berkeley: University of California Press, 1984.

Tan, R. "The Domestic Architecture of South Bali." *Bijdragen tot de Taal-, Land- en Volkenkunde* 123, no. 4 (1967): 442–475. http://www.kitlv-journals.nl.

Tao Xinlei. "Wenming limao pian: Wenming zai shengji shimin zai xingdong" (Civilizing Manners: To Improve Decorum, People Must Take Action). *Jin yang wang* (Jin Yang Express), August 8, 2007. http://2008.163.com/07/0808/10/3LC96DF000742437.html.

"Tianjin Tuanbo New Town, China." Halcrow: Development, Planning and Design. http://www.halcrow.com/dpd/projects/?id=0000000026.

Tong Jun. "Foreign Influence in Modern China." *T'ien Hsia Monthly*, May 1938.

Tourgout, James. "High East Street in the Far East." *This Is Dorset*, July 27, 2007. http://www.thisisdorset.net/news/1577194.high_east_street_in_the_far_east/#.

Trilling, Lionel. *Sincerity and Authenticity*. Cambridge, MA: Harvard University Press, 1972.

"Urban and Rural Population in China, 1952–1997." *China Statistical Yearbook* (Beijing, 1998). http://www.iiasa.ac.at/Research/SRD/ChinaFood/data/urban/urban_5.htm.

Waldmeir, Patti. "China's Mandarin Mamma Mia!" *Financial Times*, September 16, 2011. http://www.ft.com/intl/cms/s/2/0b05d818-de75-11e0-a2c0-00144feabdc0.html#axzz1oAkuBaLv.

Wang, Fei, and Yan Wang. "Simulacra." Chinese Archimage Phenomena. http://caipcaip.blogspot.com/search/label/Simulacra.

Wang Qian. "Short-Lived Buildings Create Huge Waste." *China Daily*, March 6, 2010. http://www.chinadaily.com.cn/china/2010-04/06/content_9687545.htm.

"Wanke diwuyuan: Guzili de zhongguo" (Vanke's Fifth Garden: Chinese at Its Core). Sales brochure on Fifth Garden published by Vanke. Retrieved from Fifth Garden realty office, Hangzhou, October 2008.

"Wen Jiabao zhuchi guowuyuanhui tingqu Beijing aoyun chouban jinzhan huibao" (Wen Jiabao Briefed on Preparations for Beijing Olympic Games at State Council Meeting). *Sina.com*, February 22, 2006. http://news.sina.com.cn/c/2006-02-22/18158275699s.shtml.

"Who Are China's Middle Class?" *China.org.cn*, January 23, 2010. http://www.china.org.cn/china/2010-01/23/content_19293900.htm.

———. "China: Retailers Tap into Hierarchy of the Nouveau Super-Riche." *Financial Times*, June 4, 2007. http://www.ft.com/cms/s/1/95718032-1021-11dc-96d3-000b5df10621,dwp _uuid=c2f336f6-093a-11dc-a349-000b5df10621.html.

Wong, Chia-Peck. "China Property Sales Rise 75.5% to 4.4 Trillion Yuan." *Businessweek*, January 18, 2010. http://www.businessweek.com/news/2010-01-18/china-s-2009-property-sales-rise -75-5-to-4-4-trillion-yuan.html.

Wu, Fulong, ed. *Globalization and the Chinese City*. New York: Routledge, 2006.

Xiao Tong. *Wen Xuan: Selections of Refined Literature*. Translated by David R. Knechtges. Princeton, NJ: Princeton University Press, 1987.

Xiaozu Wang. "State-Owned Enterprise Reform and Corporate Governance of China." School of Management, Fudan University, 2003. http://coe21-policy.sfc.keio.ac.jp/ja/event/file/s1-6.pdf.

Xijing zaji (I: 3a–b). Quoted in Sugimura Yuzo, *Chugoku no niwa*, 24. Tokyo: Kyuryudo, 1966.

Xin Zhigang. "Dissecting China's 'Middle Class.'" China Daily, October 27, 2004. http://www .chinadaily.com.cn/english/doc/2004-10/27/content_386060.htm.

Xu Gu, ed. *Jiedu Anting xinzhen* (Reading of Anting New Town). Shanghai: Tongji daxue chubanshe, 2004.

Xue, Charlie Q. L. *Building a Revolution: Chinese Architecture since 1980*. Hong Kong: Hong Kong University Press, 2006.

Xue, Charlie Q. L., and Zhou Minghao. "Haiwai jianzhushi zai Shanghai 'yi cheng jiu zhen' de shijian" (Overseas Architects in Shanghai's "One City, Nine Towns" Plan). *Jianzhu xuebao* (Architectural Journal), March 2007: 24–29. Yang Ziyun. "Rhapsody on the Tall Poplars Palace." In Xiao Tong, *Wen Xuan*, vol. 2, *Rhapsodies on Sacrifices, Hunting, Travel, Sightseeing, Palaces and Halls, Rivers and Seas*.

Yu, Yali. *Gardens in Suzhou*. Stuttgart: Edition Axel Menges, 2003.

Yuan, Haiwang. *The Magic Lantern and Other Tales from the Han Chinese*. Westport, CT: Libraries Unlimited, 2006.

Zhang Fan. "Chengshi zhi lishi xingtai bijiao yanjiu—Yi ge lishi chengshi leixing zaisheng" (Comparative Study of Historical City Form—The Regeneration of a Type of Historical City). In Xu, *Jiedu Anting xinzhen*, 75–83.

Zheng Shiling. "Contemporary Architecture and Urbanism." In Balfour and Zheng, *Shanghai*, 119–133.

"Zhonggongzhongyang jueding jiyu Cheng Liangyu kaichudangji kaichu gongzhi chufen" (Communist Party Revokes Cheng Liangyu's Party Membership, Expels Him from His Position). *Xinhua wang* (Xinhua net), July 26, 2007. http://news.xinhuanet.com/2007-07/26/content_6435299 .htm.

Zhou Jian, "Zhongguoshi zaocheng de gainian renshi" (Understanding the Concept of Constructing the Chinese City). *Chengshi zhonguo* (Urban China), September 19, 2005. http://www .urbanchina.com.cn/Magstall/mag050915_WMC.html.

Zhuang He. "China Real-Estate Investment Rose 16.1% in 2009, Ministry Says." *Bloomberg*, March 8, 2010. http://www.businessweek.com/news/2010-03-08/china-s-2009-housing-investments -rise-16-1-percent-update2-.html.

Zhuangzi. *The Complete Works of Zhuangzi*. Translated by Burton Watson. New York: Columbia University Press, 1968.

INDEX

Page numbers in **boldface** refer to illustrations.

advertising. *See* branding; marketing

agricultural land, 122–123. *See also* sustainability

Air Garden Babylon (Chongqing), 60

amenities, in simulacrascapes, 2, **5**, 61–65. *See also* festivals; religious houses of worship

Amsterdam Central Station, replication of, **15**, 46, 48

amusement parks. *See* theme parks

Andersson, Johan Gunnar, 75

Andreu, Paul, 89

Anting Town (Shanghai), 37, 54, 58, 98; environment of, 107; German festival in, 63; "green" building practices in, 80; sales in, 99, 101

Arata Isozaki, 124

architects, 12–14, 78, 84; Chinese, 21, 72, 73, 75, 80; foreign, 10, 43, 49, 53–54, 74, 79, 92, 99, 124, 125. *See also specific names*

architecture, Chinese, 75, 80–82, 83, 88–89; early foreign influence on, 9–12; "green" design, 80, 119, 124–126, 131; ideological, 10, 80, 89–92; Mao Zedong and, 71–73, 80; neotraditional, 127–129; in simulacrascapes, 71–76; Soviet influence, 10, 72, 80. *See also* prototypes for replication

Arena of Nîmes, replication of, 47–48, **56**

aristocracy, 48, 59, 60, 104–105, 117

art, 28; exhibits at simulacrascapes, 63; forgery of, 21, 24, 51; painting theory, 24–27; theory concerning replication of, 20–21, 51

authenticity: of simulacrascapes, 34, 41, 43, 48, 50, 61, 84, 90, 109, 111; theory of, 20, 22–23, 28–30, 51, 90

Balfour, Alan, 83

basements, 44–45

Baudrillard, Jean, 22–23

Beijing, 5, **6**, 59, 89; Cathay View in, 127, **128**; Chateau Zhang Laffitte in, **11**; contemporary architecture in, 89; Linked Hybrid in, 125, **126**; Modern MOMA in, 125, **126**; neotraditional Chinese architecture in, 127–128; Orange County in, 42–43, 49; Palais de Fortune in, 42, 60, 80, 83, 102–103, **105**; Palm Beach Villas in, 60; Upper East Side in, 95; Venice Gardens in, 111–112; Watermark-Longbeach in, 49; Xuanyi Jiayuan in, 128; Yi Jun Villas in, 127

Beverly Hills (Chongqing), 41–42, 60

Bhalotra, Ashok, 43

Blue Cambridge (Shanghai), 54–55, 73, **77**, 103–104

bourgeoisie, 34, 65, 95, 102–104

branding, 37, 39, 58–61, 76–80, 83, 103–104, 109. *See also* marketing

Breakers, The (Newport, RI), 7

British Town (Chengdu), 48, 56–57, 61, 85

building materials, 42, 43, 87

Campanella, Thomas, 8, 129–130

Canadian Maple Town (Shanghai), 49, 80

Capitol Building, U.S., **16**, 38, 73, 85, 91

cars. *See* transportation

Cathay View (Beijing), 127, **128**

Champs Elysées Square, 1, 56

Changsha, 57–58

Charpentier, Jean-Marie, 61

Chateau Comte de Sunac (Chongqing), **78**, **83**

Château Maisons-Laffitte, replication of, **11**, 104

Chateau Zhang Laffitte (Beijing), 11

Chen Liangyu, 97

Chengdu, 1; British Town in, 56–57, 61, 85; Dorchester, England, in, 1, 48, 56–57, 85; neotraditional Chinese architecture in, 127; Tsinghua House in, 128

Chinatowns, 7

China Vanke, 5, 41, 69, 100, **101**, 128–129

Chinese dream, 14, 17, 95, 101–103

Ching, Dora C.Y., 122

Chongqing: Air Garden Babylon in, 60; Beverly Hills in, 41–42, 60; Chateau Comte de Sunac in, **78**, **83**; Chrysler Building in, 38, 86, 91; "New York, New York" in, 38, **86**

Chrysler Building (Chongqing), 38, 86, 91

churches. See religious houses of worship

Citta di Pujiang (Shanghai), 98

class divide, 9, 99, 104–105, 117, 121. See also middle class; upper class

communal living, 96

Communist Party of China, 70, 86–87, 90, 96, 103, 116; corruption in, 69–70, 97; simulacrascape projects led by, 38, 69, 85, 91, 97–99. See also British Town; "One City, Nine Towns"

corruption, in government. See Communist Party of China

courtyards, 43, 51, 52, 102, 124

cultural immersion, in simulacrascapes, 63–64, 65–66, 112–117. See also amenities

Cultural Revolution, 87, 131

culture: government and, 116–117; simulacrascapes and, 55–58, 65–66, 110–112, 119

danwei, 105

Dao, 27–30

Dao de jing (Laozi), 29

décor, 42–43, 58, 84, 103, 110–112

Deleuze, Gilles, 23

democracy, 117

Deng Xiaoping, 59, 110, 117, 131

Dian Kingdom, invasion of, vii

Disneyland, 21, 24, 49, 66

Doge's Palace, replication of, 45–46

domestic life, 44–45, 51, 52, 55, 58, 64–65, 96, 104, 110–112

Dorchester, England, replication of, 1, 48, 56–57, 85

Eaton Town (Suzhou), 59, **82**

Eco, Umberto, 21, 22–23, 24, 80

economy, Chinese, 87; and cultural changes post-Reform, 67–68, 85–86, 96, 107; disparities, 99, 105–106; growth, 5, 8–9, 70, 120, 121, 127

education of architects, 71–75; studying abroad, 49

Eiffel Tower, replication of, 1, **2**, 47, 55–56, **96**

emigration, 109–110

English County (Kunshan), **12**, 43, 44, **45**, **68**, **84**

etiquette, 113, 115–116

evictions, 69–70

Fengcheng Town (Shanghai), 98, **99**

Fengjing Town (Shanghai), 98

fengshui, 45, 51, 52, 54, 99

festivals, in simulacrascapes, 63–64

Fifth Garden (Shenzhen), 128

films, influence of, 49, 50, 111. See also World, The

floor plans, 54–55, 102–103

Fontainebleau Villas (Shanghai), 106, 122, 123

Fontaine des Quatre Parties du Monde, replication of, 56

food: Chinese, 93, 110–112; importation of, 123; Western, 2, 61, 64–65. See also amenities

Forest Manor (Shanghai), **64**, **93**

Foucault, Michel, 93–94

Frampton, Kenneth, 91

Future City (Shanghai), 124, **125**

Future of the Past, The (Stille), 25

Fuyang, 38, 85

Galaxy Dante (Shenzhen), 65, 100, 103, **104**

Garden of Monet (Shanghai), **59**

gardens, 30; container gardens, 27–28; imperial parks, 31–33, 34–35, 89–92; private gardens, 33–35; within simulacrascapes, 43, 52–53, 83, 111, 122–123. See also landscaping in themed communities

Germany Villas (Suzhou), 38

"get rich is glorious," 59, 110, 117

Glory Vogue (Beijing), 59

government, 85, 87, 97–99; Chinese dream and, 95–97; culture and, 116–117; land ownership by, 69–70, 77–78

Goya development (Hangzhou), **13**, 111

Great Leap Forward, 71–76, 123

"green" building practices, 80, 119, 125, 131

Guangsha Development Company, 74–75

Guangzhou, 38, 91; Le Bonheur in, 38; Majesty Manor in, 59; Tsinghua House in, 128

guanxi, 69

Hallstatt, Austria, replication of, 47, 49

handan xue bu ("Learning how the Handan residents walk"), 118

Han dynasty, 9, 14, 31–32; gardens in, 30, 35; place names and, 34

Hangzhou, 120; Goya development in, **13**, 111; Mount Rushmore in, 91; Tianducheng in, 47–48, 49, 50, 55–56, 63, 74–75, **96**, 107, 113, **115**; Venice Water Town in, **3**, 11, 45–46, 47; Versailles Palace in, 2, 56, 91–92; Washington Monument in, 91

Harbin Pharmaceutical Group, 91–92

Haussmann, Georges-Eugène, 1

Herzog and de Meuron National Stadium (Beijing), 89

heterotopias, 94–95. *See also* Foucault, Michel

HNPoly Villas (Changsha), 57–58

Holland Village (Shanghai), **8**, 11, 43, 44, **108**

home design, in simulacrascapes, 41–42, 45, 54–55, 84, 102; Chinese influence on, 51–55; effect on neighborhoods, 64. *See also* décor; floor plans

homeowners' associations, 41, 117

Huis ten Bosch (Nagasaki, Japan), 6

Huizhou, 47, 49

Hyde Park (Nanjing), 38

hyperreal, 21, 23, 80

ideological architecture, 10, 80, 89–92

imagineering, 34, 66

individualism, 4, 17, 60, 93–97, 100–107, 110, 119

intellectual property, 25

iPhone, 25, 83

Jameson, Frederic, 22–23

Japan, 6, 8

Jia Zhangke, 87, 109

Jiande World Villas (Shanghai), 52–53, 56–57

Jiangxi Province, 122

Jiu Jian Tang (Shanghai), 124

Kattenbroek (Amersfoort, The Netherlands), 43–44

KCAP. *See* Kuiper-Compagnons

Kennicott, Phillip, 13, 90

King, Anthony, 126

kitsch, 3, 13, 51

Koolhaas, Rem, 89, 92

Kowloon Mountain Resort (Pinghu), **74**

Kuang Xiaoming, 75, 87, 88–89

Kuiper-Compagnons (KCAP), 43

Kunming Lake, vii–viii, 34

Kunshan: English County in, **12**, 43, 44, **45**, **68**, **84**; Scenic England in, **40**

land: agricultural, 122–123; government ownership of, 69–70, 77–78; government restrictions for, 123; leasing of, 77–78

landscaping in themed communities, 15, 38, 47, 52–53, 55–56, 106, 121–123. *See also* gardens

Laozi, 29

Le Bonheur (Guangzhou), 38

Ledderose, Lothar, 26, 30, 31

leisure, 31, 33–34, 63–65, 108–109. *See also* tourism; vacation homes

Le Vau, Louis, 124

Li Qiang, 69

Linked Hybrid (Beijing), 125, **126**

Liu, Cary, 32, 122

Long Island Villas (Wuhan), 57

Luodian Town (Shanghai), 34, 37, **71**, 80, **97**, 106; *fengshui* in, **54**; landscaping in, 52–53; troubles of, 98, 99

Majesty Manor (Guangzhou), 59

Malaren Lake, 34, 37

management, of simulacrascapes, 41–42, 64, 97–100

Mao Zedong, 9–10, 51, 72, 80

marketing, of simulacrascapes, 5–6, 41–42, 58–61, 79, 83, 98. *See also* branding

Meier, Richard, 124

middle class, 9, 18, 55, 68, 81, 103, 107; architecture and, 119; changing tastes of, 124; residential construction and, 70

Milani, Fred, 6

Ming dynasty, 30, 35, 111

Minhang People's Court (Shanghai), 16

Minmetal Land, 47

Modern MOMA (in Beijing), 125, **126**

monuments replicated. *See names of individual landmarks*

Nanjing, 38, 91

National Theater (Beijing), 89

New Amsterdam (Shenyang), **15**, 46, 48, 50

New Songdo City (South Korea), 77

"New York, New York" (Chongqing), 38, **86**

New York City, 6, **86**, 87, 91, 119

Ning Qiang, viii

Noordeinde Palace, replication of, 46

Northern Dynasties, 34

Notebook on Cities and Clothes (Wim Wenders), 23

OCT Properties, 124

"Of Other Spaces" (Foucault), 94

Olympic Games, Summer 2008, 89, 116, 129, 130

"One City, Nine Towns" (Shanghai), 1, 74, 97–98, 99, **125**

"Open Door" policy, 104

Opium Wars, 10, 81

Orange County (Beijing), 42–43, 49

ordinances, 40–41, 43, 49, 77–78

"Oriental Paris," 1

Original Mediterranean Villas (Shanghai), 52, **122**

Palace on Rare (Shanghai), 60

Palais de Fortune (Beijing), 42, 60, 80, 83, 102–103, **105**; floor plans of, 102–103; high-density of, 83; security at, **105**

Palm Beach Villas (Beijing), 60

Palm Springs (Shanghai), **120**

Paradiso, The (Foshan), 38

Paris: in Hangzhou, 47–48, 55–56, 113; "Oriental Paris," 1

Parthenon, replication of, 6

pastiche, 21, 48, 59

Peace Palace of The Hague, replication of, 46, 48

Pentagon, replication of, 73

Pinghu, **74**

place names, 6–7, 34–35, 57, 59, 79, 125

Pleasantville (Ross), 61

postmodernism, 21–22, 23

Poyang Lake, 122

"Preface on Painting Mountains and Water" (Zong Bing), 26

privacy, 64–65, 95–96, 110

"Problem of Forgeries in Chinese Painting, The" (Wen Fong), 21

prototypes for replication: British, viii, 1, **12**, 37, **38**, 40, 41, 48, 54, 56–57, 58, 59, 61, 62–63, 64, 69, 78, 81, **82**, 85, 95, 99, 100, 109, 110, 113, 114; Canadian, 49, 80, 98; Chinese, 127–130; Dutch, **8**, 11, **15**, 43, **44**, 46, 48, 50, **108**; French, 1, **2**, **11**, 38, 42, 47–48, 49, 50, 55, 56, 59, 60, 78, 80, 83, 91–92, **96**, 102–103, **105**, 113, **115**; German, **5**, 37, 38, 54, 58, 98, 99; Italian, **3**, 11, 37, 38, 45–46, 74, 98, 111–112; North American, 16, 38, 41–43, 49, 57, 60, 73, 85, **86**, **88**, 91, 95, 100, **101**, 120; Spanish, 6, **13**, 38, 49, 96, 98, **99**, 111, 112; Swedish, 34, 37, 38, 51–52, 52–53, 54, 71, 80, 97, 98, 99, 106

Pujiang Town (Shanghai), 37

qi, 27, 29–30, 45, 52, 90

Qin Shihuangdi, vii

Qing dynasty, 14, 27, 30, 32, 35

Rancho Santa Fe (Shanghai), 39, 100, **101**

real estate developers: short-term approach of, 77–78; simulacrascapes by, 69–71; success of, 100–101. *See also individual companies*

real estate market, 5, 37, 96, 100, 103, 120; comparison with U.S., 127; competition in, 77–80; construction of simulacrascapes for, 5, 40, 47, 49, 51, 78, 125; foreign investment in, 4; government involvement in, 69–71, 85, 97–100, 120; pressure to complete developments,

77–78; private property ownership in, 5, 25, 72, 95, 117; speculation in, 120–121

Red Guards, 96

religious houses of worship, 37, 55–56, 87, 113–115

residential construction, 4–6, 70, 80, 83

residential covenants, 40–41

"Rhapsody on the Tall Poplars Palace" (Yang Ziyun), 32

Rockefeller family, 6

Roman Vision (Nanjing), 38

Russia, 6, 10, 115. *See also* Soviet Union

rustication, under Mao Zedong, 72

Saint Mark's Campanile, 46

Saint Mark's Square, replication of, 45–46, 47

San Carlos (Shanghai), **17**, 41, 52, **76**

san dai tong tang (three generations living together), 52

Scandinavia Stroll (Shanghai), 51–52, 54

Scenic England (Kunshan), **40**

second homes. See vacation homes

security, in simulacrascapes, 40, 103, 105–106, 117, 121; themed uniforms of, 37–38

Shanghai, 73, 74, 89, 91; Anting Town in, 37, 54, 58, 63, 80, 98, 99, 107; Blue Cambridge in, 54–55, 73, **77**, 103–104; Canadian Maple Town in, 49, 80; Citta di Pujiang, 98; Communist Party and, 90, 97; corruption in, 97; Fengcheng Town in, 98, **99**; Fengjing Town in, 98; Fontainebleau Villas in, **106**, 122, 123; Forest Manor in, **64**, **93**; Future City in, 124, **125**; Garden of Monet in, **59**; Holland Village in, **8**, 11, 43, 44, **108**; Jiande World Villas in, 52–53, 56–57; Jiu Jian Tang in, 124; Little White House in, 88; Luodian Town in, 34, 37, 52–53, **54**, **71**, 80, **97**, 98, 99, 106; Minhang People's Court in, **16**; "One City, Nine Towns" in, 1, 74–75, 97–98, 99, **125**; Original Mediterranean Villas in, 52, **122**; Palace on Rare in, 60; Palm Springs in, **120**; Pujiang Town in, 37; Rancho Santa Fe in, 39, 100, **101**; San Carlos in, **17**, 41, 52, **76**; Scandinavia Stroll in, 51–52, 54; *shikumen* in, **81**; Stratford in, 41, 60, 100; Thames Town in, viii, 37, **38**, 54, 58, 60, 61, 62–63, 64, 69, 78, 81, 95, 99, 109, 110, 113, 114; Tuanbo New Town in, 52; U.S. Capitol Building in, **16**, 91; Vienna Gardens in, **79**; Weimar Villas in, **5**, 37, 52, 61; Windsor Gardens in, 40; World Financial Center in, 89

Shanghai Art and Crafts Museum, **88**

Shanghai Songjiang New Town Construction and Developing Company, 69

Shanglin Park, 31

shanzhai, 25

Shenyang, 15, 46, 48

Shenzhen, 72, **110**; Fifth Garden in, 128–129; Galaxy Dante in, 65, 100, 103, **104**; Vanke Town in, 61; White House in, **88**

shikumen, 43, **81**, 96

siheyuan, 43, 83, 96, 127–128

Silbergeld, Jerome, 27, 122

Silk Road, 9

Silverstone, Roger, 106–107

simulacrum, 4–5, 34–35; inspiration for, 69–71; motivation for, 67–92; originality and, 20–36; philosophy of, 22–24

SinoCEA, 49

Sino-centrism, 10, 90, 121, 130

Sino-Japanese War, 81

Six Dynasties period, 33

"socialism with Chinese characteristics," 67

Southern Dynasties, 34

South Korea, 77

Soviet Union, viii, 10, 72, 80

Special Economic Zones, 4

Spiritual Civilization Steering Committee, of Communist Party, 116

state-owned enterprises (SOEs), 69, 99–100

Stein, Rolf, 27, 32–33, 90

Stille, Alexander, 25

Stratford (Shanghai), 41, 60, 100

street commitees, 41, 64–65

styles of architecture, in simulacrascapes: Art Deco, 7; Baroque, **17**, 42, 49, 63, 67, **76**, 80, 93, 104, 124; Bauhaus, 104; Beaux Arts, 7, 104, 124; Brutalist, 104; Futurist, 104; Gothic, 6, 7, 45, 55; Greek Revival, 6, 52, 55, 104; International, 104; Mediterranean, 6, 7, **13**, 52, **59**, **61**, **78**, **120**, **122**; Neoclassical, 10, 41, 60, 81, **106**; Neotraditional Chinese, 127–129; Queen Anne, 7, 41, 57, **64**, 78, 112; Rococo, 6, 52, 104, 124; Tudor, viii, 7, 57, 96; Victorian, **83**, 104

suburbs, viii, 43, 76, 83, 98, 106–107

Supreme Forest, 31–32, 34

sustainability, 76; "green" design and, 80, 119, 125, 131; water pollution and, 121–122

Suzhou, 59, 38, 82, 128, **130**

Tang dynasty, 112

taste, 51, 103, 104, 107

Thames Town (Shanghai), viii, 37, **38**, 58, 60, 61, 62–63, 78, 81, 95, 109, 110, 113, 114; *fengshui* and, 99; floor plans in, 54; privacy in, 64; SOEs and, 69; as tourist attraction, 109; weddings in, 113, 114

theme parks, viii, 3, 12, 13, 24, 87–88, 109; comparison with simulacrascapes, 15, 66

Tiananmen Square, 132

Tianducheng (Hangzhou), 47–48, 49, 50, 55–56, 63, 74–75, **96**; environment of, 107; festivals in, 63, 113; land auction, 69; weddings in, 113, **115**

Tianjin, 10, 11, 52, **88**

tianjing (sky well), 128

Tianlun Suiyuan (Suzhou), 128, **130**

Top Aristocrat (Beijing), 59

tourism, 50, 94, 108–110; difficulty traveling abroad for purposes of, 94

traditional Chinese building. See *shikumen*; *siheyuan*

transportation: car ownership, 93, 103, 110, 121; commuting, 98, 121; public transporation, 98, 121

Travels in Hyperreality (Eco), 23–24, 80

Treaty of Nanjing, 10

Treaty Ports, 10

trends, 95–97; and appeal of the West, 80, 82, 103–104

Trilling, Lionel, 20

Tuanbo New Town (Shanghai), 52

Tumushuke, viii

TV shows, influence of, 50. See also films, influence of

United Arab Emirates (UAE), 6, 8

United States: architectural influence of, 49, 75, 126; Capitol Building of, 16, 38, 73, 85, 91; China's competition with, 88, 91; comparison with China's simulacrascape-building movement, 6, 7, 66; economy of, 120, 127, 131; Pentagon of, 73; White House of, 6, 16, 85, **88**, 89–92

upper class, viii, 52, 55, 68, 81, 103, 104

Upper East Side (Beijing), 95

urbanization, 4–5, 16, 72–76

vacancies, 97–99, 121

vacation homes, 18, 107, 120

Vanderbilt, Cornelius, 7

Vanke Town (Shenzhen), 61

Venice Gardens (Beijing), 111–112

Venice Water Town (Hangzhou), **3**, 11, 45–46, 47

Versailles Palace, replication of, **2**, 42, 47, 56, 60, 91–92, 102–104

Vienna Gardens (Shanghai), **79**

villas, 84. See also specific developments

Wang Jian, 27

Wang Xufei, 49

Washington Monument, replication of, 91

water: pollution of, 121–122; in simulacra-scapes, 52, 121–122. See also sustainability

Watermark-Longbeach (Beijing), 49

weddings, 113–115. See also religious houses of worship

Weimar Villas (Shanghai), **5**, 37, 52, 61

Wen Fong, 20–21, 24–25, 51

Wen Qiang, 69

Wenders, Wim, 23

Wenling, 91

Wen xuan, 31–32

White House, replication of, 6, **16**, 85, 88, 89–92

Windsor Gardens (Shanghai), 40

World, The (Jia Zhangke), 87, 109

World Bank, 122

World Financial Center (Shanghai), 89

Wright, Frank Lloyd, 124

Wu (emperor), 31–32, 34

Wuhan, 57

Wuxi, **88**, 91

Xianyang, vii

Xing Ruan, 52, 75, 84

Xuanyi Jiayuan (Beijing), 128

Yang Ziyun, 32

Yi Jun Villas (Beijing), 127
Yi xian zhuan (Wang Jian), 27
Yoji Yamamoto, 23
Yung Ho Chang, 91

Zhang Yuchen, 11
Zhang Zhian, 85
Zhejiang Guangsha Development Company, 69
Zheng Shiling, 72
Zhuangzi, 28
Zi Huayun, 116
Zong Bing, 26–27

ABOUT THE AUTHOR

Bianca Lencek Bosker is a graduate of Princeton University. Elected to Phi Beta Kappa and graduating summa cum laude, she was awarded the prestigious Marjory Chadwick Buchanan Prize for the most outstanding senior thesis in Princeton's East Asian Studies Department. She is the co-author of a book on the cultural history of bowling entitled *Bowled Over: A Roll Down Memory Lane* (Chronicle Books). In 2007, she was the recipient of the *Wall Street Journal*'s Robert L. Bartley Fellowship for Editorial Journalism, which she completed at the *Far East Economic Review* in Hong Kong. Her articles, book reviews, and editorials on technology, international affairs, economics, and Asian culture have been published in the *Far East Economic Review*, the *Wall Street Journal*, and *Fast Company*, among other publications. Bianca lives in New York City, where she is the Senior Tech Editor at *The Huffington Post*. She oversees and writes for the site's tech section, which she helped launch in 2009 and draws millions of readers monthly.